Baedeker

MUNICH

Imprint

109 illustrations, 34 maps, plans and drawings, 1 large map at end of book

Original German text: Johannes Kelch, Helmut Linde, Rainer Eisenschmid, Carmen Galen-schovski, Prof. Dr Hans-Dieter Haas, Dr Christina Melk-Haen, Dr Roland Metz

Cartography: Gert Oberländer, Munich; Mairs Geographischer Verlag, GmbH & Co., Ostfildern-Kemnat (large map)

General direction: Dr. Peter Baumgarten, Baedeker Stuttgart

Original English translation: James Hogarth
Additional text and updating: Wendy Bell, Alec Court, Brenda Ferris
Editorial work, English language edition: Margaret Court

Following the tradition established by Karl Baedeker in 1844, sights of particular interest and hotels and restaurants of particular quality are distinguished by either one or two asterisks.

To make it easier to locate the various places listed in the "A to Z" section of the Guide, their co-ordinates on the large city map are shown at the head of each entry.

Only a selection of hotels, restaurants and shops can be given; no reflection is implied therefore on establishments not included.

In a time of rapid change it is difficult to ensure that all the information given is entirely accurate and up-to-date, and the possibility of error can never be entirely eliminated. Although the publishers can accept no responsibility for inaccuracies and omissions, they are always grateful for corrections and suggestions for improvement.

2nd English edition 1994

© Baedeker Stuttgart
Original German edition

© 1994 Jarrold and Sons Limited
English language edition worldwide

© 1994 The Automobile Association
United Kingdom and Ireland

Distributed in the United Kingdom by the Publishing Division of the Automobile Association, Fanum House, Basingstoke, Hampshire RG21 2EA

Licensed user:
Mairs Geographischer Verlag GmbH & Co., Ostfildern-Kemnat bei Stuttgart

The name *Baedeker* is a registered trade mark
A CIP catalogue record of this book is available from the British Library

Printed in Italy by G. Canale & C.S.p.A – Borgaro T.se –Turin

Published in the United States by:
Macmillan Travel
A Prentice Hall Macmillan Company
15 Columbus Circle
New York, NY 10023

Macmillan is a registed trademark of Macmillan, Inc.

ISBN US and Canada 0–671–89685–7

Contents

The Principal Places of Tourist Interest at a Glance

Preface

This pocket guide to **Munich** is one of the new generation of Baedeker guides.

Baedeker pocket guides, illustrated throughout in colour, are designed to meet the needs of the modern traveller. They are quick and easy to consult, with the principal features of interest described in alphabetical order and practical details about location, opening times, etc., shown in the margin.

This city guide is divided into three parts. The first part gives a general account of the city, its topography, climate, population, culture, economy and transport, famous people and history. A brief selection of quotations leads in to the second part, where the principal places of tourist interest are described. The third part contains a variety of practical information designed to help visitors to find their way about and to make the most of their stay. Both the sights and the Practical Information section are given in alphabetical order.

Baedeker pocket guides, which are regularly updated, are noted for their concentration on essentials and their convenience of use. They contain many coloured illustrations and specially drawn plans, and at the back of the book will be found a large plan of the city. Each main entry in the A to Z section gives the co-ordinates of the square on the plan in which the particular feature can be located. Users of this guide, therefore, should have no difficulty in finding what they want to see.

Facts and Figures

General

Munich is the capital of the Free
State of Bavaria and of the administrative district of Upper Bavaria.
The third largest German city, it is
sometimes called "the secret
capital of Germany".
Munich is the headquarters of the
European and of the German
Patent Offices and the Federal
Finance Court is located in the city.
It has two universities, several
colleges and academies and
renowned research institutes as
well as a broad spectrum of
theatres, popular museums and
galleries; all these ensure that the
influence of Munich as a cultural metropolis extends far beyond the boundaries of Bavaria.

Munich is twinned with Edinburgh (Scotland), Bordeaux (France), Verona
(Italy) and Sapporo (Japan).

The centre of the city (Frauenkirche – Church of Our Lady) lies at latitude
48°8'23" north and longitude 11°34'28" east. The highest point in the city
area is the Warnberg (579m/1900ft) in the south of Munich (Solln). The
lowest point is in the Isar meadows in the north-east of the city at
482m/1580ft. Munich lies in the middle of the gravel plain of the same
name. The southern parts of the city have a more pronounced relief pattern
and merge into the glaciated foothills of the Alps.

Topography

To the south-west of Munich two lakes, the Ammersee and the Starn-
bergersee, both surrounded by forests, present a charming landscape.

The territory of the Bavarian capital is traversed by the River Isar from the
south-east to the north-east. As a result of the build-up of deposits and of
erosion the river has formed terraces, and here can be seen the nuclei of old
villages, which are in danger of being swamped by the mass of houses of
the modern conurbation.

The new airport is situated on moorland in the north of the city.

For administrative purposes the city is divided into 41 districts (see map on
page 11).
Munich is governed by a directly elected senior burgomaster, two burgomasters chosen from the members of the city council and thirteen full-time
consultants, each of whom is responsible for a specific administrative
department. According to Bavarian local regulations the senior burgomaster is not only the highest responsible representative of the city but is
also the head of administration. In the city council are 80 honorary councillors who meet in committees and in full sessions. The period of office for
the burgomasters, consultants and councillors is six years.

City districts

◄ *Marienplatz with New City Hall; in background towers of the Frauenkirche*

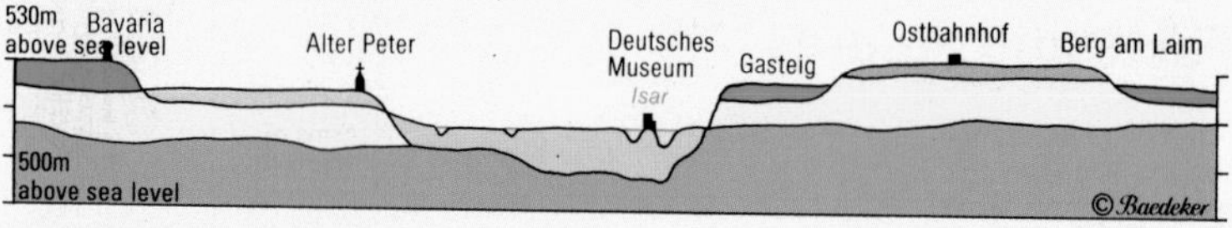

Geological Profile

- Tertiary Flint
- Gravel of First Ice-Age
- Gravel of Second Ice-Age
- Old Silting up
- Recent Silting up
- Clay and Loess
- Waters

Climate

Munich lies on the boundary between the west European maritime and the east European continental climatic zones. In addition the weather is influenced by the nearness of the Alpine range and is often very changeable. The average annual temperature is 7·6°C/46°F. The warmest months are June, July and August, when occasionally maxima of more than 30°C/86°F can be reached. The coldest months are December, January and February. On cloudless nights in the heart of winter the temperature occasionally falls to below −25°C/−13°F. Average precipitation is about 1000mm/39·4in. Most rain falls in the months of May, June and July, when storms occur quite often, sometimes accompanied by torrential rain and hail. In autumn and winter there are occasional long periods of weather-inversion which favours the build-up of smog, and in the winter months considerable amount of snow is not unusual

Föhn

A special feature of the climate of Munich is the föhn, a dry, warm, katabatic wind from the south, which can occur at any time of the year. It disperses the cloud over the Alpine foreland of Upper Bavaria. Its relatively low humidity and the clarity of the air make possible an exceptional clear view, so that on many days the impression is created that Munich is situated on the edge of the Alps.
The exact effect of the föhn on the human organism has not yet been fully researched; when the föhn is blowing people often suffer from attacks of migraine, circulation problems and extreme mental depression.

"Beer snow"

A speciality of Munich is the so-called "beer snow". This arises when very damp emissions from the large Munich breweries condense at temperatures below freezing and crystallise into a frost-like white precipitation. It lies like icing-sugar on roofs, roads and squares.

Ozone

On sunny days in summer when pressure is high there is a severe increase in the ozone level. This has a detrimental effect on many people.

Population

Inhabitants

In 1854 there were only 120,000 inhabitants in Munich, but on January 1st 1991 there were 1,278,000. The increase in population has been most marked since the 1890s, when as a consequence of industrialsation very many country-dwellers streamed into the city.
Until 1939 the population increased to 829,318. The decrease during the Second World War (in 1945 there were only 480,447) was short-lived, principally because of the influx of refugees and exiles. In 1950 Munich had more than 850,000 inhabitants and in 1957 the million mark was passed. Foreign workers from the south-east and south of Europe contributed to a

City Area

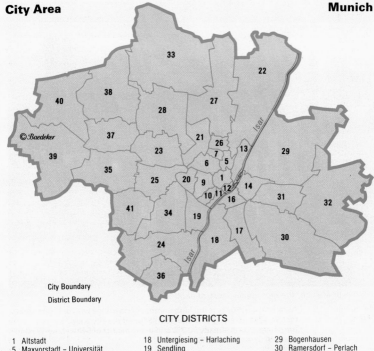

City Boundary

District Boundary

CITY DISTRICTS

1 Altstadt
5 Maxvorstadt – Universität
6 Maxvorstadt – Königsplatz
   – Marsfeld
7 Maxvorstadt – Josephsplatz
9 Ludwigsvorstadt
10 Isarvorstadt – Schlachthofviertel
11 Isarvorstadt – Glockenbachviertel
12 Isarvorstadt – Deutsches Museum
13 Lehel
14 Haidhausen
16 Au
17 Obergiesing

18 Untergiesing – Harlaching
19 Sendling
20 Schwanthalerhöhe
21 Neuhausen – Oberwiesenfeld
22 Schwabing – Freimann
23 Neuhausen – Nymphenburg
24 Thalkirchen – Obersendling
   – Forstenried – Fürstenried
25 Laim
26 Schwabing-West
27 Schwabing-Nord – Milbertshofen
   – Am Hart
28 Neuhausen – Moosach

29 Bogenhausen
30 Ramersdorf – Perlach
31 Berg am Laim
32 Trudering
33 Feldmoching – Hasenbergl
34 Waldfriedhofviertel
35 Pasing
36 Solln
37 Obermenzing
38 Allach – Untermenzing
39 Aubing
40 Lochhausen – Langwied
41 Hadern

further increase in 1972 to 1,338,924 (the highest total so far). Since that time some 50,000 people have either moved to more attractive residential districts in the surroundings or have returned to their own countries. Between 1989 and 1991, following the dissolution of the German Democratic Republic, Munich received many incomers from that former country and also many immigrants from east and south-east Europe. The influx from the east continues. After Berlin and Hamburg, Munich is the third largest city in the German Federal Republic. At present about 11% of the population of the Free State of Bavaria live in Munich, and the population density is about 4125 per square kilometre (10,867 per square mile).

Currently some 214,000 foreigners, some 16% of the whole population of the city, live in Munich. The largest groups are people from the former Yugoslavia (54,000), Turks (44,000), Austrians (25,000), Italians (21,000) and Greeks (18,000).

Föhn over Munich; the Alps appear close at hand

One-person households	A statistical curiosity is the high number of dwellings with only one inhabitant. In 1961 barely 15% of the population of the city were "singles"; now the percentage is already 50·7% and in the district of Schwabing-West this quota has reached 63·6%
Religion	The majority of the inhabitants of Munich are traditionally Roman Catholic (currently some 56%). About a fifth are Protestant (evangelical) and barely a quarter members of other religious groups.

Culture

Munich has many institutions concerned with all spheres of cultural activity and a number of them enjoy international fame. The Bavarian State Opera, the State Playhouse, the State Theatre in the Gärtnerplatz and the Munich Studio Theatre (Kammerspiele) annually attract audiences of more than 1·3 million. Museums with exceptional collections and effective presentation enjoy continuous popularity. Among the leading museums are the Deutsches Museum, the Old and the New Pinakothek, the Munich City Museum and the Municipal Gallery in the Lenbachhaus. The large exhibitions in the Haus der Kunst (House of Art) are very popular. A considerable element in the cultural life of Munich is the Gasteig Cultural Centre, the home of the Munich Philharmonic Orchestra (Münchner Philharmonie), the Münchner Volkshochschule (people's academy) and the Städtische Bibliothek (Municipal Library), Musical events are essentially provided by the Munich Philharmonic Orchestra, the Radio Symphony Orchestra, the Radio Orchestra, the Musica Viva and the Musical Academy. Musical events with guest artistes, and concert series take place in the pleasant surroundings of a number of castles and country houses.

Among the numerous libraries in the city the Bavarian State Library (Bayerische Staatsbibliothek) is the largest, with over 7½ million books and manuscripts.

Measured by the number of students (over 63,000) the Ludwig Maximilian University is the second largest university in Germany (only surpassed by the Free University of Berlin). It was founded in 1472 by Duke Ludwig the Rich in Ingoldstadt and moved by Kurfurst Max Joseph IV in 1800 to Landshut. It owes its name to these two princes. In 1826 Ludwig I transferred the university to Munich. Friedrich Gärtner designed the large prestigious university building in Romanesque style between 1835 and 1840 and it was subsequently extended on several occasions. It is situated in Ludwigstrasse at the "Forum der Wissenschaften" (Forum of Science) at the Geschwister-Scholl Platz.

Ludwig Maximilians University

The Technical University was founded in 1868 as a technical college of surveying, engineering, architecture and agriculture; it was a development from earlier specialist technical institutions. At present it has over 23,000 students.

Technical University

There are a number of research institutes of the Technical University which are situated in Garsching, 13km/8 miles north of Munich.

Economy

During the last decades Munich has become the greatest industrial city in Germany and one of the most important economic centres of Europe. In 1986 there were some 800,000 jobs. Siemens, BMW, MAN and Linde are but a few of the well-known industrial firms. In addition the Bavarian capital is the leading publishing centre in Germany (more than 300 establishments producing books, newspapers and periodicals are located in the city), and also a fashion centre (including Loden-Frey, Bogner). Munich has a considerable reputation in the spheres of finance and credit. With about 170 insurance firms the city occupies the leading place in the Federal Republic and is only surpassed in the field of banking by Frankfurt-am-Main.
In many respects Munich has the leading place in the north–south axis of Germany. In the sphere of the old federal provinces the city was the community where most established firms had a balance of over 100 million Deutschemarks. Since the re-unification of Germany the large number of industrial enterprises, insurance offices and banks now concentrated here can scarcely be matched by any other city in the country. Of the sixteen largest German cities Munich can claim the greatest industrial growth in the past twenty years. At the beginning of the 1960s Munich occupied sixth place as far as industrial activity is concerned; in 1990, in spite of having the most expensive site costs in Germany, Munich had 179,000 industrial workers, more than Berlin (164,000) and Hamburg (137,000).
Even in the statistics for unemployment Munich's position is far more favourable than that of German cities farther north. During the recession between five and six per cent of workers in Munich were unemployed, while the figures for Dortmund, Bochum and Cologne were more than twice as high. This leading position within the Federal Republic is not only the result of the structure of the firms located here. A large number of those employed in industry in the conurbation of Munich are concerned with research and development. In a rapid change of direction more and more traditional jobs are being replaced by senior positions in the fields of development and research, and in management.

Technologically orientated Economic System

The unmistakable mixture of art, culture, joie de vivre and business activity leaves its mark on the statistics for tourism. In more than 350 hotels, inns and holiday homes Munich has currently some 35,000 beds available. In 1990 there were about 3.6 million overnight stays by 1.7 million visitors (principally from the USA, Japan and Italy). Since then the number of overnight stays has reached the seven million mark. Not included in the above figures are those for visitors who have been accommodated by relatives and friends.

Tourism

With over 50 million day-visitors annually, Munich is one of the leading destinations for tourists in Europe.

Communications

Local Transport

The U-Bahn (underground), S-Bahn (suburban railway), the Strassenbahn (trams) and almost all buses in Munich form part of the city's combined transport services (Münchner Verkehrs- und Tarifverband). Timetables are integrated. On weekdays the number of passengers carried by the MVV transport undertaking greatly exceeds 650,000.

At present the U-Bahn covers a total network of 69km/15 miles; 15km/9 miles are under construction and a further 17km/10½ miles are in the planning stage. The first line (U 6) was opened in 1971. It runs in a north–south direction and at Marienplatz connects with the S-Bahn. For the Olympic Games in 1971 the "Olympia Line" to the Olympic Centre was opened. Since 1980 there has been a line from the Olympic Centre to Perlach, via the Main Station. Two new lines from the Main Station were completed in 1983, one to Rotkreuzplatz and the other to Westpark where the International Horticultural Exhibition was held. Meanwhile a line has been opened which provides speedy communication between the west end through the inner city to Arabella Park in Bogenhausen.

The S-Bahn network, which serves the area in all directions, has a total length of some 410km/254 miles. Its nucleus is the 4.2km/22½ mile long tunnel from the Main Station right through the Old Town to the East Station, with connections to the U-Bahn (Marienplatz, Hauptbahnhof) and to the tramway network (Stachus). 40 of the 135 S-Bahn stations are within the city area. A connection to the new airport has been completed and further extensions are in progress.

The new ICE train in Munich Main Station

In the area of the most important S- and U-Bahn stations there is parking for 13,000 cars and 24,000 bicycles.

In the near future modern buses, with low gangways and ramps for wheelchairs will replace the existing fleet.

Hauptbahnhof

The main station of Munich is a junction for international, national and regional services. Munich can be reached by direct trains from all the more important European cities. Since 1991 the ICE high-speed train has been running on the route between Munich, Stuttgart, Frankfurt-am-Main and Hamburg.

Airport

The new Munich Franz-Josef-Strauss International Airport, opened in 1992, is situated 30km/18 miles north-east of the city centre in the Erdinger Moos. It has two runways, each 4km/2½ miles long and offers direct services to and from the principal European capitals and connections to most international routes. Up to 14 million passengers can be dealt with annually at the new airport. Munich airport holds third place in Germany for the number of arrivals. More than two dozen airlines and some 80 charter companies provide weekly services to all parts of the world.

Motorways
(Autobahnen)

Munich can be reached on motorways from every direction.
A 8 Stuttgart (west; E 52)
A 8 Rosenheim, Salzburg (east; E 45/52)
A 9 Nuremberg, (north; E 45)
A 95 Garmisch-Partenkirchen (E 533), branch A 952 to Starnberg; south
A 96 Gilching – Unterpfaffenhofen (E 54; to the Ammersee)
A 99 Part of ring motorway, connecting motorways to Nuremberg and
   Salzburg

National
highways

B 2 Fürstenfeldbruck–Augsburg–Donauwörth/Weilheim–Garmisch-
   Partenkirchen
B 11 Landshut/Deggendorf/Wolfratshausen–Mittenwald
B 12 Mühldorf–Passau/Landsberg–Kempten
B 13 Ingolstadt–Eichstadt/Bad Tölz–Sylvensteinspeicher
B 304 Wasserbur–Traunstein
B 388 Vilsbiburg–Eggenfelden

Famous People

Albrecht (Albert) V
(29.2.1528–
24.10.1579)

Duke Albert I, the Magnificent, reigned from 1550. A resolute opponent of the Reformation, he summoned the Jesuits to Munich to restore the Catholic faith in the city. With his Kumquat (cabinet of art) and Antiquarium (see A–Z, Residenz), the first museums in Germany, he established the reputation of Munich as a city of art and culture.

Egid Quirin Asam
(1.9.1692–
29.4.1750)
Cosmos Damian
Asam
28.9.1686–
10.5.1739)

The Asam brothers, Egid Quirin, sculptor, stucco artist, painter and architect, and Cosmos Damian, painter and architect, were the founders and principal representatives of the Bavarian Rococo school.
Both studied in Rome and were influenced by Bernini, and between them they created the interiors of many Munich churches – the Church of the Holy Ghost, the two churches of St Anne, Trinity Church, the Asam Church and St Mary's in Thalkirchen.
Visitors to Munich can still see the house occupied by Egid Quirin Asam, with his rich stucco ornamentation on the façade.

François de
Cuvilliés the
Elder (1695–
1768)

François de Cuvilliés, a native of Hainaut (which then belonged to Austria) and a dwarf – indeed he began his career as Duke Maximilian Emanuel's court dwarf – was the greatest architect and decorator of the South German Rococo. After receiving a thorough training in Paris he became Court Architect in Munich in 1725. His principal works are the Cuvilliés Theatre in the Residenz, the Amalienburg and the façade of the Theatinerkirche. His son, François de Cuvilliés the Younger, was also an architect in Munich.

Rudolf Diesel
(18.3.1958–
29.9.1913)

Rudolf Christian Carl Diesel, who was born in Paris, studied in Munich at the Technical University and at first worked in the field of refrigeration. The high-pressure combustion engine, named after Diesel and patented by him, is self-igniting with a particularly high thermo-dynamic working temperature and economical fuel consumption.
Rudolf Diesel also spent the last years of his life in Munich. In 1901 he had a fine villa built in the elegant suburb of Bogenhausen by the celebrated architect Max Littmann.
Diesel was drowned, in mysterious circumstances, during a sea crossing from Antwerp to Harwich.

Albert Einstein
(14.3.1879–
18.4.1955)

Born in Ulm but brought up in Munich, Albert Einstein settled in Switzerland in 1894 and became a Swiss citizen in 1901. He was a professor at the Universities of Zurich and Prague and at the Prussian Academy of Science.
After the Nazis seized power he resigned his academic posts in Germany and emigrated to the USA, remaining there until his death. Much of his work revolutionised modern physics, in particular his Theory of Relativity (1914–16). In 1916 he received the Nobel Prize for Physics. Although he was a lifelong convinced pacifist he gave a warning after the Second World War of the dangers of nuclear weapons.

Elisabeth (Sissy)
(24.12.1837–
10.9.1898)

Elisabeth Eugenie Amalie, the second daughter of the Bavarian Duke Maximilian Joseph, was born in Munich. In 1854 she married the Emperor Franz Joseph I of Austria. "The beautiful girl from Munich" was greatly loved, especially in Hungary, a country of which she was particularly fond. Empress Sissy, as she was affectionately called by her subjects, did not take kindly to the restrictions of the court and often embarked on her travels. Count Andrássy, the Hungarian president at that time, made use of her popularity for political purposes.
In 1898 Empress Elizabeth was killed by an Italian anarchist. Her life has been the subject of several films.

Franz von Lenbach

Oscar von Miller

Carl Spitzweg

Friedrich von Gärtner was trained as an architect in Munich, and after a study tour in Italy, where he became familiar with the forms of classical architecture, he succeeded Leo von Klenze as architect reponsible for the development of the Ludwigstrasse in 1827 (though officially not appointed until 1832). An architect of the Romantic/Christian school, he achieved a synthesis of neo-classical principals of proportion and historical forms (Romanesque, Byzantine, Gothic, Renaissance). His major works in Munich were the State Library, the Ludwigstrasse, the University, the Feldherrnhalle and the Siegestor.

Friedrich von Gärtner (10.12.1792– 21.4.1847)

After a period of training under Giovanni da Bologna in Florence, Hubert Gerhard worked as a sculptor in bronze in Augsburg, Munich and Innsbruck. As the principal representative of the South German school of bronze sculpture about 1660, he played a leading part in the development of sculpture from Mannerism to Early Baroque. He created the figure of St Michael and the dragon on the façade of St Michael's Church and the figure of the Virgin as Patroness of Bavaria on the Mariensäule in the Marienplatz.

Hubert Gerhard (c. 1550–1620)

Hans Krumper, a native of Weilheim in Upper Bavaria and a pupil of Hubert Gerhard, worked at the Bavarian court as a sculptor in bronze, interior decorator and architect from 1592. Influenced by Dutch and Italian Mannerism, he played a major part in the development of an independent school of Early Baroque sculpture in southern Germany. His principal works were the figure of the Virgin as Patroness of Bavaria on the façade of the Residenz, the Wittelsbach Fountain in the Residenz, the tomb of Ludwig the Bavarian in the Frauenkirche and the Temple in the Hofgarten.

Hans Krumper (c. 1570–1634)

Franz von Lenbach, as the leading portrait painter of the Gründerzeit (the period of rapid economic development in the early 1870s), was a dominant figure in the artistic life of Munich during the latter part of the 19th century. His palatial villa now houses the Municipal Gallery (see A–Z, Lenbachhaus).

Franz von Lenbach (13.12.1836– 6.5.1904)

The son of the culture loving King Maximilian I, Joseph became ruler of Bavaria in 1825. King Ludwig I was a supporter of the very liberal Bavarian constitution of 1818. Full of determination he carried out the reconstruction of the royal capital of Munich which was intended to become an important metropolis. In 1826 he moved the provincial university from Landshut to Munich. With great sympathy he furthered the struggle for freedom by the Greeks, who were ruled by his son Otto.
After 1830 his policies revealed a backwards-looking tendency and his attachment to the dancer Lola Montez was regarded with suspicion. Her elevation to the rank of Countess of Landsberg in 1847 caused a crisis in the

Ludwig I King of Bavaria (25.6.1796– 29.2.1868)

Famous People

government of Bavaria. The affair with Lola Montez and the confusion of the March Revolution of 1848 led to the abdication of Ludwig I.

**Ludwig II
King of Bavaria
(25.8.1845–
13.6.1886)**

Born in Schloss Nymphenburg and brought up in Schloss Hohensch-wangau, he was from childhood fascinated by German legends. His first contact with Richard Wagner's "Lohengrin" was a landmark for his future. Ludwig II, King of Bavaria from 1864, was an enthusiastic admirer and patron of the composer of romantic operas. Shielded from the outside world, the king had a passion for building, and the "fairytale" castles of Neuschwanstein, Linderhof and Herrenchiemsee were constructed at great expense, far from the Bavarian capital. Increasing signs of mental disorder led to the certification of the king and the Prince Regent Luitpold took over responsibility for affairs of state. Ludwig was taken to Schloss Berg on the Starnberg Lake, where in unexplained circumstances he and his physician Dr Gudden were drowned.

**Thomas Mann
(6.6.1875–
12.8.1955)**

The author Thomas Mann was born in Lübeck and came with his family to Munich after the death of his father. In 1894 he became a trainee with a Munich insurance company. From 1898 to 1899 he was the editor of the satirical magazine "Simplicissimus". He married in 1905 and lived in Munich until 1933. Here he developed into one of the most celebrated German storytellers, receiving the Nobel Prize for Literature in 1929.
He had great problems with the emerging National Socialists and in 1933 did not return from a lecture tour. He then went to live in southern France and later in Switzerland. While abroad he protested against the power-grabbing Nazis. In 1938 his essays entitled "Europe, Beware" were published. In 1939 he went to the USA as a visiting professor and acquired American citizenship in 1944. After the war he visited Germany in 1949 where he was to receive the Goethe Prizes from the cities of Frankfurt-am-Main and Weimar. He finally returned for good to Europe in 1952 and in 1954 settled at Kilchberg on Lake Zurich.

**Oskar von Miller
(7.5.1855–
9.4.1934)**

The Munich engineer Oskar von Miller was a pioneering inventor and organiser in the field of power production (Walchensee hydro-electric station, Bayernwerk power station). In 1882 he achieved the first transmission of electric power in the world (from Miesbach to Munich). In 1903 he founded the German Museum.

**Lola Montez
(25.8.1818–
17.1.1861)**

Lola Montez, the daughter of a Scottish officer and a Creole mother, was born in Limerick in Ireland. During an adventurous life as a dancer she came to Munich, where she succeeded in gaining the favour of King Ludwig I. Her influence over the king became stronger and stronger, and in 1847 he made the "Bavarian Pompadour" Countess of Landsberg. The entire Bavarian cabinet resigned in protest. In 1848 Lola Montez was banished. His attachment to Lola was one of the reasons why the king was forced to abdicate in 1848.

**Carl Orff
(10.7.1895–
29.3.1982)**

Born in Munich, the composer Carl Orff spent the greater part of his life in his native city, working successfully as a composer, conductor and music teacher.
In 1924 he founded, together with Dorothee Günther, a school for gymnastics, rhythm and artistic dance. He devised new theories of teaching music and concerned himself with the creation of a new percussion orchestra, in which simple instruments, such as drums, xylophone, etc., played a leading role. He was also concerned with the therapeutic power of music.
His best-known musical work is "Carmina Burana", a suite first performed in 1937, which is based on medieval satirical songs and dances.

**Jan Polack
(1435–1519)**

A native of Cracow, Jan Polack came to Munich about 1470 and became civic painter, creating numerous frescoes and altar-pieces. He ranks as the most important Munich painter of the Late Gothic period. Among his surviving works are the paintings for the old High Altar of St Peter's Church,

Richard Strauss *Empress Elisabeth* *Lola Montez*

the altar-pieces in the chapel of Blutenburg Castle and the wall-paintings in the Pippinger Kirchl.

Carl Spitzweg, a native of Munich, was originally a pharmacist but taught himself to paint and in 1836 became a member of the Munich Artists' Union. He painted landscapes, but is best known for the pictures in which he depicted in irony and mockery the foolishness, naïvety and narrow-mindedness of the good Munich townsfolk of his day, and the serene world of the Biedermeier period. In 1840 he began to work as an illustrator for the humerous journal "Fliegende Blätter". One of his best-known pictures "The Poor Poet" is in the Neue Pinakothek.

Carl Spitzweg (1808–85)

Straub was born in Swabia but received much of his education in Vienna where he became acquainted with the Austrian Baroque style. From 1736 he worked in Munich as Court Sculptor. He created tabernacles, altars and pulpits in the Rococo style and later under the influence of the Renaissance. However, his forte was wood-carving; like Ignaz Günther he is considered a leading Munich sculptor of the 18th century.

Johann Baptist Straub (25.6.1704– 15.7.1784)

The composer and conductor Richard Strauss, one of the leading exponents of German Late Romanticism, was born in Munich and from 1886 to 1898 was Kapellmeister (musical director) of the city. Then he became Court Kapellmeister and later General Director of Music in Berlin. With F. Schalk he conducted at the Vienna State Opera from 1919 until 1924. As a composer and guest conductor he worked with almost all the important European orchestras. His most famous symphonic works are: "Don Juan" (1889), "Salome" (1905), "Elektra" (1908), "Der Rosenkavalier" (1911) and "Ariadne auf Naxos" (1912). His earliest opera "Guntram" received its first performance in Munich.

Richard Strauss (11.6.1864– 8.9.1949)

Born in Italy, the son of a Flemish painter, Sustris brought Dutch and Italian Mannerism to Munich where he worked as a painter, decorator and architect. In 1580 he became "Artistic Director" to the court of King William V. He designed the Grottenhof (grotto court) in the Residenz, the Jesuit college, now known as the Old Academy, and played an important part in the construction of St Michael's Church.

Friedrich Sustris (c. 1540–92)

Karl Valentin (real name Valentin Ludwig Frey) was in his day famous throughout German-speaking countries. A "character" in Munich, his performances, generally accompanied by his partner Liesl Karlstadt, in cabarets, small theatres and inns were comical, droll and even absurd. His puns, sketches and extemporary comedy as well as his critical comments on contemporary topics are legendary. Even Bertolt Brecht was

Karl Valentin (4.6.1882– 9.2.1948)

impressed by Valentin's nonsensical logic. Karl Valentin films are still very popular.

Numerous mementoes of Valentin can be found in the Valentin Museum (see A–Z, Isartor).

Richard Wagner
(22.5.1813–
13.2.1853)

Born in Leipzig, Richard Wagner grew up in Dresden. After leaving school he studied and worked as an orchestral and choral director. In 1843 he returned to Dresden and was appointed Hofkapellmeister (director of music at the court) for life. Because of his implication in the May uprising in 1849 he was forced to leave Dresden. During his time in that city the first performances of "Rienzi" (1842), the "Flying Dutchman" (1843) and "Tannhäuser" (1845) took place. Also at this time Wagner laid the foundations for his controversial theoretical writings.

In 1864 he found in King Ludiwig II of Bavaria a great patron who called him to Munich. One year later "Tristan and Isolde" received its first performance in the Bavarian capital. After tension with the Bavarian cabinet the great composer left Munich and went to Tribschen near Lucerne which was to be his permament residence until 1872. King Ludwig II continued to support him. In 1868 the first performance of Wagner's "Die Meistersinger von Nürnberg" was given in Munich.

In 1872 Wagner inaugurated the Bayreuth Festival with the production of "The Ring of the Nibelungen".

Enrico Zucalli
(c. 1642–
8.3.1724)

Born in Switzerland, Enrico Zucalli was one of the most important representatives of Italian Baroque in Bavaria. From 1673 he worked in Munich as Court Architect. He completed the Theatinerkirche and from 1680 he was largely engaged in the decoration of the new Residenz. Among his other noteworthy masterpieces are: Schloss Lustheim, the sketch for the new Schloss Schleissheim and the Palais Porcia (later rebuilt by Cuvilliés).

History of Munich

First evidence of human settlement	New Stone Age
Celtic settlement	500–15 B.C.
Bavarian settlement in the Munich area (hence place-names ending in -ing, such as Pasing, Sendling, Schwabing, Aubing (all now districts of Munich).	From A.D. 530
Monks from Tegernsee settle on the banks of the Isar. Their settlement is called "Munichen" (at the monk's place). The origin of the town is still recalled in the coat of arms of Munich, which depicts a monk in a black habit edged with gold.	10th–11th c.
Foundation of a town by the Guelf duke Henry the Lion. The Duke of Saxony and Bavaria destroys the Bishop of Freising's toll-bridge downstream from the town and in its place builds a bridge and establishes a market and a mint at the monkish settlement of Munichen, protecting them with a circuit of walls.	1158
Henry the Lion outlawed by the emperor. Bavaria passes into the hands of the Wittelsbachs.	1180
Munich becomes the Wittelsbachs' capital.	1255
Munich is capital of the empire.	1314–47
St Peter's Church is built	1368
The first buildings of the Residenz are erected.	1385
The guilds revolt against the patricians	End of 14th c.
Munich suffers several disastrous fires.	15th c.
Duke Albrecht IV enacts the "Preu Aid" (Munich purity law). Good Munich beer may only be produced from barley, hops and water.	1487
Munich becomes the capital of Bavaria	1505
Munich is the principal base of the Counter-Reformation.	1563
The Hofbräuhaus is built	1589
Foundation of the Catholic League	1609
Thirty Years' War. Munich is fortified. In 1632 the town has to yield to King Gustavus Adolfus of Sweden. The last encounter of arms of the war takes place in 1648 between Allach and Dachau.	1618–48
A third of the population dies of plague	1634
The Theatiner Church and Nymphenburg Palace are built.	1663
Munich receives a post station.	1664
Munich is occupied by Austrian troops during the War of the Spanish Succession. Setting up of an imperial administration under a governor (Statthalter).	1704–14

History of Munich

Dec. 25th 1705	A rising by Bavarian peasants is bloodily repressed just outside Munich
1721	Execution of the last witch
1742	Munich is de jure the imperial capital. Occupation by Austria.
1789	The English Garden is laid out.
1791	Considerable parts of the town walls are pulled down.
1800	The French occupy the town.
1805	Napoleon marches into the town as an ally.
1806	Establishment of the Kingdom of Bavaria. Munich becomes capital of a much enlarged state with a rigidly centralised government. In the following decades large-scale extensions of the town take place; the Maxvorstadt, Ludwigvorstadt and Isarvorstadt districts are developed.
1810	The first October Festival takes place, celebrating the marriage of Crown Prince Ludwig and Princess Therese of Sachsen-Hildburghausen.
1816	Treaty of Munich. By cession and allocation of territory the Bavarian state attains approximately the size it is today.
1818	Munich becomes the seat of the Bavarian State Council and of the newly created bishopric of München-Freising.
1826	Munich becomes a university town.
1839	The Russian Czar Nicholas visits Munich. Opening of the railway from Munich to Lochhausen.
1846	The population reaches 100,000.
1857	The Munich "white sausage" is created.
1866	Bavaria takes the side of Austria against Prussia. There are further political disputes in Munich.
1867	The new Rathaus (town hall) is built.
1873	A severe epidemic of cholera breaks out in the town.
1876	The first trams run in Munich.
1879	The Munich professional fire-brigade is formed.
End of the 19th c.	Industrialisation does not come fully into force until the end of the 19th c. It causes a massive influx of workers from the country districts. New suburbs arise (e.g. Haidhausen), and others are extended.
Turn of the century	Georg Hirth publishes the magazine "Die Jugend", which is to give its name to the German Jugendstil (Art Nouveau). At the turn of the century Munich becomes one of the centres of this art form.
1900	After Berlin and Hamburg, Munich is the third largest German city, with over 500,000 inhabitants. Foundation of FC München Bayern, a football club which is soon to become the largest German sporting union. Lenin lives in the town until 1902 and edits periodicals.
1905	The Gau Südbayern of the German motorcycle union is founded; this forms the origin of the present-day ADAC (the German equivalent of the British AA).

First World War. Munich is attacked by French aircraft. 1914–18

Beginning in Munich of the German November Revolution by Kurt Eisner. 1918
Creation of the Free State of Bavaria.

Kurt Eisner is shot. The anarchistic, then communist soviet republic is 1919
ruthlessly crushed by imperial troops.

First mass meeting of the National Socialist German Workers' Party 1920
(NSDAP).

Attempted Nazi putsch, March to the Feldherrnhalle. 1923

Inauguration of the Deutsches Museum 1925

In Dachau the first concentration camp on German soil is constructed. 1933

Munich is the "Capital of the Movement". 1935–45

Second World War. The first air attack on Munich occurs as early as 1940, 1939–45
and until 1945 there are another 70. Until 1945 more than 22,000 members
of the armed forces are killed or wounded. In addition 6632 civilians are
killed and some 10,000 are missing.
At the end of the war 82,000 dwellings have been destroyed.

On April 30th US troops march into the city. Dr Karl Scharnagl, a member of 1945
the CSU, is installed by the occupying forces as senior burgomaster

The presidential conference of German provinces breaks up; the repre- 1947
sentatives of the east zone withdraw early.

Thomas Wimmer becomes the new senior burgomaster. 1948

The population of Munich reaches the million mark. In the next few years 1957
several satellite towns are established.

Dr Hans Jochen Vogel is elected senior burgomaster. 1960
The 37th World Eucharistic Congress.

The city gets a modern U-Bahn (underground railway) and S-Bahn (subur- 1966–72
ban railway) system.

The foundation-stone for a new satellite town (Perlach) is laid. 1967

20th Summer Olympic Games in Munich. Arab terrorists attack the Israeli 1972
team in the Olympic Village, taking hostages; an attempt to free them on
Fürstenfeld military airfield fails.
Georg Kronawitter (SPG) becomes senior burgomaster. Opening of the
pedestrian zone in the city centre.

World football championship: In the final Germany defeats the Nether- 1974
lands 2:1.

Pope John Paul II visits Munich. 1980
The European Patent Office opens.
A bomb attack during the October Festival causes twelve deaths.

Opening of the Neue Pinakothek (art gallery). 1981

International Garden Exhibition. 1983

Georg Kronawitter is re-elected senior burgomaster. 1984

History of Munich

1985	The Gasteig Cultural Centre opens its doors.
1987	The pope canonises the Jesuit priest Rupert Mayer.
1989	Many emigrants from eastern Europe and people from the former German Democratic Republic settle in Munich.
1990	Georg Kronawitter becomes senior burgomaster for the third time.
1991	World figure-skating championships are held in Munich. A new railway-age begins in Munich (and Hamburg). On the route between Munich–Stuttgart–Frankfurt-am-Main–Hamburg the first regular ICE (high-speed trains) come into service.
1992	The new Franz-Josef-Strauss Airport comes into operation after decades of preliminary work and violent legal battles. Leading diplomats and specialists meet at the Munich world trade summit.

Munich in Quotations

When I got to know the people of Munich, who at first had seemed somewhat dull and blunt, then I learned to respect both the city and the people. The people are hospitable, charming. artistic, colourful and happy.
I arrived in the city in a carefree mood but left it with a heavy heart. In this city, where piety combines strangely with worldliness, where you think you can hear the gods of love giggling in the dark recesses of a church, the fragrant fresh Alpine air mingles with the soft enticing breezes coming from Italy.
(*c.* 1870)

Felix Philippi
(1851–1918)

The people of Munich are probably the most naïve in Germany, almost as naïve as the Parisians. This is also the reason why art prospers and thrives so well in Munich. Naïvety is the fertile soil of art and unaffectedness its first principle. Life is always the prototype of art. The joy of living, the joy of the people in themselves, everybody as uncritical as possible, trying to get the utmost personal pleasure from whatever they are doing, unconcerned about the opinions of other people or what others think of them, this is what makes Paris an inexhaustible source of new artistic ventures. Munich, with its beer, its not too noisy but nevertheless more highspirited carnival, its pretty girls who are so scrupulous in the slightest things and elegant in their appearance, all this reveals a great deal about Munich, but it would never occur to any of its citizens that they should behave like Parisians.

Frank Wedekind
(1864–1918)

Avenues of broad white houses,
Basking in the noontide glare; –
Streets, which foot of traveller shrink from,
As on hot plates shrinks the bear; –

Elsewhere lawns, and vista'd gardens,
Statues white and cool arcades,
Where at eve the German warrior
Winks upon the German maids; –

Such is Munish; – broad and stately,
Rich of hue, and firm of form;
But, towards the end of August,
Unequivocally *warm.*
Verses and Translations 1861

Charles Stuert
Calverley

Bavaria

Bavaria is too humid, too green and lush, and mountains *never* move – they are always there. They go all different tones and colours – but still, they are always there.
Letter to A. W. McLeod, May 1913

D. H. Lawrence
(1886–1930)

NEUHAUSEN
**MUNICH
(MÜNCHEN)**

250 m

©Baedeker

Kreittmayrstraße

Linprun-straße

Erzgießereistraße

Dachauer Straße

Gabelsberger-straße

Schelß-straße

heimer Str.

Augustenstraße

Theresien-straße

Heß-straße

straße

**Neue
Pinakothek**

Luisen-straße

straße

**Technical
University**

**Alte
Pinakothek**

**State Mi...
Coll...**

Nymphenburger Straße

Stiglmaier-platz

Brienner Str.

Lenbachhaus

Gabelsberger-

Karl-

Sandstraße

Dachauer Straße

Karl-

Augustenstraße

straße

straße

Glyptothek

Propyläen Königs-platz

**Music
Academy**

Arcis-straße

Barer Straße

straße

Mars-

straße

Rundfunk-pl. Mars-

straße

Seidl-straße

**Bavarian
Radio**

Augustenstraße

**State Antiques
Collection**

Brienner

Karolinen-platz

**Basilika
St. Bonifaz**

Meiserstraße

**Staatl.
Graphische
Sammlung**

Barer Straße

Max-Joseph-Str.

Straße

Arnulf-

Sophien-straße

Luisen-straße

Karl-straße

straße

Old
Botanical Garden

Barer straße

Otto-

**Wittels-
bach
Fountain**

Maximiliansplatz

Starnberger
Station

straße

Elisen-hof

Elisenstraße

**Triumphal
Arch**

Lenbach-platz

**Trini...
Chur...**

Prome...

Paul-Heyse-Unterführung

Main Station

Prielmayerstr.

**Palace of
Justice**

Karlsplatz
(Stachus)

**Carmelite
Church**

Maxburgstraße

Löwe...

Holzkirchner
Station

straße

Karlstor

Neu-

**Bürger-
saal**

St. Michael

Frau...
pla...

Bayer-

Neuhauser-

Herzog-

**German Hunting
Museum**

**Frauenk...
...Cathe...**

Laufing...

Schwanthaler-

Heyse-Straße

Goethe-

straße

straße

Sonnen-straße

Herzogspitalstraße

Wilhelm-

**Deutsches
Theater**

**St. Anna
(Damenstifts-
kirche)**

Farber...
...graben

St. Paul

Landwehr-

Josephspitalstr.

**Holy Cross
Church**

**St.-Johann-
Nepomuk
(Asamkirche)**

**Munich
Mus...**

Pettenkoferstraße

Georg-
Hirth-Pl.

Paul-Straße

Schiller-

Mathildenstraße

straße

Sendlinger-
Tor-Pl.

Sendl.

Sendl. Tor

Ober-

anger

St.-Ja...

Pettenkofer-

straße

University

Nußbaumstraße

**St Matthew's
Church**

Roßmarkt

St. Ja...

Bavaria ring

Kaiser-straße

Beethoven-platz

Hospitals

Lindwurmstraße

Müller-str.

Blumen-

Unter-

str.

**Theresien-
wiese**

Beethoven-
Ludwig-Pl.

Goethe-

Herzog-Heinrich-

Maistraße

Augsburger Str.

straße

Fraunhofer-str.

Thalkirchner str.

Frauenlobstr.

St. Stephan

Pestalozzistr.

Holzstr.

Hans-
Sachs-Str.

Goethe-
pl.

Schloß Nymphenburg

Trade Fair Grounds

University
Geschw.-Scholl-
Platz
Prof.-Huber-
Platz

Monopteros

Turkenstraße
Amalienstraße
Ludwigs-straße
Schellingstraße
Königinstraße
Kaulbachstraße

St. Ludwig
(Ludwigskirche)

E n g l i s c h e r

Bavarian State
Library

Schwabinger Bach
Elsbach

Haupt-
staatsarchiv

lark's
rch

G a r t e n

- v. - Miller- Ring

Von- der- Tann- Straße

Japanese
Tea House

Königinstraße

State Prehistoric
Collection

Oettingen-straße
Emil-Riedel-Str.

Prinz-Carl-
Palais

Galeriestraße

Haus der Kunst
(State Gallery of
Modern Art)

Bavarian
National
Museum

Odeons-
platz

Neue
Staatskanzlei

Prinzregenten-

Lerchenfeld-

Neue
Sammlung

str.
Widenmayer-

Schack-
galerie

ner
Straße
der Opfer
tionalsoz.

Theatiner-
kirche

Hofgarten

Krieger-
denkmal

F.-J.-Strauß-Ring
Seitzstr.
Unsöld- straße
Oettingen-straße
Liebigstraße

Salvator-
kirche

ors-traße
sing-
s

Feldherrn-
halle

straße

Liebigstraße

Liebigstraße

Residenz

St. Anna
Pfarr-
kirche

Residenz-
theater

Kloster-
kirche

Thiersch-
platz

Max-
Joseph-
Pl.
National-
theater

Maximilian-

straße

Marien-
hof
Neues
Rathaus

Alter
Hof

Schauspielhaus
(Kammerspiele)

Maximilianstraße

Stern-

Widenmayer-

Maximilians-

Marien-
atz

Altes
Rathaus

Hofbräuhaus

Orlandostr.

Karlstraße

Museum of
Ethnology
Knöbelstr.

Max-
monument

Maximiliansbrücke

Maxi-
millaneum

St.
Peter

Heilig-Geist-K.

Tal

Hochbrücken-
straße

Knöbelstr.

Thomas-

Thierschstraße

LEHEL

Alpenvereins-
haus

anlagen

Viktualien-
markt

Isartor

Isartor-
platz

Thierschstraße

St. Lukas

str. Frauen-

Rumford-
str.

Zweibrücken-straße

Steinsdorf-

Maximiliansbrücke

Rum-
bach-
Reichen-fordstraße
bachplatz

Klenzestr.

Patent Office

Ludwigsbrücke
Rosen-

Innere Wiener Str.

Müllersches
Volksbad
Am
Gasteig
Keller-straße

Preysingstraße

Gärtner-
platz

Baader-
platz

Forum für Technik

Cultural
Centre

Theater
am
Gärtner-
platz

European Patent
Office

Bader-

Corneliusstraße

Erhardt-

Deutsches
Museum

Isar

Zeppelinstraße

HAIDHAUSEN

———☐——— S-Bahn   ———○——— U-Bahn

Sights from A to Z

Suggestions for making the most of a short visit to Munich will be found under the heading "Sightseeing" in the Practical Information section of this guide. — Short visits

Suggestions for making the most of a short visit to Munich will be found under the heading "Sightseeing" in the Practical Information section of this guide.

Short visits

Akademie der Bildenden Künste (Academy of Art)   42 56

The Academy of Art, which provides training in painting, graphic art, sculpture and art education, lies at the Siegestor.
This extended range of buildings (230m/755ft in length) with projecting wings, was built between 1874 and 1885 by Gottfried von Neureuther, in the style of the Italian High Renaissance. In a manner typical of the architecture of the Gründerzeit (the period of rapid expansion in the early 1870s) the design is concerned only to achieve an effect of imposing grandeur on the main (south) front.

Location
Akademiestr. 2

U-Bahn
U3, U6
(Universität)

Allerheiligenkirche am Kreuz (All Saints Church at the Cross)   41 54

All Saints, formerly the cemetery church of St Peter's parish, was built about 1478 by Jörg von Halspach (known as Ganghofer), architect of the Frauenkirche. Secularised after the closing of the cemetery in 1789, it is now the church of Munich's Ukrainian Catholic community.
The Gothic building, oriented to the south, is constructed of brick without plaster or other facing. The semicircular apse dates from the Baroque remodelling of the church in 1620.
Notable features of the interior: painting on the high altar, "The Virgin appearing to St Augustine" by Johann Rottenhammer (17th c.); tabernacle of the school of J. B. Straub (1770); fragment of a Gothic fresco of Christ in a mandorla above the east doorway (now walled up); wooden Crucifix by Hans Leinberger (1520) above the west doorway; monument ("Raising of Lazarus") to the banker Goetz by Hans Krumper (1627).

Location
Kreuzstr. 10

U-Bahn
U1, U2, U3, U6
(Sendlinger Tor)

Alte Akademie (Old Academy)   41 54

In the heart of the Pedestrian Zone, adjoining Michaelskirche (see entry), is the Old Academy, a large complex surrounded by four courtyards. Now occupied by the Bavarian Statistical Office, this Renaissance building was erected between 1585 and 1597 for a Jesuit college and school.

After the expulsion of the Jesuits in 1773 it housed the Court Library and Archives (1774–1885), a school of painting and sculpture (hence the designation Academy) and, from 1826 to 1840, the University. Destroyed during the Second World War it was rebuilt in 1954.

Location
Neuhauser
Str. 51

S-Bahn
S1–S7
(Karlsplatz/Stachus)

U-Bahn U4, U5
(Karlsplatz Stachus)

**Alte Pinakothek (Old Picture Gallery)   41 55

The Alte Pinakothek, one of the world's largest and finest picture galleries, was built by Leo von Klenze between 1826 and 1836, replacing the older

Location
Barer Str. 27

◀ *A Munich landmark – the Theatiner Church*

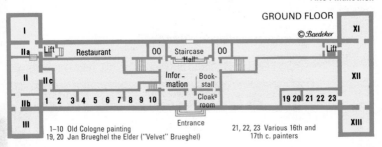

GROUND FLOOR

© Baedeker

1–10 Old Cologne painting
19, 20 Jan Brueghel the Elder ("Velvet" Brueghel)
21, 22, 23 Various 16th and 17th c. painters

I Old Bavarian and Frankish masters before Dürer
II South Tyrolean painting

IIa Late Gothic and Early Renaissance portraits
IIb B. Strigel

III Swabian painting
XI, XII, XIII Various 16th and 17th c. masters

gallery by the Hofgarten which had become too small for the steadily increasing Royal Collection. The building was so badly damaged by air attack in 1944–45 that demolition was contemplated; but between 1953 and 1963 it was restored, and the gallery's treasures, which had been stored elsewhere for safety, could again be put on display.

Opening times: Tue.–Sun. 9.15am–4.30pm; also 7–9pm Tue. and Thur. Entrance fee (Sun. and public holidays free)

U-Bahn
U2 (Königsplatz)

Tram
18 (Schellingstr.)

Bus
53 (Schellingstr.)

This "masterpiece of architectural proportion" (Wölfflin) is modelled on the Renaissance palaces of Venice. It was the largest gallery built in the first half of the 19th c. and as such became the model for others in Rome and Brussels. It is a massive structure, 127m/417ft long with short side wings (37m/121ft from front to rear). The 24 statues (by Ludwig Schwanthaler) of famous painters on the south front and the frescoes (by Peter Cornelius) in the interior were destroyed in the wartime bombing.

Further restoration work was carried out in the late 1970s.

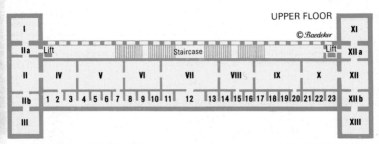

UPPER FLOOR

© Baedeker

I, IIa Old Dutch and Flemish painting
II, IIb, III Old German painting
IV Florentine early Renaissance
V Venetian painting
VI Anthonis van Dyck
VII, VIII Peter Paul Rubens
IX Dutch painting
X Italian Baroque painting
XI, XII, XIIIa French painting of the 17th c.
XIIb Venetian veduta
XIII Spanish painting

1–6 Venetian 16th c. painting
7 Anthonis van Dyck
8 Peter Paul Rubens
9 Van Dyck, Rubens
10 Adriaen Brouwer
11 German painters c. 1600
12 Flemish painters
13–15 Dutch painters
16 Rembrandt van Rijn
17–22 Dutch painters
23 Italian Baroque painting

◀ In the Pinakothek – Titian: "Emperor Karl V"

Alte Pinakothek

The Old Pinakothek, rebuilt after heavy damage by bombing

Paintings

All European schools of painting from the Middle Ages to the beginning of the 19th c. are represented in the Alte Pinakothek. The nucleus of the collection was a series of historical pictures painted for Duke Wilhelm IV of Bavaria about 1530.

The famous pictures by Dürer were acquired by the Elector Maximilian I (1623–51). During the 18th c. valuable collections were acquired from Düsseldorf, Mannheim and Zweibrücken, including works by French and Dutch painters (Rubens, Van Dyck). Altarpieces came from secularised churches and religious houses. The collection was further extended by purchases in the 19th and 20th c.

A selection of the most notable works on the ground floor

Medieval German painting

15th/early 16th c. (I–III, 1–10):
Hans Balding-Grien, "Count Palatine Philipp"
Master of St Veronica, "St Veronica with the Veil"
Stefan Lochner, "Mary with the Infant Jesus by a Grassy Bank"

Historical pictures from the collection of Duke Wilhelm IV of Bavaria and his wife Jacobaea of Baden, including Hans Schöpfer's "Story of Suzanna".

Flemish and Dutch painting

16th/17th c. (XII–XII, 19–23):
Cornelius van Dalem, "Landscape with a Farm"
Marinus van Reymerswaele, "A Tax Collector and his Wife"
Jan Brueghel the Elder, "Bunch of Flowers"
Pieter Brueghel the Elder, "Land of Cockayne", "Head of an Old Peasant Woman"

Some notable works on the upper floor

15th/early 16th c. (I–IIa):
Roger van der Weyden, Altar of the Three Kings (Columba Altar)
Dirck Bouts, winged altar, the "Pearl of Brabant"
Hans Memling, "The Seven Joys of Mary"
Jan Grossaert, "Danae"
Lucas van Leyden, "Madonna and Child with St Magdalena and a Patron"

Medieval Dutch and Flemish Painting

15th/16th c. (II–III):
Matthias Grünewald, "SS Erasmus and Maurice"
Albrecht Altendorfer, "Alexander's Battle" (see also historical paintings on the ground floor, 4–7)
Albrecht Dürer, "The Four Apostles", "Self-Portrait"
Lucas Cranach the Younger, "Venus and Cupid"
Michael Pacher, Altarpiece of the Four Fathers of the Church

Medieval German Painting

14th–18th c. (IV, V, X, XIIb, 1–6, 23):
Giotto, "The Last Supper" (fragment of an altar panel with various scenes from the life of Christ), after 1306
Leonardo da Vinci, "Virgin and Child", *c.* 1436
Raphael "Madonna Tempi", *c.* 1507
Sandro Botticelli, "The Mourning of Christ", after 1490
Fra Filippo Lippi "Virgin and Child", *c.* 1465
Titian, "Crowning with Thorns", "The Emperor Charles V"
Tiepolo "Adoration of the Magi", 1753

Italian Painting

16th/17th c. (11):
Adam Elsheimer "The Flight into Egypt", "Troy Burning"

German painting

17th c. (VI–VIII, 7–10):
Adriaen Brouwer, "Hearing"
Jakob Jordaens, "Satyr with Peasant"
Jan Silberrechts, "Women Sleeping in a Pasture"
Van Dyck, "Rest on the Flight"
Rubens, "Rubens and Isabella Brant in the Honeysuckle Arbour" (wedding picture), "Rape of Leukippos's Daughter", "Meleager and Atalante"

Flemish painting

17th c. (IX, 13–22):
Frans Hals, "Willem van Heythuysen"
Jan van Goyen, "Village by the River"
Abraham van Beyeren "Still life with Lobster"
Rembrandt, "Self-Portrait", "Passion Cycle for Prince Frederik Henrik of Orange"
Jacob van Ruisdale, "Forest with Rising Storm"

Dutch painting

17th and 18th c. (XI–XIIa):
Claude Lorrain, "Seaport with Rising Sun", "Banishment of Hagar"
Nicolas Poussin, "The Mourning of Christ"
François Boucher, "Madame Pompadour"
Jean Baptiste Chardin, "Servant girl scraping vegetables"

French painting

17th c. (XIII):
El Greco, "Disrobing of Christ"
Velázquez, "Young Spanish Nobleman"
Bartolomé Estebán Murillo, "Boys eating Melons and Grapes"

Spanish painting

Alter Botanischer Garten (Old Botanic Garden)   41 54/55

From 1814 to 1909 this park, just north of the Old Law Courts (see Karlsplatz), was the municipal Botanic Gardens. A whole range of trees, some of them quite exotic, are a reminder of its former glories. The area became a public park in 1935–37 since when it has provided an oasis of peace amid the rushing traffic of the city centre.

Location
Eisenstr./
Sophienstr.
(north-east of
the main railway
station)

Alter Hof

S-Bahn
S1–S7 (main
railway station,
Karlsplatz)

U-Bahn
(U1, U2, U4, U5
(main railway
station),
U4, U5
(Karlsplatz)

Neuer Botani-
sche Garten

The gardens were originally laid out in 1808–14 by the landscape gardener Ludwig von Sckell. The Neo-Classical gate in Lenbachplatz (see entry) was erected in 1812 by Joseph Emanuel Herigoyen. The Neptune Fountain (1935–37) was the work of Joseph Wackerle.

In 1854 a "Crystal Palace" was erected on the north side of the garden for the first international Industrial Exhibition.

The steel and glass structure – progressive for its day – was destroyed by fire in 1931. An exhibition of works by major German Romantics was lost at the same time.

See Botanischer Garten

---

*Alter Hof (Old Court) 42 54

Location
City centre (not
far north-east
of Marienplatz)

S-Bahn
S1–S7
(Marienplatz)

U-Bahn
U3, U6
(Marienplatz)

The Alter Hof, formerly also known as Ludwigsburg, was the first Munich residence of the Wittelsbach family (1253–1474). Built by Duke Ludwig II after the division of Bavaria (1255), its most brilliant period was in the reign of the Emperor Ludwig the Bavarian, who ruled the Holy Roman Empire from here between 1328 and 1347. By the end of the 14th c. the building had become too small, antiquated and unsafe, and the Dukes began to build a new fortified residence (see Residenz). From the 17th c. the Alter Hof was used only for administrative purposes; it is now occupied by a tax office. The handsome inner courtyard is open to the public, but not the interior. The four ranges of buildings surrounding the courtyard were much altered and enlarged in later centuries. At the beginning of the 19th c. St Lawrence's Chapel (Lorenzkapelle) in the north wing and the gate-tower at the south end were pulled down (though the tower was later rebuilt in its original form).

After the Second World War the whole building was restored. The lozenge

Alter Hof: window ornamentation . . .   *. . . and south tower*

pattern painted on the walls of the courtyard dates from the 15th c.; it was renewed in the 1960s following the uncovering of fragments of the original decoration in 1963.

A feature of particular interest is the beautiful Late Gothic oriel in the courtyard, known as the Affenturm (Monkey's Tower). Legend has it that a monkey from the Royal Menagerie carried the infant Prince Ludwig, later the Emperor Ludwig the Bavarian (1314–47), from his nursery and on to the pointed roof of the oriel, bringing him back safely only after much coaxing. During the summer the Alter Hof provides an impressive backcloth for open-air theatre and musical events.

Open-air theatre

---

*Altes Rathaus (Old Town Hall)   42 54

Munich's Gothic Town Hall, known since the 19th c. as the Old Town Hall, was built by Jörg von Halspack (known as Ganghofer) between 1470 and 1480 (an earlier building, the first town hall to stand on the east side of the present Marienplatz, is known to have been under construction in about 1310). After undergoing modification in accordance with the taste of the day in the Late Renaissance and Baroque periods, the Altes Rathaus was reconverted in the Gothic style in 1861–64. It was badly damaged during the Second World War, restoration beginning shortly afterwards. The archway and passage for pedestrians date from the 19th c.

Location
South-east side of Marienplatz

S-Bahn
S1–S7
(Marienplatz)

U-Bahn
U3, U6
(Marienplatz)

The 55m/180ft tower of the Old Town Hall, rising prominently in the south-east corner of the Marienplatz, was rebuilt in 1975 after its destruction by wartime bombing.

The Council Chamber served additionally as the meeting-place of the Estates, as a ballroom for Munich's patrician families, a dance-hall during the Shrovetide festivities and for civic receptions. It was also used by the Wittelsbach Dukes of Bavaria for state occasions.

The interior is a masterpiece of medieval design. It has a barrel-vaulted timber roof with decorated beams and golden stars, a frieze of coats of arms (1478) and the celebrated figures of Morisco dancers by Erasmus Grasser (originals in Municipal Musuem; see entry).

The small toy museum (Ivan Steiger Collection) now established in the Altes Rathaus tower has an interesting miniature railway and a variety of other toys including lead toys and pretty dolls and doll's houses. Open: daily 10am–5.30pm. Entrance fee.

Toy Museum

Amalienpassage   42 56

The Amalienpassage cuts through a block to the rear of the University, between Amalienstrasse and Türkenstrasse. It was constructed in 1975–77 by a group of architects following a new concept of urban planning: a grey and unattractive area to the rear of the street frontages was to be opened up, replanned and redeveloped for housing. Although at first the demolition of older property and its replacement by new building at high density met with some resistance, the Amalienpassage is now widely accepted as a successful example of the rehabilitation of the old city centre and has become a popular place of resort for the people of Munich, with shops, cafés and restaurants bringing animation to its three linked courts.

Location
Amalienstr.
87–89, Türkenstr. 84–88

U-Bahn
U3, U6
(Universität)

Arabellapark   45 55/56

Arabellapark, a commercial/industrial quarter at the northern end of the smart Bogenhausen district, was developed during the 1970s and 80s, creating some thousands of new jobs.

The highly distinctive Hypo-Haus, around which cluster other futuristic

Location
4km/2½ miles
north-east of
the city centre

Asamkirche

U-Bahn
U4
(Arabellapark)

Tram
18, 20
(Effnerplatz)

Bogenhausen   See entry

buildings clad in glass and eloxal, including branches of several large industrial concerns (e.g. Siemens), is now a dominant feature of the city's skyline.

Big hotel chains are also well represented in Arabellapark, their huge "concrete palaces" – some architecturally more successful than others – catering for tourists as well as for the many visiting business people.

Asamkirche (Asam Church) 41 54

Location
Sendlinger Str.
61

U-Bahn
U1, U2, U3, U6
(Sendlinger Tor)

This beautiful Rococo church, dedicated to St John of Nepomuk, was built between 1733 and 1746 by the brothers Cosmas Damian and Egid Quirin Asam and richly decorated with stucco ornament, stucco figures, frescoes and oil paintings. It was restored at great expense between 1975 and 1982. The church's narrow façade fits unobtrusively into the line of buildings in Sendlinger Strasse. The doorway is flanked by massive columns, and above it is a figure of St John of Nepomuk kneeling in prayer.

In the interior of the church, a wrought-iron grille (1776) separates the stucco figures of the saints from the long nave with its galleries and projecting cornice under the ceiling. On the ceiling is a magnificent fresco depicting the life of St John of Nepomuk by Cosmas Damian Asam (restored 1977).

The impressive twilight effect of the interior is created by its concealed windows. When, during restoration work in the 1970s, a large window was inserted in the choir and the church was flooded with light, there was a bitter controversy among art historians about the authenticity of the change, and in the end the authorities responsible for the conservation of historical monuments decided the window should be closed up.

The most notable feature of the interior is the high altar, enclosed by four twisted columns. On the altar is a glass shrine containing a wax figure of St John of Nepomuk. The altar in the gallery depicts the Trinity, with two angels in adoration. On the cornice above the high altar is God the Father,

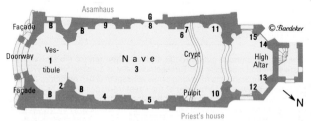

1 St Nepomuk's vision of the Virgin (ceiling fresco)
2 Zech epitaph by Ignaz Günter
3 Scenes from the life of St Nepomuk (ceiling fresco)
4 Presentation of the rosary to St Dominic (painting)

5 Adoration of the tongue relic (relief)
6 Crucifix with the sorrowing Madonna
7 Christ and Nicodemus (wall painting)
8 Christ driving out the money-changers (relief)
9 Guardian angel (painting)
10 Former Quirinus altar, statue of St Joseph

11 Former Egidius Chapel Statue of the Virgin
12 Statue of St John the Evangelist
13 Portrait of C. D. Asam
14 Portrait of E. Q. Asam

B Confessional
G Entrance to Crypt

Rich Rococo ornamentation in the Assam Church ▶

in a Papal tiara, bending over the Crucified Christ, with a dove representing the Holy Ghost in the aureole above.

Asam Haus

This 16th c. house was acquired in 1733 by Egid Quirin Asam, who decorated it with lavish stucco ornamentation, giving plastic form to the South German technique of *Lüftlmalerei* (painted decoration on the exterior walls of houses). The themes of the decoration are mankind's artistic activity and the sensuous world (lower half), and Heaven as conceived by Christianity and by classical antiquity (upper half).

Bavaria, Ruhmeshalle, Theresienwiese 39/40 53/54

N.B.

Beloved of the romantically-minded, the Theresienhöhe, with its great statue of Bavaria, and the Rumeshalle, is one of the Bavarian capital's most famous landmarks. At the foot of the Bavaria statue lies the Theresienwiese, venue of Munich's famous annual Oktoberfest (October festival).

*Bavaria Statue 39 53

Location
Theresienhöhe

U-Bahn
U4, U5
(Theresienwiese)

Opening times
Tue.–Sun.
10am–noon and
2–6pm

The colossal 18m/60ft-high statue of Bavaria, a female figure in the old German style, was modelled by the Munich artist Ludwig Schwanthaler and cast in bronze by Ferdinand von Miller in 1844–50. Weighing 792kg/1560cwt it is the largest bronze figure ever cast.

Bavaria stands clad in a long garment and a bearskin, her raised left hand holding a garland of oak leaves, her right hand a sword. Beside her sits a lion, the heraldic animal of Bavaria.

A flight of 126 steps leads up inside the statue to the head, from which there is an extensive view over the city.

*Ruhmeshalle 39 53

Location
Theresienhöhe

To the rear of the statue can be seen the Ruhmeshalle (Hall of Fame), an open Doric portico with two side wings, built by Leo von Klenze in 1843–53. It houses 80 busts of notable Bavarians superbly executed by the artist Ludwig Schwanthaler.

Theresienwiese, Oktoberfest 39/40 53/54

Location
South-west of
city centre

U-Bahn
U4, U5
(Theresienwiese),
U3, U6
(Goetheplatz,
Poccistr.)

Bus
31, 32

Extending from the foot of the Bavaria statue (see above) is the Theresienwiese (Therese Meadow) where, on October 17th 1810, horseraces were held in celebration of the marriage of Crown Prince Ludwig of Bavaria, later King Ludwig I, to Therese von Sachsen-Hildburghausen. It was these celebrations which gave rise to Munich's famous Oktoberfest, the biggest popular festival in the world, taking place every autumn.
In 1811 the horseracing was augmented by an agricultural show. Then in 1818 swings and rides made their appearance for the first time. From 1820 onwards numerous other attractions were added, including show booths, roundabouts, troupes of performing artists and the so-called "anatomical wonder". On September 26th 1980 a terrorist bomb claimed twelve lives (memorial at entrance).

**Oktoberfest

In terms of both the area covered and the number of visitors (about 6 million) the Munich Oktoberfest, held annually on the Theresienwiese (or "Wies'n" for short) at the end of September/beginning of October,

The "Bavaria" outside the Ruhmeshalle

At the October Festival

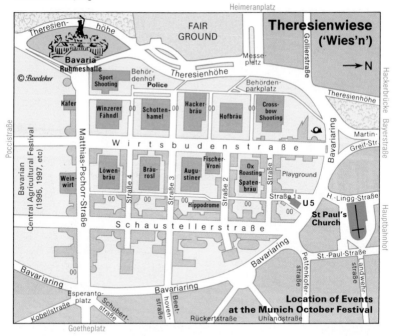

Location of Events
at the Munich October Festival

ranks as the biggest and best-known popular festival anywhere in the world. Preparations start months in advance with the erection of huge marquees and other facilities. Year after year a host of attractions – vast but welcoming beer tents, a fun-for-all show and great variety of pleasure booths, traditional swings and roundabouts, hurtling roller-coasters and breathtaking fairground rides, prove totally irresistible to foreigners and locals alike, irrespective of age-group. Swept along by the crowd they try their hand at everything, collecting in the process all manner of odd "trophies" and other curiosities. Amidst much merriment they have their fortunes told and enjoy the lights, the bustle and the noise. There is no opportunity to go hungry and even less to go thirsty, with traditional Hendl and Steckerlfische (grilled chicken and fish) in plentiful supply, washed down, naturally, with equally lavish quantities of German beer. Every year sees the establishment of a new Hendl-eating record!

---

*Schloss Blutenburg (Blutenburg Castle)   33 57

Location
Obermenzing,
Würmtal

S-Bahn
S2 (Obermenzing)

Bus
73, 75, 76

Pluedenburg (Blütenburg/Blossom Castle) was built on the banks of the Würm by Duke Albert II in 1438–39 as a hunting-lodge, replacing an older castle burned down in war. Its original defences included a ring wall, towers and a moat. After being destroyed during the Thirty Years' War it was again rebuilt in 1680–81 as a plain rectangular structure.
The castle now houses the International Youth Library, a collection of literature for children and young people in 110 languages, at present totalling some 400,000 volumes.

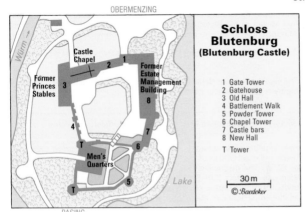

OBERMENZING

Schloss Blutenburg (Blutenburg Castle)

Castle Chapel

Former Estate Management Building

Former Princes Stables

Men's Quarters

1 Gate Tower
2 Gatehouse
3 Old Hall
4 Battlement Walk
5 Powder Tower
6 Chapel Tower
7 Castle bars
8 New Hall

T Tower

30 m

© Baedeker

Lake

PASING

The castle chapel (1488), dedicated to St Sigismund, is a unique jewel of Late Gothic architecture, both the building and its furnishings being preserved in their original form. The fragments of frescoes on the exterior walls give some idea of what the external painting (now lost) of Munich's Late Gothic churches was like.

Features of particular interest: altarpieces by Jan Polack (c. 1490); paintings on the High Altar (Christ as Judge and Baptism of Christ, to right; Coronation of Virgin, to left); wooden figures of the Twelve Apostles and

Blutenburg Madonna

Blutenburg Castle

the famous Blutenburg Madonna (beside the tabernacle) by the unidentified Master of the Blutenburg Madonna; stained glass (16 scenes, from Annunciation to Passion; Wittelsbach coats of arms) by Martin the Glazier.

Castle courtyard

A modern fountain in copper by G. J. Kroiss adorns the castle courtyard.

Master concerts

Throughout the year Schloss Blutenburg provides a venue for a series of highly regarded master concerts.

BMW (Bayersiche Motorenwerke/Bavarian Motor Works, Head Office) 40/41 58/59

Location
Dostlerstr.

Four gigantic silver cylinders soaring skywards above Munich's rooftops house the Head Offices of the Bayerische Motorenwerke AG, better known as BMW. The distinctive 99m/325ft-high building is the creation of the Viennese architect Karl Schwanzer. The cloverleaf arrangement of the towers around a central shaft allows novel exploitation of the work space on individual floors. At the foot of the skyscraper are the company's extensive vehicle works and multi-storey car parks.

*BMW Museum

Location
Petuelring 130

U-Bahn
U2, U3
(Petuelring)

Opening times
Daily 9am–5pm
Entrance until
4pm

Entrance fee

The BMW Museum is housed in a windowless silver-coloured concrete bowl, 41m/134ft in diameter, the effect of which is in striking counterpoint to the adjacent skyscraper and sprawling factory buildings.

The museum exhibition, re-modelled every few years by the well-known film designer Rolf Zehetbauer, is currently titled "Zeithorizont" (Time Horizon). By means of gently ascending ramps visitors re-enter the motoring world of yesterday. Almost every vehicle produced by this long-established automobile manufacturer is represented, from the "Dixi" – popular in the twenties – to

BMW Starmotor

the showy sports and racing models of the 1950s and 1960s, and the R 32 motor cycle of 1932 to the world record-breaking machine of 1955. The section devoted to the present day includes not only BMW's current models but also demonstrations of modern production methods.

The Future ("Zukunft") is assigned a platform to itself, focussing on new forms of propulsion and futuristic designs and transport systems.

Bogenhausen 43–45 54–56

Location
North-east of
the city centre,
on the right
bank of the Isar

U-Bahn
U4

Tram
18

The Bogenhausen district lies across the Isar to the north-east of the inner city. The area between the Princeregentstrasse and Arabellapark (see entries) was already favoured by prosperous Munich people, including the engineer Rudolf Diesel (see Famous People) and the prince of painters Franz von Stuck, in the later decades of the 19th c. A great number of very attractive buildings from the early industrial years and the Munich Jugendstil (Art Nouveau) are found here, of which Stuck Villa and Hildebrand Haus (see entries), now the Monacensia Bibliothek/Library, are particularly fine examples.

Bogenhausen's original village nucleus remains reasonably easy to identify, and something of the district's former elegance can still be felt today – as witness the several galleries, luxury shops and gourmet delicatessen (such as Feinkost Käfer).

The BMW administration "cylinder"

In the BMW museum

St George's Church in Bogenhausen . . .

. . . and the pulpit

Bonifatiusbasilika

*St Georg

This small Rococo church, picturesquely situated on the right bank of the Isar, was built in 1766–68 by Johann Michael Fischer. The choir however is Late Gothic – a survival from an earlier, originally Romanesque, church. The theatrical high altar, with figures of St George on Horseback, St Donatus and St Irene, was the work of Johann Baptist Straub. The pulpit and the right-hand side altar, with a figure of St Corbinian in the centre, are by Ignaz Günther; the left-hand side altar, with a Virgin enthroned (c. 1628) is by unknown artists. There are notable ceiling-paintings in the chancel and at the east end of the nave (by Helterhof, 1770), "St George Received in Heaven" and "Martyrdom of St George".

Cemetery

Among several well-known persons who lie buried in the pretty little cemetery are the conductor Hans Knappertsbusch, Liesl Karlstadt (Karl Valentin's comic partner), the Franco-German writer Annette Kolb, and the writer Erich Kästner. Also found here are the graves of actor Walter Sedlmayer, art historian and political commentator Wilhelm Hausenstein, and the actors Rudolf and Peter Vogel.

Arabellapark

See entry

Bonifatiusbasilika (St Boniface's Church)   41 55

Location
Karlstr. 34

S-Bahn
S1–S7
(Hauptbahnhof)

U-Bahn
U2 (Königsplatz)

The Benedictine Monastic Church of St Boniface, which is also the parish church of the Maxvorstadt, was built in 1834–47 in Byzantine style to the designs of Georg Friedrich Ziebland. Following its destruction in the Second World War Hans Döllgast rebuilt the south end and porch, and later a modern conventual building was constructed on the ruins of the north end and apse.

In the aisle on the east side (to the right of the main entrance) is the tomb of King Ludwig I.

Former monastery

The old conventual buildings originally linked the building which now houses the State Collection of Antiquities (see Staatliche Antikensammlungen) with the apse of the church – a bringing together of religion (the Church), learning (the monastery) and art (the museum) which appealed to the Romantic educational ideal of the first half of the 19th c.

Börse (Stock Exchange)   41 55

Location
Lenbachplatz 2

S-Bahn
S1–S7 (Karls-platz/Stachus)

U-Bahn
U4, U5 (Karls-platz/Stachus)

The Bayerische Börse (Bavarian Stock Exchange), a palatial turn-of-the-century edifice, was opened in 1896. The size of its quoted list (with more than 4000 fixed interest stocks alone) makes the Exchange one of the largest institutions of its kind in Germany, in addition to which it is the "home" Börse of such well-known companies as BMW, Siemens AG, Allianz Versicherungen AG, the Münchner Ruckversicherungs AG, Löwenbräu AG, and other major firms.

The Visitors Service (Mon.–Fri. 11.30am–1.30pm) welcomes some 40,000 members of the general public every year, all keen to have a taste at first-hand of the hectic activity on the trading floor.

Architecture

The Neo-Baroque building with its complicated ground-plan was erected in 1896–98, the magnificence of Albert Schmid's design being a worthy acknowledgement of the financial power of the Exchange. With splendid façades on three sides the Börse forms the principal link between the Karlsplatz/Stachus and Lenbachplatz (see entries).

*Botanischer Garten (Botanic Gardens) 36 57

The present Botanic Gardens, covering an area of more than 20ha/49 acres on the north side of Nymphenburg Park, was laid out between 1909 and 1914, the previous gardens near the Karlsplatz having suffered increasingly from environmental damage. The range of plants – some 15,000 in all, about half growing out of doors – and exceptional landscaping ensure the Munich Botanic Gardens a place among the very finest in Europe.

The Botanic Gardens also have an important role to play in the University's teaching and research activities. Between the café and the ornamental court (seasonally replanted) are sections devoted to ecological and genetic research. Here botanists study the ability of plants to adapt to changes in the environment and investigate the laws governing heredity.

Adjoining to the west is a large arboretum with a very extensive selection of deciduous and coniferous trees.
Other special areas are devoted to the flora of moorlands, steppes and dunes. The heather garden is especially impressive in late spring/early summer when the broom is in flower, also in late summer when the erica (Calluna vulgaris) is in bloom.
Delightful too is the large pond with its typical water-plants and reed fringe.

The alpine garden boasts specimens from some of the highest mountains in the world. Laid out according to geographical origin and altitude, it is at its loveliest in the summer months (corresponding to the mountain spring) when the blue gentian, orange hawkweed and dwarf alpine poppy are in bloom.
The fern gorge is another of the Gardens' gems, at its best in spring when the new growth begins to shoot amidst the sandstone boulders.

Location
Nymphenburg, Menzinger Str. 61

U-Bahn
U1 (Rotkreuz-platz), then tram

Tram
12

Alpine garden

Alpinum in the Botanic Garden

Botanischer Garten

Hawkweed

Enzian

Delphinium

Hibiscus

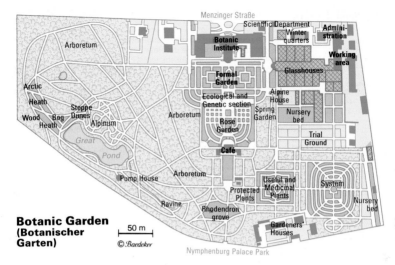

**Botanic Garden
(Botanischer
Garten)**

50 m

© *Baedeker*

Nymphenburg Palace Park

More than 200 different varieties of rhododendron flourish in the lime-free soil of their grove (flowering end of May to June).

The rose garden is yet another highlight, and not only on account of its wealth of colour and pervasive scents. – The protected species section ("Geschützte Pflanzen") adjacent to the rhododendron grove emphasises just how urgent conservation has become.

There is also an interesting section devoted to the more important varieties of plant exploited for human needs. These include various strains of cereals, fruit-wood, fibre-producing and medicinal plants and spices.

As well as flowering stone-plants, agaves, aloes and dragon trees the 5000sq.m/54,000sq.ft of hothouses include a magnificent orchid house – a panoply of exotic shapes and glorious colours. South-east Asian pitcher-plants, which trap and digest insects, make a further fascinating display.

Other major features include the Grosses Tropenhaus (Large Tropical House) with its screw-palms, bananas palms and bamboo plants growing alongside such widely cultivated tropical species as coffee, cocoa, rice, sugar cane and mahogany.

In summer "Victoria amazonica", queen of water-plants, is to be seen flowering in the Victoria House.

Yet more hothouses contain cacti, arum lilies, pineapple plants and various ferns (including palms and stag's horn ferns).

Nov.–Jan. daily 9am–4.30pm; Feb., Mar. daily 9am–5pm; Apr.–Sept. daily 9am–6pm; May–Aug. daily 9am–7pm (the hothouses always shut half an hour earlier). Midday closure: 11.45am–1pm. – Entrance fee.   **Opening times**

See entry   Alter Botani-
scher Garten

47

Brienner Strasse   41/42 55

Location
North-west
edge of the
Altstadtring

U-Bahn
U3, U4, U5, U6
(Odeonsplatz)
U2 (Königsplatz)

Tram
18 (Karolinen-
platz)

Brienner Strasse was laid out at the beginning of the 19th c. in the reign of King Maximilian I as part of the development of the Maxvorstadt, Friedrich von Sckell being responsible for the initial design. Also involved were the architects Karl von Fischer and, following his death, Leo von Klenze. The street opens into a series of magnificent squares: Wittelsbacherplatz, Karolinenplatz and Königsplatz (see entries). The houses, originally Neo-Classical and Neo-Renaissance in style, were occupied by aristocratic families, leading citizens and prominent artists. The Brienner Strasse suffered badly during the Second World War, and afterwards from alterations wrought by various banks and insurance companies. The busy Altstadtring (the ring of wide boulevards encircling the Old Town), which crosses the Brienner Strasse at the Platz der Opfer des Nationalsozialismus (Square of the Victims of National Socialism), has further eroded the original unity of conception. In recent years several of the façades have been restored and a more sympathetic approach adopted in the design of new buildings. Some high-class shops, galleries, and the luxurious premises of major companies provide a glimpse of former glories.

Almeida Palais

This mansion (Brienner Str. 14), in strict Neo-Classical style, designed by Jean-Baptiste Métivier, a pupil of Leo von Klenze, is a typical example of the original architecture of the Brienner Strasse. It was built for Sophie Petin, who was granted the title of Baroness von Bayrstorff in 1823 and married her lover Prince Carl, Ludwig I's brother, in 1834. Count d'Almeida was her son-in-law. Note the iron lanterns adorning the drive.

Globusbrunnen

Another exceptionally attractive feature is the Globus Fountain in front of Brienner Strasse 24.

Fine buildings in the Brienner Strasse and the Globe Fountain

*Bürgersaal   41 54

The Baroque Bürgersaal (Burghers' Hall), a "double" church with a prayer hall above and lower "under church" beneath, was the meeting-place and place of worship of the Marian Congregation (a community under Jesuit direction). It was built in 1709–10 to the design of Giovanni Antonio Viscardi and has been in use as a church since 1778. It was destroyed during the Second World War and rebuilt in 1945–46.

Location
Neuhauser Str. 48

S-Bahn
S1–S7 (Karls-platz/Stachus)

U-Bahn
U4, U5 (Karls-platz/Stachus)

The façade with its double pilasters is still in its original condition, apart from the side doors, which were later insertions. In a niche over the main doorway is a figure of the Virgin and Child on a crescent moon.
The interior stucco-work is by Josef Georg Baader (1710). Above the windows are fine painted medallions (c. 1774) glorifying the Mother of God; below the windows are depictions by Joachim Beich of various Bavarian places of pilgrimage (c. 1710).
Also to be seen in the upper hall are some works by Ignaz Günther, including a Guardian Angel group (1763) beneath the organ gallery and remnants of figures from a pulpit. A wooden relief of the Annunciation by Andreas Faistenberger (c. 1700) embellishes the high altar.

The windowless lower church (originally used to house the Bürgersaal's printing presses) contains the tomb of Rupert Mayer (1876–1945), a Jesuit priest who worked for the Resistance against the Nazi régime. He was beatified by Pope John Paul II in 1987.

Lower church

Damenstiftskirche St Anna (St Anne's Church)   41 54

St Anne's Church, once attached to a convent for gentlewomen, which is now a girls' secondary school, was built by Johann Baptist Gunetzrhainer in 1732–35. During the Second World War it was destroyed by bombing, leaving only the outer walls and the façade, but was rebuilt in its original form in the 1950s.

Location
Damenstiftstr. 1

S-Bahn
S1–S7 (Karls-platz/Stachus)

U-Bahn
U4, U5 (Karls-platz/Stachus), U3, U6 (Marienplatz)

The façade, with a wide middle section flanked by narrower lateral sections, is broken up by pilasters on tall bases.
The interior, consisting of a porch (with gallery), a square nave, short transepts and a rectangular chancel, is divided into bays by wide arches and roofed with shallow domes. It is attractively decorated in pink, blue, white and gold.
The altars have been reconstructed, incorporating figures which survived the bombing. The high altar has a painting by Joseph Ruffini of the Virgin and Child with St Anne; in front is a "Last Supper" with life-size figures (18th c.).

On the right-hand side altar is a painting by Balthasar Augustin Albrecht, "Glorification of St François de Sales"; on the left-hand side altar a "Visitation" by Georges Desmarées.

Right-hand side altar

The stucco-work by Egid Quirin Asam has been restored; the frescoes, in tones of grey, by his brother Cosmas Damian have been repainted (chancel: "Homage of the Angels"; nave: "Glorification of St Anne and the Virgin"; porch: "Angels' Concert").

Stucco-work

In Damenstiftstrasse are two handsome secular buildings – at No. 4 a house in Neo-Classical style (c. 1800) and at No. 8 the Rococo Palais Lerchenfeld (by A. Gunetzrhainer, 1726).

Damenstift-strasse, Palais Lerchenfeld

Deutsches Museum (German Museum)

The German Museum for Master-Works of Science and Technology is the world's largest museum of technology, covering an area of more than 50,000sq.m/59,800sq.yd and displaying some 17,000 exhibits. The collections are constantly being expanded by the addition of the latest technological developments.

The museum was founded in 1903 and directed in its early years by Oskar von Miller. Since 1925 it has been housed in a large complex built by Gabriel von Seidl on an island in the Isar, later supplemented by a library, conference hall and other such extensions.

The original conference hall, now housing the Forum der Technik (see entry) which always attracts crowds of visitors, was for decades one of Munich's principal venues. It was here that the Christian Socialist Union (CSU) was founded in November 1945 and the German trade union federation was formed in 1949. Many well-known artists also appeared at the hall.

The various departments in the museum are excellently arranged, with particularly clear explanations enabling visitors to follow the development of each scientific discipline and field of technology. Up-to-the-minute methods of presentation are used, incorporating scientific apparatus, demonstrations of experiments, machines and machinery, models, and picture displays.

The museum library, a reference library in science and technology, has some 750,000 volumes, 4500 periodicals and collections of technical journals, plans, patents, catalogues and manuscripts and other documents. The "Libri Rari" section contains 5000 or so scientific and technological source works printed before 1750 (information: tel. 217 92 24).

The museum has its own research institute for technology and the history of science, collaborating closely with the Institut für Geschichte der Naturwissenschaften (History of Science) at the Ludwig-Maximilians-Universität and the Zentralinstitut für Geschichte (History) at Munich's Technical University. Regular seminars and lectures are held (information: tel. 217 93 01).

The museum's Kerschensteiner College provides courses on the history of technology and related topics for teachers and instructional staff from industry (information: tel. 217 92 43).

The extensive study collection includes historical scientific instruments, machines and models. Access is by appointment only and is restricted to bona fide researchers in the relevant fields.

The museum boasts several special collections and well-endowed archives relating to the history of science and technology. Of the latter the air and space travel archive is particularly interesting and comprehensive (information: tel. 217 92 20).
Affiliated to the museum is a film and photographic library with a collection of some 40,000 negatives.

Location
Museumsinsel

S-Bahn
S1–S7 (Isartor)

U-Bahn
U1, U2
(Fraunhoferstr.)

Tram
18 (Deutshes Museum),
20 (Isartor)

Opening times
Daily 9am–5pm

Closed
New Year, Shrove Tue., Good Fri., Easter Sun., May 1st, Whit Sun., Corpus Christi, Nov. 1st, Xmas Eve and Xmas Day

Entrance fee

Kerschensteiner-Kolleg

Studiensammlung

Special collections, archives

Museum courtyard

Pride of place in the museum courtyard is taken by a Dornier Do 31 transport aircraft, the prototype of a vertical take-off design developed for military purposes. Also in the courtyard are a number of the highly efficient type of water-driven turbines used in hydro-electric power generation.

◄ *Shipping section in the Deutsches Museum*

Deutsches Museum

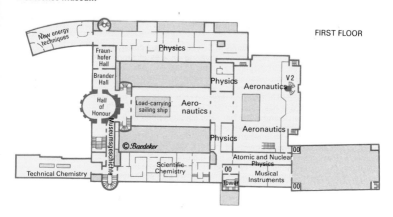

FIRST FLOOR

New energy techniques

Fraunhofer Hall

Brander Hall

Hall of Honour

Museumsgeschichte

© Baedeker

Physics

Load-carrying sailing ship

Aeronautics

Physics

Physics

Aeronautics

Aeronautics

V2

00

Technical Chemistry

Scientific Chemistry

Tower

Atomic and Nuclear Physics

Musical Instruments

00

00

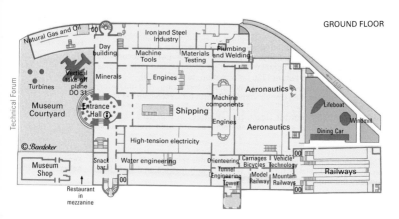

GROUND FLOOR

Technical Forum

Natural Gas and Oil

Turbines

Museum Courtyard

© Baedeker

Museum Shop

Restaurant in mezzanine

Day building

Vertical take-off plane DO 31

Minerals

Entrance Hall

Snack bar

Iron and Steel Industry

Machine Tools

Engines

Machine components

Engines

High-tension electricity

Water engineering

Materials Testing

Plumbing and Welding

Shipping

Aeronautics

Aeronautics

Orienteering

Tunnel Engineering Tower

Carriages Bicycles

Model Railway

Vehicle Technology

Mountain Railways

Lifeboat

Windmill

Dining Car

Railways

00

00

00

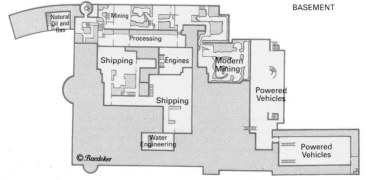

BASEMENT

Natural Oil and Gas

Mining

Processing

Shipping

Engines

Modern Mining

Shipping

Water Engineering

Powered Vehicles

Powered Vehicles

© Baedeker

Deutsches Museum

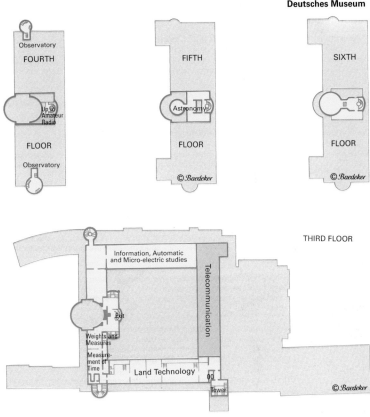

Observatory

FOURTH

Up to Amateur Radio

FLOOR

Observatory

FIFTH

Astronomy

FLOOR

© Baedeker

SIXTH

FLOOR

© Baedeker

THIRD FLOOR

Information, Automatic and Micro-electric studies

Telecommunication

Exit

Weights and Measures

Measurement of Time

Land Technology

Tower

00

© Baedeker

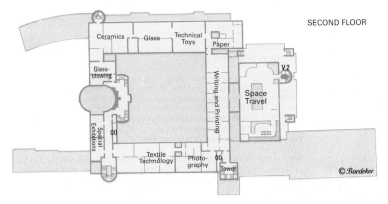

SECOND FLOOR

Ceramics

Glass

Technical Toys

Paper

Glass-blowing

Writing and Printing

V2

Space Travel

Special Exhibitions

00

Textile Technology

Photo-graphy

Tower

00

© Baedeker

Ground floor and basement

Minerals	Minerals, crystals and rocks, seams and mineral deposits.
Natural gas, oil	Prospecting and extraction, drilling at depth, oil refining, pipelines and other transport systems, storage, energy use, petrochemicals, environmental problems.
Mining	Shaft-drilling, transport underground, ore extraction, pit surveying, safety, salt-mining, processing, coke and briquette production.
Open-cast mining	Extraction methods; lignite mining.
Metalworking	Crude iron and steel, blast furnaces, the Bessemer converter, electric steel furnaces, forging, rolling, drawing, casting and moulding, bell founding, cutting.
Welding and soldering	Soldering, pressure-, electron beam-, thermite-, gas-arc and other forms of welding, welding robots.
Machine tools	Development of machine tools from a reconstruction of a 4th millennium B.C. bow-drill to original 19th c. transmission lathes, drilling and milling equipment, CNC-driven machines and a model of the computer-controlled factory of the future.
Powered machinery	Various muscle power machines, windmills, water-mills, steam engines, steam turbines, water-driven turbines, Otto engines, diesel engines, engine parts, rotary-piston engines, gas turbines, jet-propulsion engines.
Electrical power technology	Development of DC, AC and three-phase current technology, static converters, power stations, energy distribution, high-tension systems. Daily demonstrations (11am, 2pm, and 4pm) include experiments with high-tension AC current and simulated lightning strikes.
Hydraulic engineering	Urban water-management, river regulation, canal construction, harbours (e.g. Hamburg), coastal protection.
Shipping	Sailing ships, steam and motor vessels, boats, warships, submarines, navigation and diving techniques.
Road and bridge construction	Development of road-building illustrated by models (section of a Germanic plank roadway c. 180 B.C.; different types of bridge construction in timber, stone, iron, steel and concrete).
Tunnelling	Rock-drilling machinery, shoring, sections of tunnels (Simplon Tunnel, Munich Underground tunnel).
Railways	History of rail transport, operating systems, track laying (with educational film), signals and safety systems, steam engines including a Puffing Billy (1814) and Bavarian express locomotive S 3/6 (1912). Electric trains, among them the world's first electric powered locomotive built by Siemens in 1879, diesel locomotives including e.g. the V 140 (1935), mountain railways (rack-, cableway and cable-car railways); 40sq.m/430sq.ft model railway lay-out (demonstrations throughout the day).
Coaches, bicycles	Six coaches, among them a Berlin and a mailcoach, handcarts, etc., three-wheelers, history of the bicycle (Baron Karl von Drais' 1817 velocipede, early bicycles, penny-farthings, sprung-wheeled bicycles, military folding bikes, racing bikes).

Pre-1900 motor cars including an 1885 Daimler and Maybach and 1886 Benz automobile, 1881 Serpollet steam car, electric cars, classic automobiles, touring cars such as the 1914 Audi, racing cars (e.g. a 1936 16-cylinder Auto Union), utility vehicles (1935 Magirus turntable-ladder), motor-assisted bicycles, motor-cycles, motor scooters, automobile technology (chassis design, propulsion, bodywork, crash-testing, aerodynamics and prototypes), vehicle production (BMW robot assembly line); films on various aspects of automobile history. *(Motor vehicles)*

First floor

Hall of Fame honouring leading German inventors, engineers and entrepreneurs (paintings, busts, reliefs, etc.). *(Ehrensaal)*

Scientific instruments used by G. F. Brander (1713–83) who was one of the founders of the Kurbayerische Akademie der Wissenschaften (Academy of Sciences). Specially noteworthy is an azimuth quadrant made in 1761. *(Brander-Raum)*

Collection of scientific instruments belonging to Joseph von Fraunhofer (1787–1826), Georg von Reichenbach (1772–1826) and Joseph Liebherr (1767–1840), in particular a prism spectroscope, heliometer and astronomical universal theodolite. *(Fraunhofer-Raum)*

The nature of energy, main energy sources, energy from uranium, energy saving, renewable energy sources (wind energy, the tides, geothermal energy, biomass). *(New energy technology)*

Different branches of physics, history of mechanics, forces, freely falling bodies, Galileo Room, mass, liquids, gases, oscillation, heat and cold, measurement of temperature, electro-static, magneto-static, electric currents, X-rays, gas discharge, electro-magnetism, optics.
There are several pieces of apparatus of great interest including Otto von Guericke's Magdeburg hemispheres (1663), the first opthalmoscope, made by Helmholtz in 1851, valves produced by C. F. Röntgen (1896), and equipment used by Heinrich Hertz in his 1889 experiments in electro-magnetism. *(Physics)*

Alchemy, 18th c. laboratory from Lavoisier's time, 19th c. laboratory of J. von Liebig (1803–73), matter, atoms, molecules, chemical reactions, chemical analysis, chemical synthesis, biochemistry, history of pharmacy (reconstruction of the pharmacy at the St Emmeran Monastery in Regensburg, c. 1800). *(Chemistry)*

Chemistry and energy, chemistry and health, chemical processes and methods, chemistry and nutrition, artificial colouring, man-made fibres, the study of carbons, various experimental set-ups, synthetic materials. *(Industrial chemistry)*

Models of atoms, quantum theory, quantum mechanics, protons, neutrons, electrons, nuclear physics. *(Atomic, nuclear and experimental physics)*

Brass and woodwind, string and plucked string instruments, reed-pipes, organs, upright and grand pianos, harpsichords, spinets, virginals, electric organs, dulcimers, Aeolian harps, musical boxes. *(Musical instruments)*

Second floor

Neolithic tools, copy of the prehistoric painting found in the Altamira cave near Santander in northern Spain. *(Altamira)*

Deutsches Museum

Ceramics	Ceramics in antiquity, Greek and Roman ceramics, ceramics in technology, manufacturing processes, glazing and decoration, preparation of raw materials, design. Drying and firing, brick-making, ceramic workshop.
Glass-making	Crude glass, hollow-, sheet- and special glass, glass manufacture and processing, glass-blowing.
Technical toys	Building-, construction- and experimental science sets.
Paper	Japanese paper manufacture, hand-made paper, the paper industry, watermarks, documents, paper machines.
Writing and printing	Development of writing, writing implements and machines, relief printing, gravure printing, flat-bed printing, book-binding, offset printing, photo-setting, photo-reproduction.
Photography	Early years of photography (e.g. 1839 daguerreotype camera, 1894 "Bosco" automatic camera), photo-technology in the 20th c., motion pictures, cine-projection, photochemistry. (The photography section is closed at present and will remain so for an extended period. It is expected to re-open in late autumn 1995.)
Textile technology	Development from craft to industrial production; the spindle, loom, spinning-wheel, spinning and weaving machines.

Third floor

Agricultural technology	Agriculture, indoor activities (milking machines; various hand-driven machines; threshing machines; comparative models of farms c. 1800 and 1960) and outdoor (machines for working land; sowing and harvesting; technological improvements over the centuries; tractors; models), milk processing (19th c. Alpine hut with cheese-making equipment; development of butter and cheese manufacture, model dairy), milling (techniques of flour production, mortars, grinders, hand mills, 18th c. corn mill, models; 18th c. oil mill), brewing (beer-making from antiquity; models of breweries; malting, various types of brewing apparatus including a Zwei-Gefässe-Hydro-Sudwerk; model of a bottle cellar; distillery (fruit distillery with three stills dating from about 1700; potato and corn distilleries with apparatus and models), sugar production (history of sugar-cane and sugar-beet extraction with geographical focus on e.g. the Caribbean; models of the first sugar-beet factory and a modern factory for comparison; various types of equipment).
Measurement of time	Sundials, water-clocks, hour-glasses and mechanical clocks (clockmaker's workshop), electrical clocks (also quartz clocks).
Weights and measures	Development of measures and measuring apparatus for length, volume and mass; weighing scales.
Computing and automation	Mathematical instruments, calculators, cryptographic devices, punched card machines, mechanical differential analysers, analog computers, early computers, working reconstruction of the "Zuse Z3" (one of the world's first programme-controlled computers, made by Konrad Zuse in 1941), modern mainframe computer ("Cray-1").
Micro-electronics	History of solid-state technology and integrated circuits; technical crystal production; chip manufacture; logic chips and memory chips; micro-electronics applications, micro-electronics and computer sciences.
Tele-communications	The physics and technology of telecommunications; cable transmission; radio engineering; telephone exchanges; radio and television broadcasting; terminals; remote control technology.

Fourth floor

History of amateur radio; ham radio organisations and activities; working amateur radio station.

Amateur radio

Astronomy

A total of nine different presentations on varying aspects of astronomy and astrophysics are found on the third and fifth floors of the museum.

N.B.

East dome: reflecting telescope (viewing by arrangement); west dome: optical telescope with Zeiss refractor, built in 1925 (lens diameter: 300mm/11.8in.; focal length 4960mm/195in.).

Observatories

A Zeiss projector (model no. 1015), installed in the main dome in 1987, displays a night sky of 8900 stars.

Planetarium

Aeronautics and space travel

Natural flight, balloons and airships, kites, early flight technology up to 1918, flight mechanics, aerodynamics.
Mementoes and memorabilia of Otto Lilienthal.

Early Aviation
Hall, first floor

Post-First World War development of propeller-driven civil and military aircraft (Junkers F 13, 1919, Messerschmidt Bf 109 E, 1938, Junkers Ju 52/3m, 1932), piston engines and propellers (BMW radial engines, large Pratt and Whitney engines).

Modern Aviation
Hall, first floor

Jet and turbo-prop engines, turbo-jet and other aircraft (the rocket-propelled Messerschmidt Me 163, 1941, Messerschmidt Me 262, 1944,

Modern Aviation
Hall, ground floor

A Dornier 31 in the museum courtyard

Lockheed F 104 "Starfighter", HFB 320 Hansa Jet, details of the Airbus A 300), helicopters (including MBB BO 105, Sikorsky S-55; rotor construction), gliders (Vampyre and sf 24 Phoenix, etc.), various test planes (e.g. Rochelt-Solair), light aircraft, full-sized model of Spacelab.

Modern Aviation Hall, first mezzanine floor	Flight control and navigation systems, panel instruments and automatic pilot, demonstration models (model airport), flight safety and airfields, cockpit of a commercial aircraft.
Modern Aviation Hall, second mezzanine floor	Aeronautical medicine, emergency rescue and safety equipment (oxygen apparatus, protective clothing, ejector seat, emergency shute, life-raft), development of model plane construction.
Modern Aviation Hall, second floor	Introductory feature "Space and space travel", development of rocket and space technology, aggregates and rocket propulsion, models of carrier rockets including A4 rockets (V2; the world's earliest large-scale rocket), manned spaceflight (dioramas of the 1971 moon-landing, reconstruction of the Mercury capsule), satellites and probes (receiving station for weather satellite pictures, prototypes of the Helios space probe built in 1974), space technology, planetary exploration.

Museum grounds

Windmill	Dutch windmill from Wiesedermeer (East Friesland), built in 1866.
Lifeboat	"Theodor Heuss", a lifeboat which went into service in 1957. On display in the grounds of the Deutsches Museum since 1987, it is a great favourite with the public.
Restaurant car	Mitropa restaurant car, built in 1928. Serves refreshments in summer.
Forum der Technik	See entry

---

*Dreifaltigkeitskirche (Trinity Church)   41 54

Location Pacellistr. 6	During the War of the Spanish Succession a young Munich woman named Anna Maria Lindtmayr prophesied that divine judgment was about to fall upon the city, which would be saved only if a vow were made to build a church. Accordingly, when in 1704 Munich was threatened with fire and plunder, representatives of the town's nobility, clergy and citizenry made a solemn vow in the Frauenkirche "to cause to be built in our city a church with several altars for the greater worship of the Most Holy Trinity".
S-Bahn S1–S7 (Karlsplatz/Stachus)	

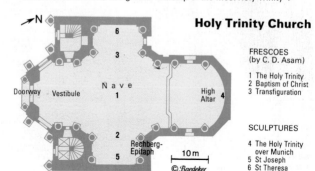

Holy Trinity Church

FRESCOES
(by C. D. Asam)

1 The Holy Trinity
2 Baptism of Christ
3 Transfiguration

SCULPTURES

4 The Holy Trinity over Munich
5 St Joseph
6 St Theresa

The church was designed by the Court Architect, Giovanni Antonio Viscardi, the foundation-stone being laid in 1711. After Viscardi's death in 1713 construction was completed by Ettenhofer and Zuccalli, including a tower which did not feature in the original plan.

U-Bahn
U4, U5 (Karlsplatz/Stachus)

Tram 19

Built at huge cost the "facciada" was the first convex church façade in Bavaria. It is notable for its plastic sense of movement, vigorous rhythm and clear articulation. In a niche on the pediment is a figure of St Michael by Josef Fichtl (1726).

Façade

The interior is cruciform, with a square central area and a longer north arm containing the choir.
The high altar (1721–28) is by Fichtl. The altarpiece by Johann Andreas Wolff and Johannes Degler (1716–17), depicting the Trinity over the city of Munich, was presented to the church by the Elector.
On the right-hand side altar are a painting of St Joseph by Joseph Ruffini (1718) and figures of St John and St Peter by Andreas Faistenberger.
On the left-hand side altar can be seen a painting of St Teresa by Degler and figures of St John of the Cross and Elijah by Balthasar Ableithner.
The impressive frescoes are by Cosmas Damian Asam (1715): in the dome the Trinity (with a self-portrait of the artist – on right, by the north-east window), in the transept the Baptism of Christ and the Transfiguration.

Interior

---

*Englischer Garten (English Garden)

42–45 55–59

The English Garden is the largest and one of the most beautiful city parks in Germany. Its naturally arranged groups of trees and plants, offering ever-changing vistas, its winding streams and its artificial lake combine to create the impression of a mature natural landscape.
In 1785, on the suggestion of Sir Benjamin Thompson (later made Count of Rumford), the Elector Karl Theodor had a Military Garden laid out on the banks of the Isar. It was intended, in his words, to "serve not only for the benefit and recreation of the military but also for general use as a public promenade." The landscaping of the garden was the work of Sir Benjamin Thompson, Baron Reinhard von Werneck and Ludwig von Sckell.
In 1789 various schools and model farms and other establishments providing training in agriculture, forestry, dairy-farming, sheep-farming and horticulture, were set up in the garden. In 1802 Reinhard von Werneck oversaw the creation of the Kleinhesseloher Lake; and in 1810–11 the garden was extended from the Hirschbau (Deer Meadow) to the Aumeisterhaus (the Huntsman's Lodge), at which time the lake was also enlarged by Ludwig von Sckell.
The English Garden still serves for the "exercise and social recreation" of the people of Munich and for their "enjoyment of free and healthy air" exactly as its founder intended; in spring and summer in particular it is a popular resort for young and old alike, who come to walk, relax, sunbathe (there are special areas for nude sunbathing), surf on the Eisbach, make music, play games, take a boat out, and drink beer (beer-gardens at the Chinese Tower and on the lake).

Location
North-east of city Centre

U-Bahn
U3, U4, U5, U6 (Odeonsplatz); U3, U6 (Universität, Giselastr., Münchner Freiheit)

Surfer

From the Monopteros, a Classical-style temple (1837–38) by Leo von Klenze, built on an artificial hill, there is a very fine view of the older part of the city. (N.B. The Monopteros tends to be a haunt of Munich's less fortunate inhabitants, particularly when the weather is good.)

Monopteros

The Chinese Tower was constructed by J. Frey in 1789–91 as an outlook tower and bandstand. Burned down in 1944, the pagoda was rebuilt in 1951. The building to the south of the Chinese Tower, now housing a café-restaurant, and the Rumfordhaus (135m/150yd north), a former officers' mess, both designed by J. B. Lechner, were erected in 1790.

Chinese Tower

English Garden: Monopteros

Chinese tower

Playing and rest areas in the English Garden

In fine weather in particular crowds of visitors from every corner of the globe congregate at the foot of the Chinese Tower, where a very large beer-garden and brass band create a permanent Oktoberfest atmosphere. Horse-drawn cabs are available to take people round the gardens.

The Seehaus (Lake House) on the shores of the Kleinhesseloher Lake, built by Gabriel von Seidl in 1883, was demolished in 1970, having fallen into a state of disrepair; in its place is a spacious new building with a restaurant and beer-garden.

Seehaus

The handsome Aumeisterhaus (Huntsman's Lodge) at the north end of the English Garden was designed by Deiglmayr and built in 1810–11.

Aumeisterhaus

Europäisches Patentamt (European Patent Office) 42 53

Since 1977 the "metropolis on the Isar" has been the home of the European Patent Office, as yet the only major European institution to have its headquarters in Germany. The Office grants patents for its eleven member countries – Austria, Belgium, France, Germany, Italy, Liechtenstein, Luxembourg, the Netherlands, Sweden, Switzerland and the United Kingdom.

The authority's ultra-modern 61,568sq.m/662,700sq.ft office block in the Bavarian capital was designed by Gerkan, Marg and Partners, the Hamburg architects. Closely spaced ribs form a structure for the impressive eloxal glass façade.

Fine works by artists from the different member countries can be seen inside and outside the complex.

The Munich office employs a staff of about 850. Together with branches in Den Haag and Berlin it processes some 62,000 patents applications annually.

Location
Erdhardstr. 27

S-Bahn
S1–S7 (Isartor)

U-Bahn
U1, U2 (Fraunhoferstr.)

Tram
18, 20

Bus
52, 56

Feldherrnhalle (Military Commanders' Hall) 42 54

The Feldherrnhalle (1841–44), a 20m/65ft open loggia designed by Friedrich von Gärtner and modelled on the Loggia dei Lanzi in Florence, closes the vista at the south end of Ludwigstrasse. Its bronze figures are by Anselm Sickinger and Francesco Sanguinetti.

Commissioned by King Ludwig I as a tribute to the Bavarian army, the loggia boasts bronze statues of the Bavarian generals Tilly (1559–1632) and Wrede (1767–1838) executed from drawings by Ludwig Schwanthaler. The Bavarian Army Memorial commemorates the Franco-Prussian War of 1870–71. The two lions on the steps were the work of W. Ruemann (1906); one is popularly said to be growling at the Residenz, the other to be keeping its mouth shut towards the church. After the failure of Hitler's attempted putsch and the subsequent "March to the Feldherrnhalle", the building became a Nazi rallying-point. – Today its excellent accoustics make it a popular venue for musicians and singers.

Location
Odeonsplatz

U-Bahn
U3, U4, U5, U6
(Odeonsplatz)

*Forum der Technik (Technology Forum) 42 53

The unique "Forum der Technik" was set up in 1992/93 in the former conference centre of the Deutsches Museum. This quite unparalleled and outstandingly successful venture in technological entertainment and edu-

Location
Museumsinsel

Forum der Technik

The Feldherrnhalle, a Munich landmark (see p. 61)

The Feldherrnhalle, a Munich landmark (see p. 61)

S-Bahn
S1–S7 (Isartor)

U-Bahn
U1, U2
(Fraunhoferstr.)

Tram
18 (Deutsches
Musuem),
20 (Isartor)

cation was made possible by enlisting the support of well-known companies such as Siemens, BMW, Rohde & Schwarz, Dyckerhoff & Widmann, Zeiss and others.

The twin centrepieces of the hyper-modern experiment in bringing science to the masses are a big, multi-functional IMAX projection room (330sq.m/3550sq.ft large-screen cinema; 30,000 watt 6-channel digital sound system) and a Space Theatre (with Carl Zeiss Model VII planetarium and laser show).

Additional facilities – including a 2000sq.m/21,500sq.ft exhibition area, five lecture-halls and thirteen seminar rooms – cater for a variety of other activities. Information: tel. 217 93 01.

Opening times: daily 9am–5pm. Closed: New Year, Shrove Tuesday, Good Friday, Easter Sunday, May 1st, Corpus Christi, Nov. 1st, Christmas Eve, Christmas Day. Entrance fee.

Deutsches
Museum

See entry

Frauenkirche (Cathedral Church of Our Lady)   41 54

Location
Frauenplatz 1

S-Bahn
S1–S7 (Karlsplatz,
Marienplatz)

The Frauenkirche has been the cathedral and metropolitan church of the South Bavarian ecclesiastical provinces since the establishment of the archbishopric of Munich and Freising in 1821.

This brick-built Late Gothic church owes its impact to its great size (109m/358ft by 40m/131ft), its high walls, its clear articulation and its lack of ornament. With its sturdy twin towers, rearing up to a height of 99m and 100m/325ft and 328ft, it is Munich's most celebrated landmark.

The Frauenkirche, the symbol of the metropolis ▶

The Frauenkirche, the symbol of the metropolis ▶

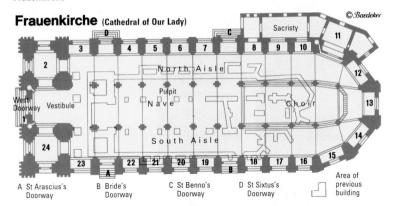

Frauenkirche (Cathedral of Our Lady)

© Baedeker

A St Arascius's Doorway
B Bride's Doorway
C St Benno's Doorway
D St Sixtus's Doorway
Area of previous building

1 Entrance to tower
2 North tower chapel
3 Apollonia Chapel
4 Chapel of St Lantpert
5 St Corbinius' Chapel
6 Seven Sorrows Chapel
7 Ecce Homo Chapel
8 Entrance to Sacristy
9 Pius Chapel
10 Chapel of the Court Brotherhood of St Anne and St George
11 Sacrament Chapel (former Sacristy)
12 St Sebastian's Chapel
13 Choir Chapel
14 Former Sacrament Chapel
15 Sacred Heart Chapel
16 Chapel of the Immaculata
17 Benno Chapel
18 Baptistry Chapel
19 Three Kings Chapel
20 Patron of Bakers Chapel (16th c.)
21 St Andrew's Chapel (formerly Chapel of the Annunciation)
22 Chapel of the Vesper Image (formerly Chapel of St Bartholomew and St Veit)
23 Memorial Chapel of the International Eucharistic Conference
24 South Tower Chapel

U-Bahn
U4, U5 (Karlsplatz/ Stachus); U3, U6 (Marienplatz)

The Frauenkirche was built in 1468–88 by Jörg Halspach (known as Gang-hofer) on the site of an earlier chapel dedicated to the Virgin. In 1525, in place of the spires originally planned by Halspach, the two towers were given their characteristic Renaissance domes, the green patina of which harmonises well with the dark red brick. The carved medallions on the five doorways were the work of Ignaz Günther (1772). – The church was se-verely damaged in 1944–45, restoration being completed in 1953.

Interior

The interior of this aisled hall-church, with 22 tall octagonal pillars in two rows, was remodelled in Renaissance style in 1601 but reconverted to a Gothic design in 1858. As rebuilt after its destruction in the last war it has a simply conceived but very effective whitewash interior.

Viewed from the porch the aisles and side windows are invisible, the octagonal pillars of the nave having the appearance of a wall; at one time the window of the choir was also obscured by the high altar. Legend has it that the Devil came to inspect the church after its completion and was so delighted that the windows had been forgotten that he stamped his foot, leaving a print in the porch that can still be seen.

In going round the church the following features should not be missed.

Porch
Larger than life-size figure of St Christopher in wood (c. 1520).

North tower chapel
Relief of the Virgin and the patron (c. 1475); Tulbeck Tomb (1476).

Apollonia Chapel
Epitaph to Cardinal Döpfner by Hans Wimmer (1981).

St Lantpert's Chapel
Re-worked Gothic figures of the Apostles and Prophets in wood from the former choir stalls, by Erasmus Grasser. Imposing marble triptych of the patrician Barth family.

Chapel of the Seven Sorrows
"The Seven Sorrows of Mary", a stained glass window by the modern artist Gitzinger (1959). Tombstone of the first chaplain, Dr Balthasar Hundertpfund.

The chapel, probably dating from the early 17th c., is by an unknown master. Epitaphian diptych from the workshop of Hans Krumper (c. 1620). — Ecco Homo Chapel

Altarpiece of the Assumption by Peter Candid (1620), previously on the high altar. — Sacristy entrance

On the altar, a mosaic of Pope Pius X by Sepp Frank (1960). — Pope Pius' Chapel

"St Anne with Mary and the infant Jesus" (c. 1520); monumental 16th c. figures of SS Rasso and George; stained glass window depicting the Annunciation (c. 1500). — Chapel of St Anne and St George

Exceptional paintings from the Memminger altar by Strigel (c. 1500). Altar, tabernacle, ambo, clergy seats and benches by Max Faller (1984). Stained glass window of the martyrdom of St Catherine (also c. 1500). — Sacramental chapel

Winged retable "The Baptism of Christ" by Friedrich Pacher (1483; wing panels by Jan Polack). Fine stained glass. — St Sebastian's Chapel

"Virgin of Mercy" with the patrons, the Sanftl family from Munich, by Jan Polack (c. 1500); stained glass by Peter Hemmel of Andlau (1493); reliefs by Ignaz Günther (1774). — Main choir chapel

Tombs of Archbishop Michael Cardinal Faulhaber (d. 1952), Joseph Cardinal Wendel (d. 1960) and Julius Cardinal Döpfner (d. 1976); memorial plaque to members of the Wittelsbach family buried near by. — Crypt

Rood altar (c. 1445); window with the life and suffering of Christ (c. 1480); Bürgermeister Karl Ligsalz's window (The Three Kings; c. 1425). — Old sacramental chapel

Altar of the Sacred Heart of Jesus (modern) by Max Lachner; late 15th c. stained glass. — Chapel of the Sacred Heart of Jesus

Bronze Immaculata by Elmar Dietz (1959); tombstone of the patrician Ligsalz family (14th c.). — Chapel of the Immaculata

Reliquaries and a silver bust of St Benno (1601); stained glass with scenes from the life of St Agnes and St Sebastian (15th c.) — St Benno's Chapel

Baroque font in red marble with, above, an early 14th c. Sorrowing Christ. — Baptistery

Altarpiece of the Magi by Ulrich Loth (1628); Late Gothic stained glass. — Chapel of the Magi

Figure of St Nicholas, probably by Erasmus Grasser (c. 1500); the Miracle of the Loaves in stained glass by Robert Rabolt (1959). — Bakers' Chapel

Wing panels of Late Gothic altar by Jan Polack; memorial to the Mandl family (1655). — St Andrew's Chapel

The Salzburg Mater Dolorosa (c. 1400). — Chapel of the Mater Dolorosa

Epitaph to Cardinal Joseph Wendel by the artist Hans Wimmer; also fine stained glass by Robert Rabold (1964). — Commemorative Chapel of the Eucharist. World Congress 1960

Free-standing monument (1619–22) in black marble by Hans Krumper, with magnificent bronze figures of Dukes Wilhelm IV and Albrecht V, also by Krumper, and, at the four corners, armour-clad standard-bearers by Hubert Gerhard (1595). — Tomb of the Emperor Ludwig the Bavarian

Freising

South tower chapel	Tomb of Jörg Halspach (known as Ganghofer), architect of the Frauen-kirche; 15th c. stained glass.
Nave	Pulpit by Blasius Spreng (1957).
Choir	High altar, ambo, by Hubert Elsässer (1971); cross in choir arch by Josef Henselmann (1954; busts and statues by Erasmus Grasser, 1502).

Freising

Location
33km/20 miles
north of Munich

S-Bahn station
Freising (S1)

Freising, an ancient bishopric and today the principal town of its district (population: 36,000; altitude: 448m/1470ft) is situated on the left bank of the Isar at the northern edge of the Munich gravel plain, straddling the little river Moosach.

Information
Fremdenverkehrsamt (Tourist Office) der Stadt Freising, Obere Hauptstr. 2, D(W)-8050 Freising, tel. (081 61) 541 22.

Sights

°Cathedral

Freising's most outstanding attraction, its Romanesque Cathedral of St Mary and St Korbinian, was constructed anew between 1160 and 1205 from remnants surviving from a fire in 1159. The five-aisle basilica was given its vaulted roof in 1480–82, and lavishly decorated by the Asam brothers in 1723–24 with stucco ornament and paintings. Since 1983 it has been co-cathedral of the archdiocese of Munich with Freising.

A Gothic porch between the twin towers leads via a stepped Romanesque doorway (figures of the Emperor Friedrich Barbarossa, Bishop Albert I and the Empress Beatrix) into the cathedral interior.

The Romanesque crypt, which survives in its original form, is one of the oldest of its kind in Germany. Among the 24 columns in three rows supporting the vaulting, with capitals of varying shape, stands a famous "animal column", made up of the intertwined bodies of men and monsters. Also in the crypt is the tomb of the church's founder, Bishop Korbinian.

Adorning the high altar is a copy of Rubens' sublime "The Apocalyptic Women" (c. 1625), the original of which has been removed to the Alte Pinokothek (see entry).

In 1723/24 the interior of the church was brilliantly refurbished in the Baroque style by the brothers Cosmas Damian and Egid Quirin Asam.

Other buildings on the Domberg

The 15th c. cloister on the east side of the cathedral was decorated in 1716 with frescoes and stucco-work by Johann Baptist Zimmermann. On its east side is a Benedictine church (c. 1340) which has a Gothic window of the Virgin (1391) and stucco-work again dating from 1716.

The Maximilian Chapel was built in 1710.

The residence of the Prince Bishops ("Bischofsschloss") was erected on the foundations of the old Agilolfinger ducal palace. It is graced by the earliest Renaissance arcade north of the Alps.

°Diocesan Museum

The Diocesan Museum on the Domberg boasts the most comprehensive collection of sacred art in Germany and provides an almost continuous history of the Catholic church from the 11th to the 19th c. The famous "Lukasbild", a quite exceptional icon from Constantinople, warrants special mention. Opening times: Tue.–Sun. 10am–5pm.

Old Town

Rising 80m/262ft above the roofs of Freising Old Town is the lovely Baroque tower of the Stadtpfarrkirche St Georg (St George's Parish Church). The Hauptstrasse-Marienplatz area includes some pleasing town houses, among them the "Zierer-Haus" in the Rindermarkt; looking around, elements of Gothic, Baroque and Biedermeier are all to be seen.

The Gothic St George's was built around 1440 by Jörg Ganghofer, later to make his name as the architect of Munich's Frauenkirche.
Opposite stands the former Prince Bishops' Lyzeum with its Baroque Asam Room decorated in 1709 by Hans Georg Asam, father of the famous brothers. The stucco and fresco ceiling is extraordinarily splendid.

Also worth visiting is the former Premonstratensian convent in the suburb of Neustift. It now houses the local administrative offices, having earlier been used, following its secularisation, first as a barracks and then a textile factory.
The parish church of St Peter and St Paul has a Late Rococo high altar (1765) with carvings by Ignaz Günther. There are also fine choir stalls.

Neustift

To the south of the market place lies the former Benedictine monastery of Weihenstephan. St Korbinian founded the first monastery on the site in 725; the earliest references to Weihenstephan however are found in documents dating from 1003, by which time the monastery had already been destroyed by the Huns and rebuilt. In 1040 Weihenstephan's Benedictine monks were granted the right to brew and serve beer, thus giving rise to a tradition of brewing unrivalled anywhere in the world.
Following the opening of the electoral "Musterlandwirtschaftschule" (Model Farming School) and "Centralbaumschule" (Central Tree School), from 1803 onwards Weihenstephan began its transformation into one of the most renowned colleges of its kind in Germany, incorporating the faculties of agriculture and horticulture and the departments of brewing, food technology and dairy science of Munich's Technical University and five specialist departments of its own.
The 5ha/12 acre "Staudensichtungsgarten" on the northern slope of Thalhauser Strasse offers pleasant walking.

Weihenstephan

Friedensengel (Angel of Peace)   43 54

The Angel of Peace, prominently situated on the upper east embankment of the Isar, was erected by the city of Munich in 1895–99 to commemorate the 25th anniversary of the Peace of Versailles (which ended the 1870–71 Franco-Prussian War) and in honour of the Bavarian Army.
The monument consists of a 23m/75ft Corinthian column surmounted by a gilded bronze figure of an angel, modelled in fact on Nike, the Greek Goddess of Victory at Olympia. At the foot of the column a double staircase leads down to an open temple portico and terrace with a fountain, designed by W. Zimmermann in 1891.
Heinrich Düll, Georg Pezold and Max Heilmeier were the sculptors, Joseph Buhlmann supervising the construction. Originally cast in 1786, the angel was beautifully restored in 1981–83.

Location
Maximilian-
anlagen (right
Isar embankment)

Tram
18

Bus
53

Immediately below the Friedensengel the Isar is spanned by the Luitpoldbrücke (formerly known as the Prinzregentbrücke). Built in 1900–01, the Theodor Fischer-designed bridge is adorned with allegorical figures representing Bavaria, Franconia, Swabia and the Palatine.

Luitpoldbrücke

See Maximilianeum

Maximiliansanlage

Schloss Fürstenried (Fürstenried Castle)   35 49

This hunting lodge in the Fürstenried district was built by Joseph Effner in 1715–17 for the Elector Max Emanuel; from 1886 to 1916 it was the residence of King Otto of Bavaria, who was insane. Since 1925 it has been a house of retreat belonging to the archbishopric of Munich with Freising.

Location
Fürstenried,
Forst-Kasten-
Allee

Schloss Fürstenried is strictly symmetrical in plan, comprising three cube-shaped blocks linked by galleries. The avenue of lime-trees in front of the castle is directly aligned with the towers of the Frauenkirche which can be seen in the distance.

U-Bahn
U3 (Fürstenried West)

Bus 34, 66

Fussgängerzone (pedestrian zone) · 41/42 54/55

After completion of the U-Bahn and S-Bahn tunnel in the Old Town, the municipal authorities resolved to limit the volume of traffic in the city centre by establishing an extensive pedestrian precinct in which people could walk about and do their shopping or window-shopping at leisure. In the centre of the zone is the Marienplatz, with the Altes and Neues Rathaus – see entries – (Old and New Town Halls). From there it extends westward along Kaufinger Strasse and Neuhauser Strasse (see entry) to the Karlsplatz (see entry). In this section are a number of department stores belonging to the major chains. In Neuhauser Strasse are the Karlstor (see Karlsplatz), Bürgersaal, Alte Akademie, Michaelskirche (see entries) and the Deutsche Jagd- und Fischereimuseum (German Hunting and Fishing Museum).

Immediately left of the Town Hall the zone extends northwards along Weinstrasse and Theatinerstrasse (see entry) to the Odeonsplatz (see entry). In Theatinerstrasse, with its elegant and fashionable shops, are the Preysing-Palais (see Theatinerstrasse) and Theatinerkirche (see entry).

The precinct also includes the Frauenplatz (around the Frauenkirche, see entry) and some adjoining lanes, the Petersplatz (round St Peter's Church) and the Viktualienmarkt (see entry) in the southern part of the Old Town.

Location
City centre

S-Bahn
S1–S7 (Karlsplatz, Marienplatz)

U-Bahn
U4, U5 (Karlsplatz), U3, U6 (Marienplatz)

Gärtnerplatztheater (Gärtnerplatz Theatre) · 42 53

The Gärtnerplatz Theatre is, after the National Theatre (see entry), Munich's second opera house (opera, ballet), and is also the only theatre in the city which puts on classical operettas and modern musicals.

Erected in 1864–65 on a triangular site where two streets converge, Franz Michael Reifenstuel's theatre is a triumph of design. Both the architecture and decoration of the building are Late Neo-Classical in style.

The loss of the rich interior decoration as a result of renovation in 1937, together with the removal of cornices, gables, round-arch windows and other decorative features from the exterior, had reduced this once splendid "Temple of the Muses" to a shadow of its former self. Today, after restoration of the interior in 1968–69 and of the sumptuous original façade in 1980–81, the theatre has recovered its earlier magnificence.

Location
Gärtnerplatz 33

U-Bahn
U1, U2 (Fraunhoferstr.)

Tram
18, 20

Bus
52, 56

---

*Gasteig (Gasteig Cultural, Educational and Conference Centre) · 43 53

Equipped with the very latest in conference technology, this modern cultural and conference centre, completed in 1985, was designed by the architects Carl F. Raue, Eike Rollenhagen, Gerd Lindemann and Günter Grossman. Located at Gasteig – from "gachem Steig", meaning steep path (to Haidhausen) – it stands near the site of the old Bürgerbräukeller, a beer-house which became notorious during the Third Reich and which boasted the largest banqueting hall in Munich.

The bunker-like building with its glazed, brick-effect façade is home to the Munich Philharmonic Orchestra, the Richard Strauss Conservatoire, the

Location
Rosenheimer Str. 5

S-Bahn
S1–S7 (Rosenheimer Platz)

Tram
18 (Gasteig)

◄ The "Angel of Peace" monument

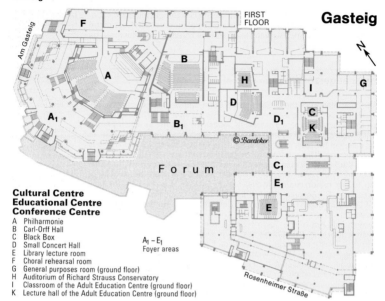

FIRST FLOOR

Gasteig

Cultural Centre
Educational Centre
Conference Centre

A   Philharmonie
B   Carl-Orff Hall
C   Black Box
D   Small Concert Hall
E   Library lecture room
F   Choral rehearsal room
G   General purposes room (ground floor)
H   Auditorium of Richard Strauss Conservatory
I   Classroom of the Adult Education Centre (ground floor)
K   Lecture hall of the Adult Education Centre (ground floor)

$A_1 - E_1$
Foyer areas

© Baedeker

F o r u m

Rosenheimer Straße

Bus 51 (Rosenheimer Platz)	Volkshochschule (adult education centre) and the City Library. Amply endowed with space the Centre offers the best in facilities for all kinds of events. It is visited by more than two million people annually. The Philharmonic Orchestra alone is always fully booked, apart from one or two days in the year.
Philharmonie	The Philharmonie, the largest and most striking of the Centre's several auditoriums, seats up to 2500 people. Highly praised for its accoustics the hall also features a built-in system of endlessly modifiable platform drops.
Carl-Orff-Saal	The Carl-Orff-Saal, with seating for audiences of between 470 and 590 persons, is intended for a variety of uses, but mainly hosts musical events.
Black Box	The 120- to 240-seat Black Box caters for the more high-brow theatrical performances, seminars and concerts.
Kleiner Konzertsaal	Although sometimes used for lectures as well, the Small Concert Hall (130–190 seats) is primarily devoted to music, with popular studio, lunch-time and evening concerts.
Other auditoriums	Library lecture theatre (136-seater), choir practice hall (230sq.m./2475sq.ft, with adjustable seating), ground floor multi-purpose hall (110sq.m/1184sq.ft), adult education centre teaching hall (ground floor; 70 seats), adult education centre lecture theatre (ground floor; 99 seats), Richard Strauss Conservatoire lecture theatre.
Foyer	The foyer, some 1300sq.m/14,000sq.ft in area, running the length of the building, is used for exhibitions, video shows and discussions as well as social events. The glazed exterior ensures a well-lit space.
Outside features	The Centre also has a number of impressive outside features, in particular the boulevard-like Forum enclosed by the building's glass façade.

The Gasteig

Comprising an area of some 3570sq.m/38,430sq.ft, it is used for a variety of events.
Adorning the Centre's south front are a 28m/92ft steel stela by Alf Lechner and an elliptical disc by Rupprecht Geiger; on the south-east side of the complex is a fountain, shaped like a huge wind instrument.

The imposing building to the east of the Cultural Centre is the Bavarian headquarters of GEMA, the organisation responsible for musical copyright, etc.

GEMA

****Glyptothek** (Sculpture Gallery)

41 55

The Glyptothek (from the Greek "glyptik" meaning sculpture, or the art of cutting stone), the oldest museum in Munich, was built between 1816 and 1830 by Leo von Klenze (1784–1864). It houses one of the foremost collections of sculpture in Europe, largely assembled in the early 19th c. by King Ludwig I, a great lover of ancient art. His agents brought back from Egypt, Greece and Italy numerous works of Greek and Roman sculpture, including the fine figures from the pediment of the Temple of Aphaia (*c.* 500 B.C.) on the island of Aegina near Athens, excavated in 1811. Opening times: Tue., Wed., Fri., Sat., Sun. 10am–4.30pm, Thur. noon–8.30pm.

Location
Königsplatz 3

U-Bahn
U2 (Königsplatz)

Tram
18

Leo von Klenze was commissioned by Ludwig to build a new gallery to accommodate the figures. The result, using plans prepared by Karl von Fischer (1782–1820), was the Glyptothek, one of the finest and most celebrated Neo-Classical buildings in Germany. Laid out round a central courtyard, it is fronted by an Ionic portico. The rooms are lit from the courtyard, the exterior walls being windowless, their bareness relieved by eighteen

Architecture

The Munich Glyptothek, like an ancient temple

Relics of the Temple of Aegina

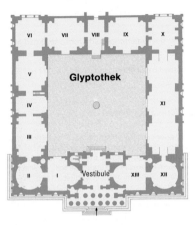

I Early Greek youth figures
II Fauns
III Diomedes
IV Mesarete tomb relief
V Irene
VI Tomb relief with hunter
VII Figures from the west pediment
   of the temple on Aegina
VIII The Sphinx
IX Figures from the east pediment
   of the temple on Aegina
X Alexander room
XI Roman effigy room
XII Apollo room
XIII Boy with goose

© Baedeker

statues in niches. The Glyptothek itself was destroyed by bombing in 1943–44, the interior frescoes by Peter von Cornelius also being lost. But its valuable contents had been removed to places of safety and survived the war undamaged.

After an extended period of rebuilding (rooms remodelled by Josef Wiedemann) the Glyptothek reopened in 1972.

Among numerous outstanding exhibits from the period 500 B.C. to A.D. 250 are:

Sculpture of Homer (antique copy); Early Greek statue of a youth; dedicatory reliefs. — Room I

"Barberinian Faun" (large statue of a satyr), named after the Palazzo Barbarini in Rome where it was found; head of the "Medusa Rondanini" (antique copy). — Room II

Statue of Diomedes; head of Athene; head of a youth. — Room III

Mnesarete tomb relief; woman's tomb, shaped like an ointment jar. — Room IV

Statue of Irene (Greek Goddess of Peace); statue of an athlete (antique copy). — Room V

Relief from a hunter's tomb; relief from a woman's tomb. — Room VI

Sculptural group from the west pediment of the Temple of Aegina, depicting the second siege of Troy by Telemon's son Ajax; coronation. — Room VII

Sphinx from the roof of the Aeginetan temple.
Museum café. — Room VIII

Sculptural group from the east pediment of the Temple of Aegina, depicting the first siege of Troy by Telamon and Hercules. — Room IX

Statue of Alexander; head of Aphrodite (antique copy);
Sculpture of Demosthenes. — Room X

Crowned bust of the Emperor Augustus (who ruled from 31 B.C. to A.D. 14); collection of Roman portrait busts; monumental relief of the marriage of Poseidon; mosaic pavement from a Roman villa in Sentinum. — Room XI

Room XII	Colossal statue of Apollo (the "Apollo Barberini"); statue of the Emperor Domitian (ruled A.D. 81 to 96).
Room XIII	Antique copies of Greek statues; boy with goose, old drunkards, head of a satyr. – Roman sarcophagi.
Courtyard	Bronze recasting of a statue of the Emperor Hadrian (ruled A.D. 117 to 138). Open-air café.

Hauptpost (Main Post Office; formerly Palais Törring-Jettenbach)   42 54

Location
Residenzstr. 2

S-Bahn
S1–S7
(Marienplatz)

U-Bahn
U3, U6
(Marienplatz)

The Palais Törring-Jettenbach, now occupied by the Main Post Office, was built in 1747–54 by Ignaz Anton Gunetzrhainer. The decoration of the interior was the work of his brother Johann Baptist; the stucco-work was by Johann Baptist Zimmermann. Nine figures in the staircase hall, now in the Nationalmuseum (see entry), were carved by Johann Baptist Straub (1744). The palace was acquired by the Post Office in 1834 for 180,000 florins. King Ludwig I had pressed strongly for the purchase, since, in accordance with the plans of his architect Leo von Klenze, he wanted to have a suitably imposing building with a proper colonnaded front in Max-Joseph-Platz opposite the Königsbau wing of the Residenz. Between 1836 and 1839 Klenze modified the palace by adding two additional windows at each end and an open portico in front. The cost of the project was the cause of considerable outcry. Klenze had estimated the cost of the alterations at 85,000 florins, and Ludwig had repeatedly stressed that this was to be the absolute maximum; however, as a result of changes regarded as "highly necessary and advantageous", the final total turned out to be more than twice the estimated sum.

Haus zur Hundskugel (Hundskugel House)   41 54

Location
Hackenstr. 10

S-Bahn
S1–S7
(Marienplatz)

U-Bahn
U3, U6
(Marienplatz),
U1, U2, U3, U6
(Sendlinger Tor)

Gaststätte zur
Hundskugel

Probably designed by Johann Michael Fischer and built in about 1740, this elegant burgher's house with its clearly articulated facade is typical of its period.

Home of the Court Sculptor Johann Baptist Straub from 1741 to 1777, the house took its name from the delightful stucco relief by Roman Boos above the left-hand entrance, showing six dogs playing with a ball (the present relief is a copy).

The Madonna figure (also a copy, the original being in the National Museum, see entry) is by Straub.

The nearby "Zur Hundskugel" on the corner of Hackenstrasse and Hotterstrasse is the oldest inn in Munich, having stood there since 1440. A typical Old Munich half-gabled house with a high pent roof, it also boasts a shallow oriel over the main entrance and a beam for a hoist in the gable.

---

* Heiliggeistkirche (Church of the Holy Ghost)   42 54

Location
Tal 77

S-Bahn
S1–S7
(Marienplatz)

This Gothic hall-church, originally belonging to the Hospice of the Holy Ghost (14th c.), was remodelled in 1724–30 by Johann Georg Ettenhofer (vaulting, refacing of pillars); in the interior can be seen fine Rococo frescoes and stucco ornament by the Asam brothers. After the demolition of the hospice buildings, in 1885, Franz Löwel added three bays at the west end of the church and gave it an imposing Neo-Baroque facade. The church suffered severe damage during the Second World War and its interior furnishings were largely destroyed; extensive rebuilding and restoration was carried out after the war.

U-Bahn
U3, U6
(Marienplatz)

Of the original Gothic church there remain only the choir buttresses and the north wall of the nave.

The tower (1730) has a lantern dome of characteristic Munich type. The Neo-Baroque façade shows a skilful use of elements borrowed from Viscardi's Trinity Church (see entry).

The interior is aisled, with an ambulatory round the choir. The nave is barrel-vaulted, with small vaults over the windows. The aisles have groined vaulting.

Among several items of considerable art-historical interest in the church are: in the porch, to left and right of the main entrance, parts of a bronze memorial made in 1608 by Hans Krumper (see Famous People) for Duke Ferdinand of Bavaria; in the chancel the high altar by Nikolaus Stuber (1730), with an altarpiece by Ulrich Loth "The Effusion of the Holy Spirit" (1661) and two flanking figures of angels by Johann Georg Greiff (1729); right aisle, a series of wall paintings (1725) by Peter Horeman illustrating the "Seven Gifts of the Holy Spirit"; in the Kreuzkapelle, a Late Gothic crucifix (1510); and, midway along the left aisle, an altar with a miraculous image of the "Hammerthaler Madonna" (15th c.).

Furnishings

The interior of the church was renovated at great expense in 1991.

Heiligkreuzkirche (Church of the Holy Cross)   36 48

This Late Gothic parish and pilgrimage church, built in the 15th c., was remodelled in Baroque style in the 17th and 18th c. (stucco-work of 1626 in nave, of 1749 in choir). The tower was given an octagonal superstructure in 1626 and a new onion dome in 1749. The church contains a valuable carved Crucifix (Romanesque, c. 1180) from Seeon Monastery in the Chiemgau. The statues of Christ and the Mater Dolorosa on the pilasters along the wall were the work of A. Fassbinder (1708). Note also the magnificent tabernacle dating from about 1700.

Location
Forstenrieder
Allee 180a

Bus
65, 66, 165

Hildebrand Haus   43 55

Hildebrand House, now occupied by the Monacensia Library, was built in 1897–98 (at much the same time, therefore, as Stuck Villa, see entry). It was the Bogenhausen studio and home of the sculptor Adolf von Hildebrand (1847–1921), among whose best known works is the Wittelsbach Fountain in the Lenbachplatz (see entry). The house, with dormer windows and staircase tower on the garden side, was designed by Hildebrand himself, clearly drawing inspiration from south German Baroque.

In addition to a comprehensive manuscript section, the Munich Library's Monacensia collection includes unpublished works by writers, artists and scientists active in the Bavarian capital. Several illustrious names appear among them, e.g. Ludwig Thoma, Ludwig Ganghofer, Frank Wedekind and Klaus Mann. Some of Hildebrand's sculptures also remain in the house. Opening times: Mon.–Fri. 8am–4pm, Thur. 10am–7pm, Fri. 8am–2.15pm.

Location
Maria-Theresia
Str. 23

U-Bahn
U4 (Prinzregen-
tenplatz)

Tram
18

---

*Hirschgarten (Deer Meadow)   37 55

Originally a tract of common woodland 35ha/86 acres in extent, the Hirschgarten, occupying a low terrace formed during the Würm Ice Age, now provides a welcome 27ha/67 acre swathe of greenery between Nymphenburg Park and the Donnersberg Bridge immediately north of the main

Location
Between Schloss
Nymphenburg and
main railway line

Hofbräuhaus

S-Bahn
S1–S6 (Laim)

Bus
32, 83,
(Steubenplatz)

railway line. Magnificent oaks, beeches and chestnuts among which several pairs of kestrels and tawny owls breed, give this protected area a parklike feel. Signs of withering afflicting some of the great trees reflects the density of urban development in the area and changes in ground-water levels.

The Hirschgarten was designated a deer-park in 1791 on the orders of the Elector Karl Theodor, whose own seat was at Mannheim. At that time several dozen larger game animals, including fallow deer and ibex, grazed the enclosed woodland, and the people of Munich much enjoyed going to see them. The head huntsman, moreover, acquired the right to sell alcohol, which made the Hirschgarten even more popular. In 1890 a fairground of sorts opened near by, eventually evolving into the largest beer garden in the world, capable of accommodating up to 8000 visitors at a time.

Today the Hirschgarten is a delightful oasis in west Munich, a place for relaxing out of doors and enjoying an al fresco meal. A children's playground, barbecues, Bavarian curling, open-air chess, and tobogganning, are among its attractions.

Magdalenendult

Every year on July 22nd the Magdalenendult takes place in the Hirschgarten, honouring St Magdalena, patron saint of Nymphenburg. There are numerous fairground-style amusements – stalls, roundabouts, swings, coconut shies, etc.

---

*Hofbräuhaus   42 54

Location
Am Platzl 9

S-Bahn
S1–S7
(Marienplatz)

U-Bahn
U3, U6
(Marienplatz)

This world-famous beer-hall in the older part of Munich, one of the city's major tourist attractions, was established by Duke Wilhelm V as long ago as 1589 in order to provide for the needs of his Court and domestic staff (Hofbräuhaus means Court Brew-House); but it was not until 1828, when the citizens of Munich were allowed for the first time to drink the excellent beer brewed for the Court, that the brewery began to operate as a beerhouse. Its fame as a place of conviviality soon spread far beyond the bounds of the city, a fame enhanced by a popular song, "In München steht ein Hofbräuhaus". In 1890 the brewery was moved out to Haidhausen, and the Hofbräuhaus, rebuilt in the Neo-Classical style, became a large and busy beer-hall.

On the ground floor is the Schwemme (literally "watering place": the equivalent, perhaps, of the public bar in an English pub), where as many as 1000 customers drink their beer at wooden tables scrubbed till they shine, to the accompaniment of a Bavarian brass band.

Upstairs are a whole range of further rooms: the Trinkstube (for up to 350 people), Schäfflersaal (for 180), Fischerstube (for 70), Jägerstube (for 45), Weihenstephanerstuben (for 30), Wappensaal (for 130), Münchner Zimmer (for 100), Erkerzimmer (for 100), and a banqueting hall capable of seating between 400 and 1300.

In summer beer is served in the colonnaded courtyard with its Löwenbrunnen (Lion Fountain).

Platzl

The Platzl ("Little Square"), world-famous on account of the Hofbräuhaus, was re-modelled in the Neo-Renaissance style around the turn of the century. The buildings surrounding it have recently been undergoing renovation, great care being taken to preserve any surviving old façades and restore traditional architectural detail. Today the square boasts several restaurants and shops, adding to the liveliness of the scene.

Among the Platzl's notable residents was the Court Composer Orlando di Lasso.

The "Platzl am Platzl", once renowned for its cabaret, is now the home of the Bavarian People's Theatre. Its repertoire of folk music and dance ranges from yodelling, "Gstanzi" (rhyming songs) and "Stubnmusi" (fireside music) to "Schuaplattln" (folk dancing), all of which can be enjoyed while sampling old Bavarian Schmankerln (delicacies) from the Platzl kitchen.

The Hofbräuhaus

*Hofgarten (Court Garden)

42 54/55

The Hofgarten, a garden in the Italian style, lies on the north side of the Residenz (see entry), enclosed on two sides by long arcades. It was laid out in its present form in 1613–17, in the time of Duke Maximilian I, and has undergone no significant alteration since then. Rows of chestnuts, limes and maples give welcome shade among the beautifully tended rose- and flowerbeds.

In the centre of the gardens stands the Temple of Diana, a twelve-sided pavilion with a low domed roof (1615; attributed to Heinrich Schön the Elder). The "Tellus Bavarica", the graceful bronze figure on the roof (originally by Hubert Gerhard, 1594), was given new attributes to make it a symbol of Bavaria by Hans Krumper.

A memorial commemorating Munich's civilian bomb victims and servicemen and women of both World Wars, is also found on the east side of the gardens.

See entry

Location
Northern edge
of the Old Town

U-Bahn
U3, U4, U5, U6
(Odeonsplatz)

War Memorial

Staatskanzlei
(Chancellory)

*Ignaz-Günther-Haus

41 54

This house, the studio and home of the sculptor Ignaz Günther (see Famous People), was opened in 1977, after extensive restoration, as a memorial to the great 18th c. exponent of South German Rococo.
On the Oberanger frontage note the characteristic Munich-style "Ohrwaschl" gable and the Madonna figure (by Günther; copy). The interior

Location
Oberanger 11

U-Bahn
U1, U2, U3, U6
(Sendlinger Tor)

77

The Hofgarten and its pavilion (see p. 77)

preserves an old barrel-vaulted timber roof and a Jacob's ladder leading up through two floors. There is an exhibition illustrating Günther's work. The house is now in the care of Munich Stadtmuseum.

*Isartor (Isar Gate)

42 54

Location
Tal,
Isartorplatz

S-Bahn
S1–S7
(Isartor)

Tram 18, 20

The Isartor, the only one of Munich's town gates that has preserved its gate-tower, formed part of the fortifications erected by Ludwig the Bavarian in the first half of the 14th c.

It consists of a tall main tower with the gateway itself in front flanked by smaller towers either side. The fresco (1835) by Caspar Neher above the gateway depicts Ludwig the Bavarian's triumphal entry following his victory over Friedrich the Handsome of Austria at the Battle of Ampfinger in 1322.

Valentin-Musäum

Kuriose

The Valentin-Musäum – the spelling is deliberate, in keeping with the irreverent spirit of the place – commemorates, with the aid of pictures, curios and humorous documents, etc., the popular actor-comedian Karl Valentin (1882–1948; see Famous People) and his comic partner Liesl Karlstadt. Very much a Munich "character", Valentin was particularly noted for his witty dialogues. Opening times: Mon., Tue., Sat. 11.01am–5.29pm, Sun. 10.01am–5.29pm. Entrance fee (as quirky as the opening times).

**Museum of
Folk Music**

In the north gate-tower there is a museum of folk music and a folk-singers' café in the style of a turn-of-the-century coffee house.

The well-preserved Isar Gate

Justizpalast (Old and New Law Courts)

41 54

The Alte Justizpalast, a monumental building with projecting wings on either side, was severely damaged in 1944 and completely renovated a few years ago. Designed by Friedrich von Thiersch and erected between 1887 and 1897, this superb example of Late Historicist architecture incorporates elements of both the Renaissance and Baroque.

The north façade of the building overlooks the Botanische Garten (see entry). The eastern end with its vaulted middle section, facing onto the Karlsplatz (Stachus), has all the effect of a richly decorated main front. The four-sided steel-and-glass dome over the central light well was a novel feature at the time of its construction.

The adjacent "new" Law Courts, a Neo-Gothic building in brick with a clock tower and stepped gables, was also the work of Friedrich von Thiersch. Built in 1906–08 it illustrates the revived interest in North European architectural forms fashionable at that time (the contrast with the Old Law Courts is striking).

Location
Prielmayerstr.
(Near Karlsplatz)

S-Bahn
S1–S7 (Karlsplatz/Stachus)

U-Bahn
U4, U5 (Karlsplatz/Stachus)

Tram
18, 19, 20, 25, 27

*Kammerspiele (Theatre)

42 54

This is the only Art Nouveau theatre in Germany. The oval auditorium (seating 727), with stalls, balcony and boxes, is decorated in a festive combination of red, green and gold. Every detail in decoration and furnishings is Art Nouveau (in Germany known as Jugendstil). The curtain is a reconstruction of the original, which was designed by Richard Riemerschmid. The foyers and entrance lobby are equally consistent in style.

The original colouring has been restored – brown and red in the lobby, blue and green in the foyer on the ground-floor, light grey, yellow and white in the upstairs foyer.

Location
Maximilianstr.
26–28

Tram
19

Built and decorated in 1900–01 by Max Littmann and Richard Riemerschmid, the theatre was renovated in 1937 and again in 1950, in a fashion that destroyed its uniformity of style and decoration. In 1970–71, however, it was restored to its original glory.

Repertoire

The repertoire of the theatre and its associated Werkraumtheater (Theatre Workshop) ranges from classical drama to classic modern plays and experimental contemporary works.

Karlsplatz (Stachus)

41 54

Location
Western edge of the Old Town

S-Bahn
S1–S7 (Karlsplatz/Stachus)

U-Bahn
U4, U5 (Karlsplatz/Stachus)

Tram
18, 19, 20, 25, 27

The Karlsplatz, outside the Karlstor, was laid out in 1791 after the demolition of the old town walls. It was named after the unpopular Elector Karl Theodor, but is familiarly known to the people of Munich as the Stachus, a name the origin of which is uncertain. It may derive from the "Stachusgarten", an eating house which, from 1755, stood on the site now occupied by the Kaufhof department store; or, alternatively, from the "Stachuschützen", marksmen who used to practice on a crossbow range near the Botanische Garten (see entry).
As a result of the development of the Altstadtring (the ring of boulevards round the Old Town) the Karlsplatz lost much of its original layout, gaining instead the doubtful reputation of being one of the busiest traffic intersections in Europe.
During the 1960s the Stachus underwent further costly redevelopment when a multi-storey complex was built incorporating the S- and U-Bahn stations, a shopping level, restaurants, a pedestrian underpass and car parking.

The elegant semi-circle of Neo-Baroque business houses on the east side of the square was the work of Gabriel Seidl, completed in about 1900. Restoration is in progress. The fountain was added in 1972.

A restored façade on the "Stachus" (Karlsplatz)

The triple-arched Karlstor at the western end of Neuhauser Strasse marks the entrance to Munich's Old Town. It formed part of the city's second ring of walls, which stood from 1319 until 1791. Known until then as the Neuhauser Tor, the gate was renamed in 1791 when the walls were demolished on the orders of the Elector Karl Theodor. After an explosion in 1861 the gate was rebuilt, but minus its central tower.

Karlstor *(right margin)*

Karolinenplatz

41 54

The Karolinensplatz, Munich's first star-shaped open space, was laid out in 1809–12 to the plans of Karl von Fischer, who probably took as his model the Place de l'Étoile in Paris. The square is one of those into which the Brienner Strasse (see entry) opens.

Location
North-east of the Altstadt-ring

The obelisk (by Leo von Klenze) in the middle of the square commemorates the 30,000 Bavarian soldiers who fell in the Russian campaign of 1812.

Tram
18

The original Neo-Classical uniformity of the square has unfortunately been damaged by later building.

Munich's America House and the Anthropologische Staatssammlung (State Anthropology Collection; viewing by arrangement) are situated on the south-west side of the square.

*Königsplatz

41 55

The plans for the Königsplatz were drawn up by Leo von Klenze in 1812 in anticipation of the city's expansion. Klenze's designs reflected the ideas of Karl von Fischer, who saw in the Königsplatz a "Forum for the Arts" comparable to the "Forum for the Sciences" represented by Ludwigstrasse. The square took 50 years to complete, the final building, the Propyläen, being finished in 1862, fourteen years after the abdication of King Ludwig I who originally commissioned the scheme.

Location
North-east of the city centre

U-Bahn
U2 (Königsplatz)

Tram
18

Between 1933 and 1935 the appearance of the Königsplatz was completely transformed when, in the hands of the architects Paul Ludwig Troost and Leonhard Gall, the square became the National Socialists's "Akropolis Germaniae" in the so-called "Capital City of the Movement". Granite paving replaced the grass and Klenze's Neo-Classical buildings acquired a new function as the setting for huge Nazi rallies. The National Socialist headquarters in Meiserstrasse/Arcisstrasse were "incorporated" into the square by the removal of trees, the buildings in question being the "Führer's Building" (now a college of music), where the Munich Treaty was signed in 1938, the offices of the NSDAP (National Socialist Workers' Party of Germany, now housing the State Graphic Collection), and two so-called "Temples of Honour", blown up in 1947 as part of the process of de-nazification. These "Temples" had replaced two Neo-Classical buildings designed by Karl von Fischer and Schnorr von Carolsfeld.
Today grass grows once more in the Königsplatz. True to its original Neo-Classical conception, the square has again taken on (since June 1988) the character of an "ancient forum", emphasised by the solitary grandeur of the three tree-framed principal buildings, the Glyptothek, Staatliche Antikensammlung (see entries) and Propyläen (see below).

Propyläen

Leo von Klenze modelled this Neo-Classical "City Gate" (1846–62) on the Propylaea on the Acropolis in Athens.
Aligned with the obelisks in the Karolinenplatz (see entry) further to the east, the Propyläen was conceived as a symbolic gateway giving entrance

Location
Königsplatz

The Propylaea by Klenze in the Königsplatz

from the old city to the new, the latter extending along the original König-strasse to Schloss Nymphenburg (see entry). The Propyläen's Doric style is in deliberate contrast to the "Ionic" Glyptothek (see entry) and the "Corinthian" Staatliche Antikensammlung (see entry).

Pediment
Sculpture

The sculpture in the pediment of the central portico glorifies the Greek struggle for independence from the Turks (1821–29) under King Otto, son of the Bavarian King Ludwig I. On his abdication in 1848 Ludwig I continued to finance the construction of the Propyläen from his private fortune, presenting the finished building to the city of Munich in 1862.

Like the reliefs of scenes of combat beneath the windows of the flanking towers, the pediment was the work of the sculptor Ludwig Schwanthaler (1802–48), also responsible for the Bavaria statue on the Theresienhöhe.

Staatliche
Antikensammlung

See entry

Glyptothek

See entry

Lehel

Location
Left bank of the
Isar between
the Isartor and
the Englischer
Garten

The Lehel district – sometimes referred to as the St-Anna-Vorstadt (suburb of St Anne's) – extends east of the Old Town as far as the Isar. Bisected by the Maximilianstrasse (see entry) and bounded to the west by the Altstadtring (Karl-Scharnagl-Ring), the area was part of the planned expansion of the city which took place in the mid 19th c.
The Lehel is principally residential, with a scattering of small- to medium-sized businesses, its houses dating mainly from the "Gründerzeit" (early

industrial period). Most eye-catching of all from an architectural point of view however are several fine Neo-Renaissance buildings. Among the many distinguished architects to leave their mark on the Lehel, in streets such as Ländstrasse and Thierschstrasse for example, were Albin Lincke, Max Littmann, Emanuel von Seidl and Karl Stöhr. The buildings in Liebigstrasse date almost exclusively from the period between 1870 and 1900. In Reitmorstrasse there are fine Biedermeier, Neo-Baroque and Neo-Classical buildings, and a lovely house (No. 23) in the Jugendstil (Art Nouveau style) by Martin Dülfer.

U-Bahn
U4, U5, (Lehel)

Tram
20

*Klosterkirche St Anna im Lehel 42 54

The Monastic Church of St Anne, built by Johann Michael Fischer in 1727–33, was the first Rococo church in Old Bavaria (i.e. Bavaria within its smaller pre-1803 boundaries). Its central plan was a novelty, the Italian pattern of a rectilinear nave with pilasters here giving place to a central oval with niches and with the chancel and porch built on at either end.
The church was badly damaged during the Second World War, and the reconstruction of the building, decoration and furnishings took many years. In the course of this work the church's beautiful Rococo façade (concealed since 1853 by a Neo-Romanesque façade built on to it) was brought to light and restored.
The fine interior decoration and furnishings (largely reconstructed) were the work of the Asam brothers and Johann Baptist Straub.
High altar: tabernacle and angels in adoration by Straub (1737); stucco figures by Egid Quirin Asam; altarpiece by Asam (reconstructed), "St Anne teaching Mary the Scriptures in the presence of St Joachim".
Front niches: altarpieces, "The last Communion of St Jerome" (right) and "St Paula of Rome with her daughter Eustachia" (left).
Side niches: Early Baroque figure of St Anthony (1682; right), altar with 17th c. "Mater Dolorosa" (left).
Frescoes: scenes from the life of St Anne (by Asam, reconstructed).

Location
St-Anna-Platz

U-Bahn
U4, U5 (Lehel)

Tram
20

Pfarrkirche St Anna 42 54

The Catholic parish church of St Anne was designed by Gabriel von Seidl and built between 1887 and 1892 in the Neo-Romanesque style. The three-aisled piered basilica was very badly damaged during the Second World War, rebuilding being completed only in 1954. The church was renovated again in 1985.
The bronze "Christ as Horseman of the Apocalypse" by Ferdinand von Miller was cast in 1910.
The Paradiesbrunnen (Paradise Fountain) gracing the terrace in front of the church was also designed by Seidl.

Location
St-Anna-Platz

U-Bahn
U4, U5 (Lehel)

Mariannenplatz 42/43 54

The Mariannenplatz, with some handsome late 19th c. buildings, is situated in the southern part of the Lehel district, south of the Maxmonument. Especially noteworthy are the Neo-Baroque west side of the square and the Evangelical Lukaskirche (1896). The latter, designed by Albert Schmidt, has Romanesque and Gothic features.

Tram
20

*Lenbachhaus (Städtische Galerie im Lenbachhaus) 41 55

Since 1929 this villa, once occupied by the celebrated 19th c. painter Franz von Lenbach (1836–1904), has housed Munich's Municipal Art Gallery. The house was built for Lenbach, in collaboration with him, by Gabriel von Seidl in 1887–91, modelled on an Italian country villa of the Renaissance

Location
Luisenstr. 33–35
(near Königsplatz)

Lenbachhaus (Städtische Galerie im Lenbachhaus)

UPPER FLOOR

7–13 19th c. Munich
     painting I
   8 Dilis, Kobell
   9 Rottmann
  13 Spitzweg
14–18 19th c. Munich
     painting II
  14 Defregger, Grützner
  15 Leibl circle
  16 Corinth, Slevogt
  17 Dachau painters
  18 Munich Art Nouveau
19–28 The Blue Rider
  19 Kandinsky 1902–07
  20 Kandinsky, Münter,
     Jawlensky 1908–10
  21 Marc, Macke 1902–10
  22 Kandinsky 1910–11
  23 New Artists' Union
     of Munich
  24 Münter, Jawlensky
  25 Kandinsky 1911–14
  26 Marc, Macke
     Campendonk 1911–17
  27 Klee
  28 Klee, Jawlensky
  29 New Functionalism
30–34 Franz von Lenbach
35–39 Contemporary art I
  37 Joseph Beuys

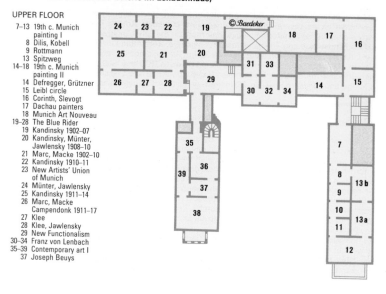

Municipal Gallery
in the Lenbach House

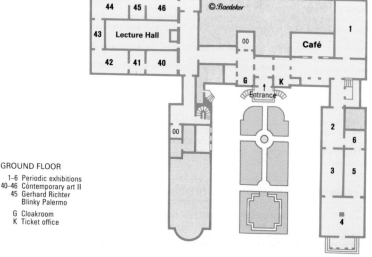

GROUND FLOOR

1–6 Periodic exhibitions
40–46 Contemporary art II
  45 Gerhard Richter
     Blinky Palermo

  G Cloakroom
  K Ticket office

The Lenbach Villa, modelled on an Italian country house

period. The artist's studios were in the south wing, constructed in 1891 and linked with the main building in 1912. The rooms in the main body of the house were badly damaged during the Second World War and now preserve little of their original rich furnishing. The north wing, designed by Hans Grässel, was added between 1927 and 1929, and the annexe on the south side in 1972.

The Municipal Gallery has particularly fine collections of 19th and 20th c. painting. Perhaps most famous of all today are works by artists of the "Blue Rider" school ("Der Blaue Reiter"), acquired by the Gallery after the Second World War. These comprise early 20th c. paintings by Kandinsky, Klee, Macke, Marc, Münter and Jawlensky. Noted 19th c. Munich artists, such as Spitzweg, Leibl, Defregger and Corinth, are also well represented, while the Gallery's collection of contemporary art contains works by Josef Beuys, Asger Jorn, Arnulf Rainer, Andy Warhol and Anselm Kiefer.

Temporary exhibitions are mounted from time to time, for which special arrangements are made. – Recorded programme information: tel. 52 82 50. – Museumspädagogisches Zentrum (MPZ), the museum's educational centre; by arrangement only: tel. 24 38 05–194, –121.

Guided tours on the theme of "Der Blaue Reiter" are organised by the Munich Volkshochschule (adult education college): Wed. 10am, Sun. 11am; fee charged.

U-Bahn
U2 (Königsplatz)

Tram
18 (Karolinenplatz)

Opening times
Tue.–Sun.
10am–6pm,
Thur. until 8pm

Entrance fee
Sun. and
holidays free

Lenbachplatz

41 54

Lenbachplatz is a typical example of turn-of-the-century urban design. The buildings are grouped with a view to picturesque effect, without any precise plan or close relation to one another.

To the south the square opens into Karlsplatz (Stachus, see entry); on its west side are the massive Old Law Courts (see Justizpalast) and the

Location
West edge of the
city centre

S-Bahn
S1–S7 (Karlsplatz/Stachus)

Franz Marc: "Blue Horse" (1911) (see p. 85)

(see p. 85)

U-Bahn
U4, U5 (Karls-
platz/Stachus)

entrance to the Botanischer Garten (see entry), with Herigoyen's Neo-Classical gate; and on the north is the palatial building occupied by the Bavarian stock exchange (see Börse).

Künstlerhaus am Lenbachplatz

Location
South side of
Lenbachplatz

The recently renovated Künstlerhaus (Artists' House) was built by Gabriel von Seidl in 1892–1900 as a meeting-place for the leading Munich artists of the day. It is a tall square building with curving gables and two lower wings

enclosing a courtyard in front of it. The lavish interior decoration, only part of which has survived in its original state, was mainly designed by the prince of painters Franz von Lenbach.
The Künstlerhaus is now occupied by the Mövenpick restaurant and a small theatre.

Wittelsbacherbrunnen (Wittelsbach Fountain)

The Wittelsbacherbrunnen (Wittelsbach Fountain; 1893–95) was erected to commemorate the completion of the new municipal water-supply system.

Location
East side of
Lenbachplatz

The fountain, the work of the sculptor Adolf von Hildebrand, is picturesquely situated on the east side of Lenbachplatz, in front of the clumps of trees in Maximiliansplatz. In its large circular basin, with a high fountain base supporting two smaller basins, are two pieces of sculpture – a youth on a water-horse hurling a boulder and a woman riding another aquatic creature pouring water from a vessel (symbolising the power and beneficence of water).

Leopoldstrasse

42 56/57

Leopoldstrasse continues the line of Ludwigstrasse (see entry) northward from the Siegestor to the square known as the Münchner Freiheit and beyond. It is both a major traffic artery and a favourite promenade for the inhabitants of Schwabing (see entry).

Location
Between Siegestor and Münchner
Freiheit

U-Bahn
U3, U6 (Giselastr., Münchner
Freiheit)

Numerous cafés tempt the passer-by to linger; and on summer evenings, by the light of candles and oil-lamps, artists, students and miscellaneous hawkers offer for sale a wide variety of arts and crafts, trinkets and trash: water-colours and oil-paintings, leather goods, articles in silver-ware, carvings and other items of varying degrees of utility.

* Ludwigskirche

42 55

Ludwigskirche, a parish church as well as the University church, was built between 1829 and 1844 during the development of the northern section of Ludwigstrasse. It was designed by Friedrich von Gärtner, an architect who took his inspiration from the Romantic school, at the behest of King Ludwig I.
The church suffered serious bomb damage during the Second World War but was later restored.
The church's relationship to its surroundings is skilfully contrived. The façade with its widely spaced towers is impressive when seen at an angle from the Ludwigstrasse, and also makes an effective termination of Schellingstrasse. Gärtner also established a relationship between his church and the Baroque Theatinerkirche at the south end of Ludwigstrasse and on the opposite side, taking over from that church its cruciform plan (with small transepts) and the pattern of the façade with its twin towers.

Location
Ludwigstr. 20

U-Bahn
U3, U6
(Universität)

On the façade, in circular niches above the porch, are figures (by Ludwig Schwanthaler, 1832–35) of Christ and the Four Evangelists. The round-headed arches of the porch are continued in the arcading on either side, which links the church with two plain square houses, the presbytery on the south side and a house on the north side, once occupied by Ludwig von Gärtner (see Famous People).

Façade

The interior of the church is dominated by a large fresco (1836–40) of the "Last Judgment" on the altar wall of the chancel. The artist, Peter von

Interior
Last Judgment

Ludwigskirche

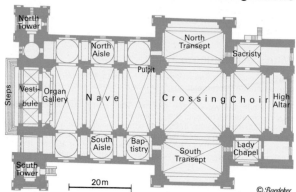

North Tower

North Aisle

North Transept

Sacristy

Pulpit

Steps

Vesti-bule

Organ Gallery

N a v e

C r o s s i n g Choir

High Altar

South Aisle

Bap-tistry

South Transept

Lady Chapel

South Tower

20m

© *Baedeker*

Cornelius, was a member of the "Nazarene" group of painters, founded in 1809, who gave fresh impetus to 19th c. monumental painting. It is the world's largest mural painting after Michelangelo's "Last Judgment" in the Sistine Chapel. The frescoes in the transepts and crossing were also the work of Cornelius.

Ludwigstrasse

Location
Between Odeonsplatz and Universität

U-Bahn
U3, U4, U5, U6 (Odeonsplatz);
U3, U6 (Universität)

Ludwigstrasse is one of Munich's two great monumental avenues (the other being Brienner Strasse, see entry), extending about a kilometre from Odeonsplatz in the direction of Schwabing (see entries). It was laid out at the behest of King Ludwig I as a prestigious street worthy of his kingdom. The general plan of Ludwigstrasse was prepared by Leo von Klenze, who also designed the buildings in the southern part of the street, adopting a rigorously Neo-Classical style modelled on Early Renaissance architecture in Italy. The northern section was built by Klenze's successor as Court Architect, Friedrich von Gärtner. An adherent of the Romantic Christian school of architecture, he favoured Neo-Romanesque.

The change in architectural style, however, did not detract from the overall impression of uniformity, for Gärtner held firmly to Klenze's basic conception of broad-fronted buildings depending on their façades for effect, and narrow streets coming in on the sides. "Europe's most monumental street" (Wölflin) has thus been able to preserve its unity, with only a few façades altered from the original plan.

The terminal point of the street at the south end is the Feldherrnhalle, at the north end the Siegestor (see entries). The architectural pattern was set by the Leuchtenberg-Palais (1816–21). The last building erected in Ludwigstrasse by Klenze was the old Ministry of War, now occupied by the Bavarian State Archive. Friedrich von Gärtner designed the Staatsbibliothek (State Library; No. 16), Ludwigskirche (No. 20) and the University.

Ludwigskirche

See entry

Staats-bibliothek

See entry

Universität

See entry

Bavarian Administrative Court of Justice   *Ludwigskirche*

Luitpoldpark

Luitpoldpark was established in 1911 by Munich citizens who, on his 90th birthday, presented the popular Prince Regent, Prince Luitpold, with 90 lime trees, planting them in rows on the north-western periphery of Schwabing. Later a wide range of facilities for sports and recreation were provided in this area.

Location
Karl-Theodor-Strasse

U-Bahn
U2, U3
(Scheidplatz)

After the Second World War the Schwabinger Schuttberg, a huge and unsightly mound of rubble from buildings destroyed by bombing, was landscaped and planted to make a pleasant hill and viewpoint known today as Luitpoldhügel (Luitpold Hill; 543m/1782ft).

Luitpoldhügel

On the west side of the park stands Bamberger Haus (1913), so called because the architect incorporated into it part of the Franconian Baroque façade of the Böttingerhaus, an old Bamberg mansion.
A popular restaurant offering modern-style cuisine, Bamberger Haus has prettily decorated rooms catering for a variety of occasions and functions. It is possible to breakfast there, or have lunch, or merely sample the excellent beer from the little brewery.

Bamberger Haus

**Marienplatz

Marienplatz has been Munich's central square since the foundation of the town. For many centuries, until 1807, it was the market square, and during the Middle Ages it was frequently the venue of knightly tournaments. The present buildings date mainly from the 19th and 20th c.

Location
City centre

S-Bahn
S1–S7
(Marienplatz)

The dominant feature of the square is the New Town Hall (Neues Rathaus; see entry), a building of overpowering proportions which occupies the

U-Bahn
U3, U6
(Marienplatz)

whole of the north side. At the east end of the square stands the Old Town Hall (Altes Rathaus; see entry), with its reconstructed tower. The massive modern department store at the south-west corner is one of the most controversial of the new buildings in Munich's Old Town.

Marienplatz, today boasting some good-sized department stores and several well-known bars, is the focus of much of the festive life of the Bavarian capital. Here processions traditionally start and end, and political parties hold their rallies. Always crowded with tourists from every part of the world, it is the stage on which buskers, mime artists and amateur acrobats choose to display their skills. Celebrations reach a crescendo on carnival Sunday when the Narren-Lindwurm (Dragon) dances over the square, also during the summer festivals and at Advent when there is a huge Christmas market.

Mariensäule

In the centre of the square rises the Mariensäule (Virgin's Column), erected in 1638 in thanksgiving for the preservation of Munich and Landshut during the Swedish occupation (1632). The red marble column bears a gilded figure of the Virgin as Patroness of Bavaria, with the infant Jesus and a crescent moon, originally carved by Hubert Gerhard for the high altar of the Frauenkirche. The four winged figures of children on the base (probably by Georg Petel) are respectively combating plague, war, famine and heresy.

Fischbrunnen

At the north-east corner of the square is the Fischbrunnen (Fish Fountain), recently erected here, with bronze figures from an earlier fountain of 1865. Until 1901 this was the scene, each year on Shrove Tuesday, of a light-hearted event known as the Metzgersprung (Butchers' Leap). Apprentice butchers, released with much ceremony from their indentures, were then required, wearing sheepskins, to jump into the fountain basin from where they threw nuts into the crowd and splashed the small boys who ran to get them.

Matthäuskirche (St Matthew's Church)   41 53

Location
Nussbaumstr. 1
(Sendlinger-
Tor-Platz)

U-Bahn
U1, U2, U3, U6
(Sendlinger-
Tor)

Matthäuskirche (St Matthew's Church), a Protestant Evangelical cathedral, stands in a dominant position in Sendlinger-Tor-Platz. Built in 1953–55 to the design of G. Gsaenger, it is an unconventional structure on a curving plan, with a curved roof which has become irreverently known as "God's bath-tub". The plain square tower housing the sacristy and parish office is in sharp contrast to the church itself.
The present Matthäuskirche replaces an earlier Neo-Classical building demolished in 1938 when construction of the U-Bahn was expected to begin.

Interior

The interior, with its six tall columns supporting the roof, is of impressive effect. On the wall of the chancel is a marble mosaic by A. Gsaenger, symbolising – in a fashion characteristic of post-war religious art – sorrow, guilt and death. The huge Crucifix over the altar is by R. Schwarzkopf.
As one of the first modern churches to be built in Munich, Matthäuskirche served as a model, pointing the way forward for other new churches.

Maxburg   41 54

Location
Pacellistr.,
Lenbachplatz

S-Bahn
S1–S7 (Karls-
platz/Stachus)

Towards the end of the 16th c. Heinrich Schön the Elder built a stronghold for Duke William V, the Wilhelminische Veste, on a site previously occupied by 54 burghers' houses. His successor, Duke (later the Elector) Maximilian Philipp, made this his residence, and it became known as the Maxburg (Max's Castle). Of the original structure only the tower on the north front survives.

While following the general plan of the Maxburg, the modern building which replaced the castle after the Second World War preserves nothing of the spirit of the original. It is occupied today by the police and criminal justice authorities.

In the courtyard is a fountain (1955) by Joseph Henselmann, "The Moses Fountain", depicting the Prophet standing on a tall crag striking water from the rock.

U-Bahn
U4, U5 (Karlsplatz/Stachus)

Tram 19

---

*Maximilianeum (Bavarian State Parliament)   43 54

The Maximilianeum, seat since 1949 of the Bavarian Landtag (State Parliament) and Senate, closes the vista at the east end of the Maximilianstrasse (see entry). This conspicuous Munich landmark on the east bank of the Isar was built by Friedrich Bürklein between 1857 and 1874. The long main front was originally designed in Gothic style with pointed arches, but at the request of Maximilian II, the architect substituted round-headed arches in Renaissance style, since Gothic arches were felt to be unsuitable for a long series of windows. The broad central block, decorated with semicircular mosaics on a gold ground and topped by a figure of an angel, is flanked on both sides by open arcades. The building was completely renovated in 1985–86.

The Maximilianeum was initially conceived as a picture gallery and a training institute for civil servants. The Maximilianeum Foundation (Stiftung Maximilianeum) still awards scholarships providing free board and lodging for gifted students (in the rear portion of the building).

In 1949 the front portion of the Neo-Renaissance complex with its terracotta-faced façade became the seat of the Bavarian Landtag and Senate. Sessions of the Landtag are open to the public (by arrangement; Bayerischer Landtag, Maximilianeum, D(W)-8000 München 85, tel. 412 63 38).

Location
Max-Planck-Str. 1

Tram
18, 19

Bus
53

The Maximilianeum, seat of the Bavarian Landtag and senate

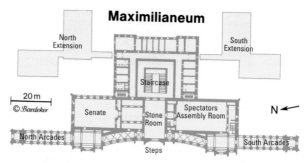

Maximilianeum

The Maximiliansbrücke, spanning the Isar in front of the Maximilianeum, was designed by Zenetti and completed in 1864. It was widened in 1906 by Thiersch. The imposing stone figure of Pallas Athene is by Drexler (1906). The balustrades of the bridge are embellished with handsome Jugendstil (Art Nouveau) ornamentation.

The Maximiliansanlagen, on the right-hand embankment of the Isar below the Maximilianeum, a garden richly endowed with old trees, was designed by Karl Effner. In 1967 this popular spot saw the unveiling of a memorial to King Ludwig II, who contemplated building a festival theatre here.

*Maximilianstrasse

42/43 54

Location
Between
Residenz and
Maximilians-
brücke

Tram
19

Maximilianstrasse, the third of Munich's prestigious 19th c. streets, starts at Max-Joseph-Platz (see entry) and runs south-eastwards to the Isar, ending at the Maximilianeum (see entry). This major thoroughfare, conceived by the architect Friedrich Bürklein and constructed in 1851–53, is the link between the Old Town and the suburbs of Lehel and Haidhausen.
Maximilianstrasse today can justly claim to be one of Germany's finest "golden miles". Here are found August Everding's Opera House and the historic Vier Jahreszeiten (Four Seasons) Hotel, the fashion designer Rudolf Mooshammer, the jeweller Bulgari, also Armani, Hermès and Guy Laroche and Charles Schumann's well-known bar.
In contrast to the rigorously controlled architecture of his father's Ludwigstrasse (see entry), Maximilian II wanted his show street to have a less formal structure: public buildings, shops, hotels, restaurants and gardens were to alternate with one another. This concept, however, was realised only in the western part of the street; the eastern section, like the Ludwigstrasse, consisted predominantly of buildings of imposing monumentality.
For Maximilianstrasse, at Maximilian's behest, a new "uniform architectural style appropriate to the circumstances of our time" was devised – the Maximilianic style, a synthesis of various styles of the past with a predominance of Gothic elements.
Half-way along its course the unity of the Maximilianstrasse is destroyed by its intersection with the Altstadtring, the ring of wide boulevards round the Old Town. In the western half are the Kammerspiele (see entry) and the world-famous Vier Jahreszeiten Hotel (1856–58). Between the intersection with the Altstadtring and the Isar, in the eastern half of the Maximilianstrasse, are the offices of the regional administration of Upper Bavaria (Regierung von Oberbayern, see entry), the Museum of Ethnology (see Völkerkundemuseum), and the Maxmonument.
The vista at the eastern end of Maximilianstrasse is closed by one of the city's most conspicuous landmarks, the Maximilianeum (see entry), on the east side of the Isar.

Maximilianstrasse

The Maxmonument

This imposing monument commemorates Maximilian II (1848–64), who built Maximilianstrasse.

Maxmonument

The bronze figure of the King stands on a tall pedestal of red marble, around which are seated bronze figures symbolising the virtues of State-craft and four children bearing the coats of arms of the four Bavarian peoples (Bavaria, Swabia, Franconia and Rhineland-Palatinate.

In 1989 a Jewish Museum was established at Maximilianstrasse Nr. 36.

Jewish Museum

Max-Joseph-Platz

42 54

Max-Joseph-Platz lies between Marienplatz and Odeonsplatz (see entries), enclosed on its north side by the rebuilt and once again resplendent royal Residenz (see entry), on its east side by the magnificent Nationaltheater (see entry) and on its south side by the Hauptpost (see entry; the former Palais Törring-Jettenbach).

Location
City centre,
near the
Residenz

S-Bahn
S1–S7
(Marienplatz)

Badly damaged in a night of bombing on April 24th–25th 1944, the buildings around Max-Joseph-Platz have all since been restored at great expense, the square thus regaining much of its original splendour.

U-Bahn
U3, U6
(Marienplatz);
U3, U4, U5, U6
(Odeonsplatz)

The square, beneath which is an underground car-park, boasts a memorial to King Maximilian I Joseph with figures by Christian Rauch from the ideas of Leo von Klenze and cast in bronze by Johann Baptist Stiglmaier of Munich.

Tram 19

93

Maxvorstadt

Location
North-west of
the city
centre

Tram
18

Bus
53

Maxvorstadt, a planned early extension of the city begun towards the end of the 18th c., lies to the north-west of the city centre, its lay-out being determined by Brienner Strasse and Ludwigstrasse. Several distinguished architects contributed to its development, among them Leo von Klenze whose magnificent designs for Ludwigstrasse have parallels here in Türkenstrasse (e.g. Kreuter, No. 4, the former Palais Dürckheim, and Schöpke, No. 30).

No. 26 Schellingstrasse, by Martin Dülfer, is also particularly fine, while Richard-Wagner-Strasse is noteworthy for the designs of Leonard Romeis. Other streets with notable buildings are Max-Joseph-Strasse, Amalienstrasse and Karlstrasse, Max-Joseph-Strasse No. 9, the former Palais Schrenck-Notzing, being by Gabriel von Seidl. The character of Maxvorstadt today is chiefly influenced by the presence of several institutes and facilities belonging to the University of Munich. Numerous shops (especially bookshops, antiquarian bookshops, galleries, etc.) and student bars add colour to the scene.

*Münchner Stadtmuseum (Municipal Museum)

Location
St-Jakobs-
Platz 1

S-Bahn
S1–S7
(Marienplatz)

U-Bahn
U3, U6
(Marienplatz);
U1, U2, U3, U6
(Sendlinger Tor)

Munich's Municipal Museum is housed in the Zeughaus, the old municipal Arsenal (a gabled building of the 15th c. with corner turrets which has preserved its vaulted Gothic hall), the adjoining Marstallgebäude (Court Stables; 15th c., reconstructed in 1977–78) and a 20th c. extension. The museum, opened in 1988, gives a comprehensive view of the city's cultural and civic history.

Brief summaries of the collections:

The museum boasts a wide variety of collections in the fields of art, small-scale plastic arts, graphic art (including a vast collection of posters), photography and film. Paintings, period rooms, toys and puppets, folk art and musical instruments are all featured. To overcome limitations of space the museum mounts periodic exhibitions in addition to its permanent displays.

Opening times: Tue.–Sun. 10am–5pm, Wed. until 8.30pm. Entrance fee (Sun. and holidays free).

Permanent displays:

Morisco dancers

Figures of Morisco dancers carved by Erasmus Grasser in about 1480 for the ballroom in the Altes Rathaus (see entry). Dainty, earthy and grotesque, they are notable examples of bourgeois art of the Gothic period. The Morisco (morris) dance was imported from Moorish Spain and was spread throughout Europe by itinerant singers and musicians. It depicts the rivalry among the costumed dancers for the favour of a fair lady.

In the same room are coats of arms (also by Grasser) carved for the barrel-vaulted roof of the municipal Council Chamber, including one with the "Münchner Kindl", the child-figure which is Munich's emblem.

Changing Munich

Views and models covering five centuries, including a very striking model of the city in about 1570.

Armoury

One the largest collections of ancient weaponry in Germany, housed in the Late Gothic Kanonenhalle (Gun Room) of the old Arsenal. The 15th c. suits of armour are rarities of their kind. A collection of armour, helmets, pikes, sidearms, firearms and artillery pieces is displayed in the large hall.

German Brewing
Museum

Exhibition entitled "Bierbrauen einst und jetzt" illustrating the historical development of brewing. Numerous documents, models, pictures and drawings, also bottles, measuring jugs, tankards, beer mugs and glasses.

The former arsenal, now the Munich Municipal Museum

A special collection based on the laboratory of Joseph von Fraunhofer, complete with his optical apparatus, and the Dr Loher Collection on the history of photography (more than 1000 cameras and several dozen projectors).
Collections by J. Breitenbach and U. Scheid focussing on the historico-cultural significance of photography.
Films – those featuring Fritz Lang, Marlene Dietrich and Karl Valentin are especially popular.

Photography and Film Museum

Films old and new are shown daily in the museum cinema (Museumskino; tel. 233–223 67 for programme information).

Museum cinema

About 2000 musical instruments from all over the world – Africa, Asia, America and Europe. Guided tours. Video presentations and orchestrion demonstrations on request (tel. 223–223 67).

Musical instruments

Puppet Theatre Collection, one of the largest of its kind anywhere, with some 50,000 items from around the world (puppets, glove puppets, marionettes, shadow-puppets, etc.).
A number of well-chosen exhibits provide historical insight into the culture of the fairground and circus showman.

Puppet Theatre Museum, Fairground and circus showmanship

Collection of 17th to 20th c. furniture arranged by period, the Biedermeier and Jugendstil (Art Nouveau) pieces being particularly fine. (The pre-1900 furniture is not at present on display.)

Period rooms

A great variety of artefacts dating from 1480 to the 20th c. including civic treasures, goblets, guild memorabilia, coins and medals; also furniture, beautiful ceramics, glassware and wonderful goldwork.

Small-scale plastic arts, applied art, coins

Devotional religious paintings, votive offerings, verre églomisé pictures and cribs. Also three centuries of bridal adornment, elaborately worked

Folk art and textiles

95

accessories, costumes, clothes and fashion jewellery. The fashion archive from the Meisterschule für Mode (Fashion College), founded in Munich in 1931, is particularly interesting.

Toys

This too is one of the finest collections of its kind in Germany. Dolls, doll's houses, toy shops, skittles, rocking horses, figures and other toys of wood and tin. A glimpse into childrens' lives of yesteryear.

Graphic art

A vast collection of graphic art documenting the cultural history of the Bavarian capital. Of special note are: the poster collection; the Parish Collection of pictures relating to the history of costume; and the Böhmer Collection of popular prints (posters, picture histories, etc.).

Paintings

A collection of more than 2000 paintings among which are works by Carl Spitzweg, including "Klausner".

Other branches of the museum

The Municipal Museum has two other branches both of which are well worth visiting. The first, known as Üblackerhäusl (see entry), records life as it used to be in the city's poorer suburbs. By way of contrast the second, the Silbersalon (see entry) in the Altes Hackerhaus, illustrates the comfortable existence of Munich's more prosperous citizenry.

Münzhof (former Hauptmünzamt; the Mint) 42 54

Location
Hofgraben 4

S-Bahn
S1–S7
(Marienplatz)

U-Bahn
U3, U6
(Marienplatz)

This building, which housed the Bavarian Mint from 1809 to 1983, was originally erected by the Court Architect, Wilhelm Egkl, in 1563–67 to accommodate Duke Albrect V's art collection and library, and the Court Stables. Consisting of four wings enclosing an inner courtyard, it was linked by arcades with the Alter Hof (see entry) and the Neuveste (see Residenz). In the 19th c. it was given a Neo-Classical west front and a Neo-Gothic north front (by the addition of arcades of pointed arches). The Mint is now the home of the Bavarian Landesdenkmalamt (the body responsible for the state's historical monuments, etc.).

The courtyard, measuring 32m/105ft by 12m/40ft, has been preserved in its original form, with arcaded galleries on all four sides on each floor level. Of importance as the first introduction into Munich of the Court architecture of the Italian Renaissance, it is far from being a mere copy. While evidently not concerned to achieve a strictly schematic arrangement of the columns and arcades, the architect succeeded in producing an informal, yet at the same time finely proportioned, masterpiece.

The Münzhof has been undergoing extensive restoration for a considerable period.

---

*Museum Mensch und Natur (Museum of Mankind and Nature) 36 56/57

Location
Schloss Nymphenburg (north wing), Maria-Ward-Str. 1b

Tram 12

Bus 41

Opening times
Tue.–Sun.
9am–5pm

Entrance fee

Room 1

The Museum Mensch und Natur was opened in the north wing of Schloss Nymphenburg (see entry) in the summer of 1990, immediately proving a major attraction to the public. It is a branch of the Bavarian State Science Collection (Staatliche Naturwissenschaftliche Sammlungen), replacing an exhibition housed from 1809 to 1944 in the Alte Akademie der Wissenschaften in Neuhauser Strasse.

The new exhibition makes inspired use of the most up to date techniques of museum presentation to bring the discoveries of modern science to an audience largely reared on a diet of television.

Covering an area of 2500sq.m/27,000sq.ft, the exhibition focusses on such topics as the history of the earth, the evolution of life, human biology, the structure and function of the human nervous system and brain, and various environmental issues.

Restless Planet Earth: planetary system, formation and inner make-up of the Earth, Earth four billion years ago (large diorama), earthquakes and volcanos, plate tectonics, continental drift, minerals and rocks, geological "study trips" from Heligoland to the Alps; video displays.

The colourful world of minerals: how minerals are formed, crystalline structures and chemistry, gemstones, quartzes, minerals from around the world.

Room 2

The story of life: the beginnings and evolution of life on Earth (fossils, illustrations; twelve dioramas with reconstructions of animals and plants from various epochs in the Earth's history).

Room 3

Nutrition and population growth: how mankind has obtained food, population growth, hunger and the Third World, geo-agrarian aspects, keeping domestic animals, plant cultivation, formation and working of the soil, soil erosion, destruction of nature, irrigation problems, use of fertilisers and plant pesticides, video presentations dealing with contemporary issues.

Room 4

Species variety: species classification and counting, the relation of the different species to one another, variety within a species.

Room 5

Learning about nature through games: a host of interesting facts about the plant and animal world revealed through interactive games (also computer games), audio-visual programmes and display cases.

Room 6

Man: biological and cultural evolution, Homo sapiens, Man – the ruler of the Earth, human organs (glass woman), embryo development.

Room 7

Nerves and brain: the structure, function and diseases of the human nervous system (interactive working models, experiments, audio-visual programme).

Room 8

Lecture hall, caféteria.

Room 9

Nationalmuseum (Bayerisches Nationalmuseum)

43 55

The Bavarian National Museum, sited on a forum-like extension of the magnificent Prinzregentenstrasse (see entry), was built in 1893–1900 by Gabriel von Seidl, who designed each section of the handsome straggling range of buildings in a different style while preserving a unified effect. Although badly damaged during the Second World War, the greater part of the museum is once again open to the public. An equestrian statue of the Prince Regent Luitpold by Adolf Hildebrand stands in the east wing (study block), extended in 1937–39 by German Bestelmeyer. The extension on the west side houses the Neue Sammlung (New Collection) and the rust-coloured building to the north the National Prehistoric Collection (Prähistorische Staatssammlung). The Bayerisches Nationalmuseum is one of the finest museums for European sculpture and applied art in Germany, most outstanding of all being its collection of medieval German sculpture and its great wealth of tapestries. There are also important collections of bronzes, posters, clocks, porcelain and glass. The museum was founded in 1855 by King Maximilian II and transferred from Maximilianstrasse to its present home in 1900.

Location
Prinzregenten-str. 3

Tram
20

Bus
53

Opening times: Apr.–Sept.: Tue.–Fri. 9.30am–4.30pm, Sat., Sun., holidays 10am–4.30pm; Oct.–Mar.:Tue.–Fri. 9am–4pm, Sat., Sun., holidays 9.30am–4pm. Entrance fee (Sun. and holidays free).

The 47 ground-floor rooms house collections on the theme of the art and cultural history of Bavaria and the south German region, arranged chronologically from the Middle Ages to the 19th c. The art and culture of neighbouring states also receives representation.

Ground floor, Cultural and art history

The rich art history collection includes works by Hans Multscher, Erasmus Grasser, Michael Pacher, Tilman Riemenschneider, Hans Leinberger,

Bavarian National Museum

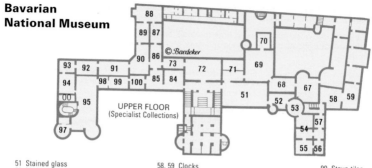

UPPER FLOOR
(Specialist Collections)

51 Stained glass
52 Miniatures
53, 54 Baroque sketches
55, 56 Ivory
57 Intarsia work

58, 59 Clocks
69 Model of the city
71–73 Special exhibitions
85–87 Porcelain

90 Stove tiles
91 Stoneware
92 Majolica
93–95 Faience
96–100 Porcelain

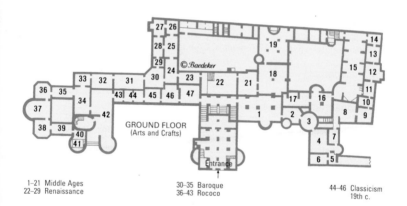

GROUND FLOOR
(Arts and Crafts)

Entrance

1–21 Middle Ages
22–29 Renaissance

30–35 Baroque
36–43 Rococo

44–46 Classicism
19th c.

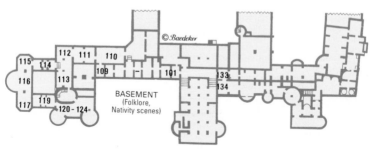

BASEMENT
(Folklore, Nativity scenes)

101–109 Rural living rooms
110 Glass, woodwork

110–117 Religious folk art

119–124 Stove-fitters implements
133 ff Cribs

Georg Petel, Johann Baptist Straub, Ignaz Günther and Franz Xaver Messerschmidt. In addition there are major works of European applied art. The Late Gothic and Renaissance furnishings in particular testify to the heights reached by bourgeois culture in southern Germany.

Among the highlights on the ground floor are:

The "Seeoner Madonna"
Sculptures by Tilman Riemenschneider and Hans Leinberger
Sculptures by Grasser and Polack
The Ignaz-Günther-Saal
The Landshuter-Zimmer
The Tattanbach-Kabinett
The Schwanthaler-Zimmer

Also noteworthy are the Augsburg weaver's room, the room containing the Flanders tapestries and, not least, the model towns (Straubing, Landshut, Ingolstadt and Munich, etc.).

The upper floor features collections of fine manufactured ware and craftwork, some from names famous throughout the world.

Upper floor
Fine manu-
factured ware and
craftwork

Pride of place goes to:

The porcelain, which includes Meissen, Nymphenburg and Ansbach as well as pieces from a number of smaller manufacturers and from French potteries

N.B.
May be closed
for alterations

The Renaissance posters (by Meister Flötner from Nuremberg, and others)
The Baroque sketches in oil in the Reuschel Collection, with works by Januarius Zick, Joseph Anton Feichmayr and Franz Anton Maulbertsch
The ivory carvings
The stained glass (including cycles from the Cistercian monastery at Seligenthal near Landshut)

Also on display are fine gold and silverwork, intarsia-work, textiles, clocks and scientific instruments.

National Museum: the exterior . . .   *. . . and interior*

Nationaltheater

Basement Folk section	Interiors from peasants' houses, pottery (Alzheimer Foundation), glass, basketry, masks, costumes, carvings and religious folklore (e.g. Kriss Collection).
Cribs	The museum possesses a celebrated collection of cribs (Nativity scenes) from Bavaria, Tyrol, Moravia, Naples, Sicily and Provence, dating from the 17th to 19th c.

**Nationaltheater (Bavarian State Opera House) 42 54

Location
Max-Joseph-
Platz 2

S-Bahn
S1–S7
(Marienplatz)

U-Bahn
U3, U4, U5, U6
(Odeonsplatz),
U3, U6
(Marienplatz)

Guided tours
Fri. 2pm

The National Theatre, Munich's world-famous opera house, originally known as the Königliches Hof- und Nationaltheater (Royal Court and National Theatre), was Commissioned by King Max I Joseph and built by Karl von Fischer in Neo-Classical style in 1811–18. Burned down in 1823, it reopened in 1825. It was destroyed again during the Second World War, when the Opera moved to the Prinzregententheater, but was rebuilt in its original form and reopened in 1963. Several more years of renovation were completed in 1988.

The portico with its Corinthian columns and the two triangular pediments are reminiscent of a Greek temple. In the pediment of the portico itself are Apollo and the Muses (by Brenninger, 1972), in the pediment of the tall main structure a coloured glass mosaic on a gold ground depicting Pegasus with the Horae (by Ludwig Schwanthaler). The interior is also predominantly Greek in style – the entrance lobby Doric, the staircase Ionic, the Royal Foyer Corinthian. The auditorium with its five tiers of seating is decorated in red, ivory, dove-blue and gold.

During the reign of Ludwig II, a fervent admirer of Wagner, the first performances of "Tristan und Isolde" (1865), "Die Meistersinger" (1868), "Rheingold" (1869) and "Die Walküre" (1870) were given in the National

The Bavarian National Theatre in Max-Joseph Platz

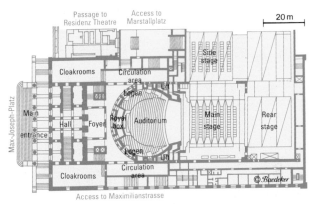

Passage to Residenz Theatre | Access to Marstallplatz | 20 m

Access to Maximilianstrasse

Bavarian National Theatre

Theatre. Among the conductors who have directed operas here have been Hans von Bülow, Bruno Walter, Clemens Krauss, Hans Knappenrtsbusch and Joseph Keilberth.

The National Theatre now ranks among the world's leading opera houses. The most brilliant event in the theatrical season is the Munich Opera Festival, held annually in summer.

Neue Pinakothek (New Picture Gallery)   41 55

The original Neue Pinakothek, built between 1846 and 1853 by August von Voit (1801–70) and Friedrich von Gärtner (1792–1847; see Famous People), suffered heavy damage during the Second World War and had to be pulled down. Thereafter for many years the Gallery's collection of late 18th and 19th c. art was housed in the Haus der Kunst (see Staatsgalerie moderner Kunst).

The new gallery, standing opposite the Alte Pinakothek and contrasting with it, was designed by Alexander von Branca and erected in 1975–80. It is 160m/525ft long by 100m/330ft deep and is the largest museum built in Germany since the last War. In spite of its great size the building is far from ponderous in effect, its bulk being relieved by the rows of narrow round-headed windows, the high glass wall of the entrance hall on the south side (in which the round-arched motif is continued), the pent-roof windows, set back above one another, and the angled end walls and staircases with copper roofs. Branca's use of traditional architectural elements such as round-headed arches, normally considered taboo in modern architecture, reflected his desire to get away from what he called "the pure schematism" of the modern style.

The building consists of two ranges of rooms: one, comprising 22 "Säle" (large rooms) and eleven Kabinette (small rooms), houses the collections of the Neue Pinakothek. The other, in the western part of the building contains the offices of the Directorate of the Bavarian State Picture Collections, a library, photographic laboratories and the Doerner Institute for the Scientific Investigation and Restoration of Works of Art.

In the basement are a room for temporary exhibitions and a video room. There is also a centre for curatorial training.

The Neue Pinakothek possesses some 550 pictures and 50 works of sculpture ranging from Rococo to Jugendstil (Art Nouveau). The foundations of

Location
Barer Str. 29
(entrance
Theresienstr.)

U-Bahn
U2 (Königsplatz)

Tram
18

Opening times
Tue.–Sun.
9.15am–4.30pm,
also Tue. 7–9pm

Entrance fee
(Sun. and
holidays free)

Collection

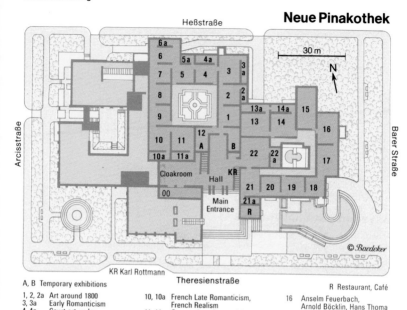

Neue Pinakothek

Heßstraße

30 m

N

Arcisstraße

Barer Straße

© Baedeker

KR Karl Rottmann

Theresienstraße

A, B Temporary exhibitions

R Restaurant, Café

1, 2, 2a Art around 1800
3, 3a Early Romanticism
4, 4a Court art under Ludwig I of Bavaria
5, 5a German neo-classicists in Rome
6 Georg Schäfer Collection
6a Small sculptures
7 Nazarenes
8, 9 Biedermeier

10, 10a French Late Romanticism, French Realism
11, 11a German Late Romanticism, German Realism
12 Kaulbach's sketches for frescoes on the original building
13, 13a Historical and genre painting
14, 14a Painting of the Gründerzeit (early 1870s)
15 Hans von Marées

16 Anselm Feuerbach, Arnold Böcklin, Hans Thoma
17 Leibl and his circle
18 French Impressionism
19 Cézanne, Gauguin, van Gogh
20 Social Realism of the 1880s and 1890s
21 German Impressionists
21a The Secession
22 Symbolism and Art Nouveau

the collection were laid in 1841 by King Ludwig I, who purchased a private collection belonging to Leo von Klenze. In 1868, the year of Ludwig's death, the gallery still had only about 400 works; it was enlarged in 1891 through the gift of Konrad Fiedler. Between 1911 and 1913 further acquisitions were made by purchase from Hugo von Tschudi, including works by Cézanne, Gauguin, van Gogh, Manet and Monet.

Neue Sammlung (State Museum of Applied Art)   43 55

Location
Prinzregenten-
str. 3

Tram 20

Bus 53

Opening times
by arrangement,
tel. 22 78 44

The Neue Sammlung, otherwise known as the Staatliches Museum für angewandte Kunst (State Museum of Applied Arts), occupies the west wing of the Nationalmuseum (see entry). Founded in 1925 it was the inspiration of the arts and crafts movement which came into being in 1907. The museum is dedicated to the preservation and exhibition of objects of any period "formative of taste and displaying excellence in design".
With about 35,000 items, most of them hand crafted, the Munich Neue Sammlung is rightly considered one of the most important collections of its kind. As well as woodwork, glass, ceramics and porcelain, textiles, wicker-work, all sorts of everyday objects, furniture, lamps and metalwork, there are also sections on photography, commercial art and book making.
The comprehensive and ever-expanding poster collection has few rivals.

The Industrial Design section is also particularly worth seeing.

Due to lack of space only part of the collection is on display at any one time, arranged in special exhibitions. Opening times: Tue.–Sun. 10am–5pm, by arrangement only; tel. 22 78 44. Currently there are plans to build a new home for the Neue Sammlung.

Opening times

**Neues Rathaus   42 54

In the mid 19th c. the municipal council resolved to build a new Town Hall to provide much-needed additional office space. A site was cleared by the demolition of 24 older buildings, including the hall in which the Bavarian Estates had met from 1554 to 1807, and a new building was designed by Georg Hauberisser. It was erected in three stages – first the brick-built eastern part (1867–74), then the extension to the rear (1889–92), and finally the western half, in limestone, with the 85m/280ft-high tower, which vies with the towers of the Frauenkirche as Munich's best-known landmark.

The main front, looking onto the Marienplatz, is decorated with a profusion of figures and ornaments – Bavarian dukes, electors and kings, fabulous creatures, saints, Munich types and characters.

The world-famous carillon and display by mechanical figures is the fourth largest in Europe. Every day at 11am (and from May to October also at noon, 5pm and 11pm) the bells play folk-tunes and the figures enact scenes from the history of Munich – the wedding in 1568 of Duke William V and Renate (Renée) of Lorraine, with a jousting-match from which the Bavarian knight emerges the victor (upper figures), and the Schläfflertanz, performed every seven years in thanksgiving for the ending of the plague of 1515–17 (lower figures). In the evening (at 9pm in summer and 7pm in winter) there appear in the oriels on the seventh tier a night-watchman blowing his horn (left) and an angel of peace blessing the Münchner Kindl, emblem of the city of Munich (right).

There are extensive views over the city from the middle gallery of the tower (open: summer Mon.–Fri. 8.30am–7pm, Sat., Sun., holidays 10am–7pm; winter daily 9am–4.30pm).

The public are admitted to council meetings by arrangement; contact the Besucherdienst (Visitor Service): tel. 233–65 77.

Location
Marienplatz 8

S-Bahn
S1–S7
(Marienplatz)

U-Bahn
U3, U6
(Marienplatz)

Entrance fee

View

Council meetings

Neuhauser Strasse/Kaufinger Strasse   54 41/42

Running between Karlsplatz (Stachus) and Marienplatz (see entries), Neuhauser Strasse and Kaufinger Strasse comprise the heart of Munich's pedestrian zone created in the Old Town area after the completion of the U- and S-Bahn tunnels.

Both are major shopping streets, with individual retailers and branches of large departmental stores. Neuhauser Strasse in particular also boasts several noteworthy buildings – Karlstor (see Karlsplatz), the Bürgersaal, the Alte Akademie, the splendid old Michaelskirche (see Sankt Michael) and the Deutsche Jagd- und Fischereimuseum (Hunting and Fishing Museum).

In fine weather the precinct takes on the character of a huge open-air stage, providing a venue for buskers of all nationalities and a colourful motley of street artists and performers of every kind.

See entry

See entry

Standing in front of the Alte Akademie, the Richard-Strauss-Brunnen (1962, by the sculptor Hans Wimmer) makes a fitting memorial to the greatest

Location
City centre

S-Bahn
S1–S7
(Karlsplatz,
Marienplatz)

U-Bahn
U4, U5
(Karlsplatz),
U3, U6
(Marienplatz)

Tram
18, 19, 20, 25,
27

Sankt Michael

Alte Akademie

Richard-Strauss-
Brunnen

Munich-born composer. The bronze column of the 6m/20ft-high fountain is decorated with scenes from Strauss's opera "Salome".

See entry

Bürgersaal

See Karlsplatz

Karlstor

The "Brunnenbuberl", a fountain by M. Gastiner which has a special place in the hearts of Munich people, is situated beside the Karstadt department store near Karlstor.

Brunnenbuberl

Nymphenburg (Nymphenburg Palace and Park)   35–37 55–57

**Palace

This vast Baroque palace on Munich's western outskirts was originally the summer residence of the Wittelsbach Electors. The impressive range of white and grey buildings, more than 600m/2000ft from wing to wing, with yellow ornamentation and red tiled roofs, was enlarged in symmetrical fashion in several phases.

The central mansion was the first part to be built, later linked to pavilions either side by low galleries above open arcades. Adjoining outer pavilions were then added, connected by wings to the large Kavaliersbau and Marstall (stables) built around a courtyard to the south and the old orangery to the north.

These extensions continue to the east in the form of the Rondell, a semicircular range of ten yellow- and whitewashed officials' houses, joined by walls, which close off the park in a charming manner. The entire ensemble is arranged on an east-west axis defined by the Nymphenburg Canal which, tumbling down a splendid marble cascade, enters the park to the west. Initially following a dead-straight course, the canal divides to pass around the main palace buildings, the two branches meeting again in a fountain-adorned pool in front of the principal façade. From there, straight as a die, it continues eastward, flanked by two avenues, the Auffahrtsalleen.

The central pavilion was a gift from the Elector Ferdinand Maria to his wife Adelaide of Savoy, celebrating the birth of an heir, Max Emanuel. The cube-shaped palace in the style of an Italian villa was constructed between 1664 and 1674 by Agostino Barelli. In 1702–04 Max Emanuel commis-

Location
North-west of the city centre

U-Bahn
U1
(Rotkreuzplatz), then tram

Tram
12 (Schloss Nymphenburg)

Bus
41

Opening times
Tue.–Sun.
10am–12.30pm and 1.30–4pm

Entrance fee

Central pavilion

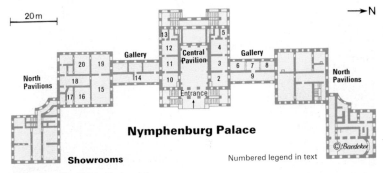

◄ The New City Hall in Marienplatz

Nymphenburg Palace, viewed from the Gardens

The painted ceiling in the Great Hall

The Great Hall (central pavilion)

sioned Enrico Zuccali and Antonio Viscardi to build the galleries and the two side pavilions. The main block acquired its present appearance in about 1715 when Josef Effner added pilasters, arched windows and a number of busts. From 1728 he continued work under the Elector Karl Albrecht, adding the outer wings and the Rondell, beyond which a town was envisaged, to be known as "Carlstadt". Schloss Nymphenburg survived the last war undamaged apart from a direct hit on the palace chapel in the north wing. The houses on the north side of the Rondell were also burned out.

The most notable features of the interior are:

The ballroom, the Steinerner Saal (1; Stone Hall), extending up through three storeys; lavishly decorated – ceiling painting by Johann Baptist and Frans Zimmermann, "Nymphs paying homage to the Goddess Flora" (1756–57), a masterpiece of Bavarian Rococo, and stucco-work by Feichtmayr. Venue for concerts during the "Nymphenburger Sommerspiele" festival in July.

Central block

Ante-room (2) with coffered ceiling (1675) and Regency décor. – Gobelin Room (3); Brussels tapestries made in 1720. – Bedroom (4), the Elector Max Emanuel's "Kleine Schönheitengalerie" ("Little Gallery of Beauties"; portraits of nine ladies who shared his exile in Paris, depicted as goddesses). – Turner's Room (5); painting of the Elector Max III Joseph at the lathe. – Max Emanuel's "Grosse Schönheitsgalerie" or "Large Gallery of Beauties" (6); five portraits of ladies from the Court of Ludwig XIV, painted by P. Gobert in 1710. – Heraldic Room (7); knotted carpets bearing the combined arms of Kurpfalz and Pfalz-Sulzbach, completed in Mannheim in 1756. – Karl Theodor Room (8); portraits of the Elector (1781) by A. Hickel and Electress (1797) by J. Hauber. – Gallery (9) with views (vedute) of Bavarian Schlösser by F. J. Beich (1722–23).

North wing

Gallery in the north wing

South wing

Ante-room (10) with white and gold panelling. – Ante-room (11); wall-coverings of red damask, superb 17th c. Italian table. – Bedroom (12); green velvet and silver bed canopy (1730). – Small Lacquer Room (13) with 17th c. Chinese coromandel lacquered panels on the walls. – Gallery (14); more views (vedute) of Bavarian Schlösser by F. J. Beich, also N. Stuber and J. Stephan (1750–60). – Old Dining Hall (15), furnished around 1807 in the Neo-Classical manner. The Old Dining Hall has assumed the mantle of King Ludwig's "Schönheitsgalerie", in place of the former banqueting hall in the Residenz (destroyed). The best known of the 36 portraits of beautiful women, from all strata of Munich society, commissioned from Joseph Stieler by the King, are those of Helene Sedlmayer, a shoemaker's daughter and later mother of nine children, and the dancer Lola Montez, the King's favourite, daughter of a Scottish officer and a Creole women. – Burr-wood Room (16), furnished in 1810, with portraits of Ludwig I and his wife (1844). – Small Room (17), painted in around 1770. – Little Gallery (18); Still Life by Jan Fyt. – Blue Salon (19), with furniture of 1810. – Bedroom (20); the room in which Ludwig II was born; mahogany furniture, again from 1810.

Palace chapel

The palace chapel is located in the second of the two pavilions on the north side, known as the "Kapellenstock". Designed by Viscardi it was built in 1713 and is provided with its own entrance.
Occupying two storeys the rectangular chapel has a rounded choir niche and oratories for the use of members of the Court built into the upper part of the west wall.

The ceiling is adorned with a wonderfully expressive painting (1759) by J. Mölck illustrating the life of Mary Magdalene.

At the altar can be seen the combined arms of Bavaria and Poland, the homeland of Max Emanuel's second wife.

*Marstallmuseum

The Marstallmuseum, one of the most important museums of its kind in the world, rivalled only by similar collections in Vienna and Lisbon, was set up in the former Court Stables (Marstall) in the south wing of the palace in 1950. Vividly evoking the glittering life of the Munich Court, the exhibits include state coaches and sleighs which belonged to the Bavarian electors and kings, also harness, saddles and other accoutrements. A particularly notable item, sumptuously decorated, is the coronation coach of the Elector Karl Albrecht (later the Emperor Charles VII). Richly carved, and equipped with harness for a team of eight, it represents a masterpiece of Parisian coachbuilding (c. 1735).

Similarly eye-catching are some splendid coaches from the time of Ludwig I and a magnificent state coach belonging to Ludwig II.

Opening times
Tue.–Sun.
10am–noon and
1–4pm

Entrance fee

*Porcelain Museum

Also housed in the south wing (upper floor) is the Porcelain Museum, opened in 1986. This provides a unique and virtually continuous record of the superlative artistry and workmanship of the Nymphenburg porcelain factory, which commenced operations here in 1761. The Bäuml Collection, on loan to the museum, is exceptionally impressive.

Opening times
Tue.–Sun.
10am–noon and
1–4pm

Entrance fee

Porcelain factory

The Nymphenburg porcelain factory, at the north end of the Schloss-rondell, was founded in 1747 and installed here in the palace in 1761. The Rococo creations of its first designer, Franz Anton Bustelli (1754–63), brought it a high reputation, which it has continued to enjoy by maintaining the old traditions.

Salesroom opening times
Mon.–Fri.
8am–noon and
12.30–5pm
(closed holidays)

Nymphenburg porcelain

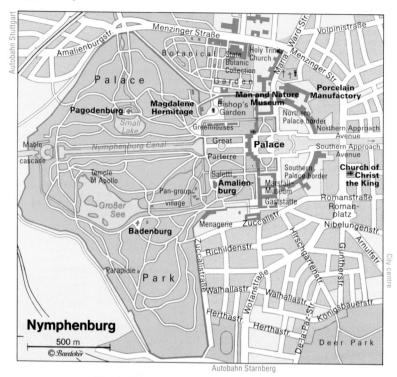

The showrooms are open to the public (groups by prior written arrangement only). Information: tel. 17 24 39.

*Nymphenburg Park

The magnificent walled park extends westwards from the palace for some 1400m/1530yd, being about 2100m/2300yd across from north to south. Begun in 1671 as a small Italian garden, it was enlarged greatly during the 18th c. and redesigned in the French manner. Between 1804 and 1823 it was landscaped in the English style by F. L. von Sckell, who cleverly preserved the main features of the original Baroque layout, the large parterre and the canal.

The Grosses Parterre on the garden side of the palace is ornamented with vases and figures of Greek gods (1769) in white Sterzing marble and, in the centre, a great fountain with a jet 10m/33ft high. The view to the west culminates after some 900m/985yd in the marble cascade at the end of the precisely centred canal.

To the north the park opens directly onto Munich's Botanische Garten. The palace hothouses on the north side of the Grosses Parterre were the most advanced of their time, the palm house boasting the first hot-water heating system installed in Germany. The maze with its Heckentheater (Hedge Theatre) is another feature of the park which should not be missed.

**Amalienburg

This single-storeyed hunting lodge was built by François Cuvilliés in 1734–39 for Maria Amalia, wife of Karl Albrecht. Regarded as the finest example of Court Rococo in Germany, it was beautifully restored to its former splendour in 1956–58. Note in particular on the exterior the charming sculpture (group) of the huntress Diana, and the busts of satyrs. The interior decoration was the work of J. B. Zimmermann and J. Dietrich together with a number of craftsmen, probably Dutch. Unique in design and colouring is the circular Spiegelsaal (Hall of Mirrors), decorated with hunting symbols in silver on a blue ground. In the Ruhezimmer (Rest Room), which is decorated in silver and yellow, are portraits of Karl Albrecht and his wife in riding costume (from the workshop of Georges Desmarées). The Jagdzimmer (Hunting Room), also in silver and yellow, has hunting scenes by G. Horemans and pictures of animals by F. Hamilton. Also worth seeing are the Hundekammer (Dogs' Room), decorated with paintings on hunting themes and furnished with gun-presses with beds for the hunting-dogs, and the Küche (Kitchen), faced entirely with blue and white and coloured Dutch tiles.

Opening times
daily 10am–noon
and 1.30–4pm

Entrance fee

Badenburg

The two-storeyed Badenburg, built by Joseph Effner in 1719–21 as a bathing pavilion for the Elector Max Emanuel, was partially remodelled in the 19th c. in the Neo-Classical style by Leo von Klenze. Restoration work carried out in 1952–53 has successfully erased almost all signs of bomb damage. The ground plan is determined by the oval reception room, which has rich stucco ornamentation (fruit and shells) and a ceiling painting by J. Amigoni, "Apollo in the Chariot of the Sun". The most notable feature of the vestibule (which also served as a games room) is its Chinese wallpaper, with a pattern of birds, flowers and butterflies. The bathing room reaches down to the basement, the bath being faced with Dutch tiles and the walls of the gallery decorated with prefabricated stucco-marble. The bedroom also has Chinese wallpaper, this time with life-size figures.

Opening times
Tue.–Sun.
10am–noon and
1.30–5pm

Entrance fee

Pagodenburg

The Pagodenburg, an elegant two-storeyed tea pavilion roughly cruciform in plan, was also built by Joseph Effner (1716–19). It was mainly used as a place for resting after pall-mall, a ball game played on a horseshoe-shaped "mall" in the Pagodenburger Tal (valley) to the north.
The exterior is decorated with stucco masks (Bacchus, Flora, Neptune, Ceres), the interior in the then popular chinoiserie. On the ground floor is the "Saletti", with a ceiling painting by G. Gumpp and walls faced with Dutch tiles. There are three rooms on the upper floor: the Chinese Salon and Chinese Cabinet have panelling lacquered in black and red, and silk wallpaper; the Rest Room is decorated in white, gold and green.

Opening times
Tue.–Sun.
10am–noon and
1.30–5pm

Entrance fee

Magdalenenklause

In keeping with the custom of the time the Magdalenenklause (Magdalene Hermitage, 1725–28) was designed as a place of prayer and meditation for the aged Elector Max Emanuel, who died however before it was completed. The architect was Joseph Effner. The single-storeyed building with two apses and two round bay windows has artificially contrived cracks in the walls and crumbling plasterwork to simulate a ruin. The chapel, occupying about half the building, was decorated with a mosaic made from imitation coral.

Opening times
Tue.–Sun.
10am–noon and
1.30–5pm

Entrance fee

Odeonsplatz

| | The ceiling paintings by N. G. Stubers are thought to portray the penitent Mary Magdalene. The crucifix, etc. are carved from a narwal tusk. The cells – three of which have heating in the form of stoves with coloured tiles – are panelled in stained oak. |

Saletti
The Saletti, an octagonal pavilion, was built for the Prince Elector Ludwig in 1799.

Temple of Apollo
The Temple of Apollo (Monopteros) was erected in 1865 to the design of Leo von Klenze. It contains a stela recording the dates of the various remodellings of the park.

Hamlet
The Dörfchen ("Hameau"/hamlet), a favourite motif in Baroque gardens, consists of a group of little houses. The machinery in the pump-room, still in operation, is a masterpiece of early technology.

Pan and the He-goat
The statue of Pan and the He-goat was executed by Peter Lamine in 1815.

Marble cascade
The cascade, designed by Joseph Effner, is constructed from nagelfluh (rock composed of slender pebbles) faced with marble. The reclining figures symbolising the Rivers Danube and Isar are by Volpini (1717). Other figures: Minerva, Hercules (1720, by Volpini); Flora, Æolus (1725, by Dubut); Mars, Minerva, Thetis (1775, by R. A. Boos); Neptune (c. 1730, by G. de Groff).

Museum Mensch und Natur
See entry

Odeonsplatz

Location
Northern edge of the city centre

U-Bahn
U3, U4, U5, U6

Odeonsplatz, at the southern end of Ludwigstrasse (see entry), one of Munich's two monumental 19th c. streets, was part of Leo von Klenze's ambitious scheme of urban expansion. Surrounded by several fine buildings it was conceived in celebration of the flourishing Bavarian kingdom, restored in 1806.

Former Odeon
The former Odeon, designed by Leo von Klenze and erected in 1826–28 as a concert hall, occupies the south-west corner of the square. It was almost completely destroyed in the Second World War, when the columns supporting the tiered interior collapsed leaving only the outer walls and courtyard. Partly rebuilt in the 1950s it now houses the Bavarian Ministry of the Interior.

Leuchtenberg-Palais
This Neo-Classical mansion (1816–21), another of Leo von Klenze's designs, here modelled on the Palazzo Farnese in Rome, set the pattern for the development of Ludwigstrasse. Count von Leuchtenberg was Napoleon's stepson Eugène de Beauharnais, for a time Viceroy of Italy, who married a daughter of King Max I Joseph of Bavaria. The palace, rebuilt after being severely damaged during the Second World War, became the headquarters of the Bavarian Ministry of Finance in 1966.

Basargebäude
On its east side Odeonsplatz is bounded by the Basargebäude (Bazaar), a long, narrow building also designed by Leo von Klenze and constructed by Johann Ulrich Himbsel. To the rear lies the Hofgarten (see entry).

Ludwig I Monument
Adorning the west side of the square is an equestrian statue of Ludwig I (1857–62), a realisation by the sculptor Max Widnmann of ideas by Ludwig von Schwanthaler.

Hofgartentor
The Hofgartentor, erected at the eastern end of Brienner Strasse in 1816, gives access to the Hofgarten (see entry).

*Olympiapark (Olympic Park)

The 20th Summer Olympic Games were held in Munich in 1972, the necessary facilities being assembled between 1967 and 1972 on an area of some 2.7 million sq.m/3.2 million sq.yd on the Oberwiesenfeld, once a training ground for the Royal Bavarian army and later an airfield. Incorporated into the site is an artificial hill almost entirely composed of rubble from the last war.

Location
4km/2½ miles north-west of the city centre

The Olympic Park is now a multi-functional recreation area with an appeal far exceeding that of the usual sports arena or tourist attraction. A variety of major events are held there (e.g. the Summer Festival in August and the Tollwood Arts Festival), attended by an ever-increasing number of visitors.

U-Bahn
U2, U3 (Olympiazentrum)

The 290m/950ft television tower, built in 1965–68, was renamed Olympiaturm (Olympia Tower) in honour of the Games. Of its two Körbe (pods), the Postkorb houses the telecommunications installations, and the Aussichtskorb a revolving restaurant and two viewing platforms affording a breathtaking panorama over the city. With a föhn wind blowing the Alps seem almost within touching distance of the tower. Open: daily 9am–11.30pm.

*Olympia Tower

The Olympiastadion, the large and small Olympiahalle, the Olympic Pool and the unusual tent roof, were all erected between 1968 and 1972, the architects being Bhenisch and Partners. The highly original roof construction was the work of the architect Frei Otto.

Olympic Stadium
Olympic Hall
Olympic Pool
**Tent roof

The oval-shaped stadium seating 78,000 spectators is used for major football matches, international athletics meetings, and other similar events including the Compaq Grand Slam Cup. The stadium is also the permanent home of FC Bayern München.

The multi-purpose Olympic Hall (seating for 14,000) provides a venue for all kinds of sporting competitions, pop concerts and conferences.

The vast 74,800sq.m/90,000sq.yd tent roof, a network of cables suspended from twelve steel masts up to 81m/265ft high, covered with translucent acrylic sheeting, was inspired by studies of the surface tension of soap bubbles. Like the roof itself the cost of its construction soared, eventually reaching DM170 million.

A carillon set up in Coubertinplatz (between the sports hall and the stadium) always attracts a large audience.

Carillon

The Olympic cycling stadium (Radstadion) with seating for 5100 spectators was built by civil engineers and architects Beier and Partners.

Cycling stadium

The Eissportstadion (Ice Stadium, seating for 7200) was the only structure apart from the Olympiaturm not built specially for the Games. Its architect was Schütze, while Ackermann designed the neighbouring skating rink.

Ice stadium,
Skating rink

The landscaping of the site included the creation of a lake on the south side, fed by the Nymphenburg canal. The lakeside Theatron, its stage projecting into the water, is used regularly for pop concerts.

Olympic Lake,
Theatron

The 52m/170ft Olympiaberg consists mainly of rubble, the remains of buildings destroyed by bombing and dumped here after the war. It was landscaped in preparation for the Olympics and now provides a popular recreation spot.

Olympic Hill

Standing in a garden to the south-west of Olympiaberg is a Russian Orthodox chapel, the Timofej-Kapelle, built after the Second World War by a Russian recluse known as "Väterchen Timofej" (Little Father Timofej).

Timofej-Kappelle

Designed by Heinle, Wischer and Partners, the Olympisches Dorf Männer (Olympic Mens Village) north of the Mittlerer Ring was later sold off as private housing.

Olympic Village

Women competitors were accommodated in low-rise buildings on the Mittlerer Ring, subsequently converted into residences for 1800 students.

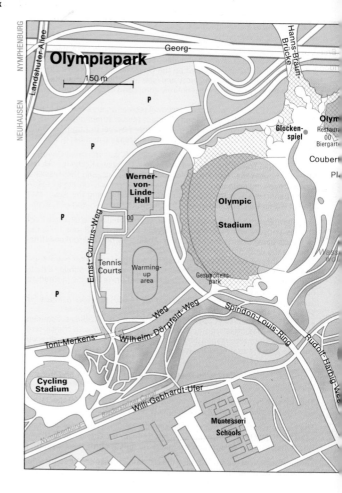

| Terrorist attack | On September 5th 1972 Arab terrorists attacked the Israeli Olympic team, killing eleven of its members. |

** Peterskirche (Alter Peter) (St Peter's Church)   42 54

Location
Rindermarkt 1
(Petersplatz)

St Peter's Church, known affectionately as Alter Peter (Old Peter), is Munich's oldest parish church and was for a long time its only one. It stands on the Petersbergl, a slight eminence which was settled by monks prior to the foundation of the town.

The church has a complicated history. It was preceded by an 11th c. Romanesque basilica (first mentioned in the records in 1169) which was

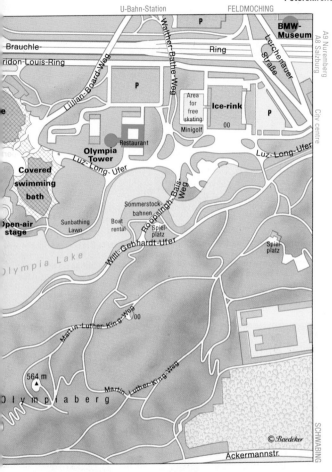

U-Bahn-Station • FELDMOCHING

Brauchle-
ridon-Louis-Ring

BMW-Museum

Ring

Walther-Battke-Weg

Leichenauer Straße

A9 Nuremberg
A8 Salzburg

City centre

P

Area for free skating
Ice-rink
Minigolf

P

Lillian-Board-Weg

Restaurant
Olympia Tower

Luz-Long-Ufer

Luz-Long-Ufer

Covered swimming bath

Open-air stage

Sunbathing Lawn

Sommerstockbahnen

Boat rental

Spielplatz

Roopsingh-Bais-Weg

Witti-Gebhardt-Ufer

Spielplatz

Olympia Lake

Martin-Luther-King-Weg

564 m

Olympiaberg

Martin-Luther-King-Weg

© Baedeker

SCHWABING

Ackermannstr.

destroyed in a great fire in 1327. The present church was built in Gothic style in 1379–86 but was subsequently altered by the addition of a Baroque choir with three apses in 1630–36, the substitution of a barrel-vaulted roof, and the remodelling of the interior in Baroque style (1641–54). Between 1607 and 1621 the tower was given a lantern dome in place of its earlier pair of Gothic spires.

The church was almost totally destroyed during the Second World War. The rebuilding, completed in 1954, kept faith both with the traditional architecture and the original furnishings.

Notable features of the interior are the font by Hans Krumper (under the tower), monuments in red marble by Erasmus Grasser (set in the west wall), the Schrenk Altar (north aisle, *c.* 1470), with sculptures of the Crucifixion and the Last Judgment, the splendid pulpit by J. Prötzner (1750) and

S-Bahn
S1–S7
(Marienplatz)

U-Bahn
U3, U6
(Marienplatz)

Interior

115

St Peter's Church (Peterskirche)

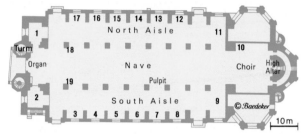

1 St Katherine's Chapel
2 Baptistry Chapel
3 Chapel of the Poor Souls
4 St Sebastian's Altar
5 Three Kings Altar
6 Johann Nepomuk Chapel

7 High Altar
8 St Anne's Chapel
9 Mariahilf Altar
10 Pötschner Altar
11 Corpus Christi Altar
12 St Martin's Chapel

13 Corbinius Altar
15 Wiess Chapel
15 Sandrart altarpiece
16 Mundita Chapel
17 Quirinus Altar
18 Aresing epitaph
19 Pötschner epitaph

the high altar (1730). The latter, 20m/65ft in height, by N. Stuber, has figures by E. Q. Asam of the Four Fathers of the Church and a figure of St Peter by Erasmus Grasser (from an altar of 1517). The panel-paintings on the choir walls are by Jan Polack.

Mariahilf-Altar

At the end of the south aisle stands a highly regarded Mariahilf-Altar (Altar of the Virgin of Mercy) with figures by Ignaz Günther (1756).

"Old Peter"

Pipping Church

The tower of Alter Peter reaches a height of 91m/298ft (including the tip of the papal cross). From the gallery, in fine weather or when the föhn wind blows, it is possible to enjoy a panoramic view of the Alps extending for more than 100km/62 miles.

Tower

The tower can be climbed (299 steps): Mon.–Sat. 9am–7pm, Sun. and holidays 10am–7pm. May be closed in bad weather.

Music is traditionally played from the gallery of the tower: June–Sept. 5.30–6pm (programme in the daily paper).

The tower of Peterskirche boasts no less than eight clock-faces. The first was positioned midway up the tower as early as 1381 while the unusual lantern was equipped with its complement of clocks in 1621.

Tower clocks

Alter Peter's famous chimes are produced by eight bells:

Bells

"Zwölferin" (1382; 650kg/1433lb, note A; which used to be rung at mid-day), "Elferin" (1665; 800kg/1764lb, note G; which used to be rung about 11 in the morning), "Angelus-Glocke" (1951; 900kg/1984lb, note E; rung thrice daily for the angelus), "Maria-Hilf-Glocke" (1958; 1100kg/2425lb, note F), "Maximiliansglocke" (1957; 1600kg/3528lb, note D), "Petrusglocke" (1720; 2250kg/4960lb, note C), "Jubiläumsglocke" (1958; 7000kg/15,435lb, note low F; one of the largest bells in Germany), "Arme-Sünder-Glocke" (14th c.; the Poor Sinners' Bell, also known as "Sterbeglöcklein" or Little Death Bell; used to be rung when the priest was called to the dying and for executions in Marienplatz).

Special chimes: Ringing in the Sabbath: Sat. 3pm; Remembrance chimes for the dead: Sun. 6pm.

By the time the rebuilding of Peterskirche was completed following the Second World War, the church had become famous all over the world. In order to help keep public donations flowing in, Bavarian Radio took to broadcasting only a truncated version of its interval signal – "Solang der Alte Pe . . . (ter, der Petersturm noch steht . . .)". When at last on October 28th 1951 the tower had been raised anew, the full version could once again be heard.

The song: "Alter Peter"

---

*Pippinger Kircherl (St Wolfgang in Pipping)

33 56

The Pippinger Kircherl, officially the Church of St Wolfgang in Pipping, is a rare example of a Late Gothic village church which has survived without modification. Unusually for the Munich area, in which almost all the Gothic churches were remodelled in the Baroque style, the interior of this church, built by Duke Sigismund in 1478–80, escaped the modernising zeal of the 16th and 17th c. The tower was rebuilt in 1794 with a steeple after being destroyed by lightning.

Location
Pipping,
Pippinger Str. 49a

S-Bahn
S3–S6 (Pasing)

Bus
73, 76

The wall-paintings in the chancel (Passion, Death of the Virgin, Prophets, Wise and Foolish Virgins) and the paintings of the Four Fathers of the Church on the stone pulpit were probably the work of Jan Polack (1479). The stained glass dates from 1478–79, the three carved altars (figure of St Wolfgang on high altar) from 1490.

**Prähistorische Staatssammlung (State Prehistoric Collection)

43 55

The State Prehistoric Collection is housed in an exceptionally well designed purpose-built museum overlooking the English Garden.

Location
Lerchenfeldstr. 2

The collection was begun following the foundation in 1759 of the Bavarian Academy of Sciences, and fostered by King Max I Joseph as well as by the very active Historical Society of Upper Bavaria. Towards the end of the 19th c. the anthropologist Johannes Ranke campaigned tirelessly for a separate museum of prehistory.

Tram
20

Bus
53

Opening times: Tue., Wed., Sat., Sun. 9am–4pm, Thur. 9am–8pm, Fri. 9am–3pm.

On display are:

Rooms I–VI
Paleolithic period: finds from the Klausen caves near Neuessing and the Weinberg caves near Mauern.
Mesolithic period: finds from Speckberg near Eichstätt, etc.
Neolithic period: stone tools and pottery, including ribbon-ware from Hienheim near Kehlheim.
Bronze Age: story of metal processing.
Urnfield culture: weapons and tools, including swords, lances and ceremonial axes.
Hallstatt period: jewellery (gold rings, amber, etc.), vessels from the Schirndorf burial site, ornaments of geometric design.
Laténe period: animal figures (from Weltenburg, Lindau, etc.), finds from the Obermenzing healer's grave, relics of the Late Celtic oppidum at Manching, various coins, small gold rainbow bowl from Irsching.

Rooms VII–IX
Roman period: weapons from Künzing Castle on the Danube, sections of mosaic pavements, Terra Sigillata, glass: reconstruction of the female grave at Wehringen near Augsburg, parts of the Roman baths at Schwangau, bronze mask from Eining near Kelheim, treasures from Straubing.

Rooms X–XII
Early Middle Ages: grave goods from Fürst, weapons, jewellery (including elaborate fibulas), items from a royal grave at Wittislingen (e.g. gold disc fibula, gold-leaf cross), model churches, model of the village of Kirchheim, medieval bog corpse.

Foyer/side room
Mosaics from Jordan.

---

*Prince-Carl-Palais
42 55

Location
Königinstr. 1

U-Bahn
U3, U4, U5, U6
(Odeonsplatz)

Bus
53

This Neo-Classical palace, now used by the Bavarian state government for receptions, etc., was built by Karl von Fischer in 1804–06. It takes its name from Prince Carl, brother of Ludwig I, who occupied it from 1825 to 1875. The façade, a model of classical proportion, is articulated by a series of colossal Ionic pilasters before which stands a portico with a high pediment. The palace was originally sited in a park to the north of the Hofgarten. At the end of the 19th c. it acquired a new function in Munich's townscape as the western terminal point of Prinzregentenstrasse (see entry).

Prinzregentenstrasse
42–44 54/55

Location
Between Prinz-Carl-Palais and Vogelweideplatz

Bus
53

This was the last of Munich's great 19th c. streets to be constructed (1891–1912). It is named after the Prince Regent Luitpold, who ruled Bavaria during the incapacity of Ludwig II and the insanity of King Otto. The street was laid out in accordance with the town-planning principles of the day, designed to secure a picturesque effect – with houses set back from the street, curves and sudden widenings so as to achieve variety and surprise. The Prinzregentenstrasse is in sharp contrast to the Ludwigstrasse (see entry), the dead straightness of which was considered dull by turn-of-the-century tastes.

Along Prinzregentenstrasse are a number of very fine buildings, such as the Haus der Kunst (see Staatsgalerie moderner Kunst; No. 1), the official residence of the Bavarian prime minister (No. 7), the Schackgalerie (No. 9, see entry), the Nationalmuseum (No. 3, see entry) and the Bavarian Ministry of Economic Affairs (No. 28).

The road crosses Luitpoldbrücke to the Friedensengel (see entry) which it makes an island. Climbing the Isar embankment and passing Stuck Villa (see entry), it reaches its culmination in Prinzregentenplatz, dominated by the Prinzregententheater (see entry).

Prince-Carl-Palace

*Prinzregententheater (Prince Regent Theatre)   44 54

The Prinzregententheater, with its splendid façade incorporating Jugend-stil (Art Nouveau) and Neo-Classical forms, was designed by Max Littmann and built in 1900–01. Initially it was the Richard Wagner Festival Theatre and later became a playhouse.

After the destruction of the Nationaltheater in the Second World War the Bavaria State Opera found refuge here.

At the end of the 1980s the theatre was renovated at considerable expense. Reconstruction of the orchestra pit and the main stage has been delayed owing to the cost. The interior of the theatre was modelled to a large extent on its great predecessor in Bayreuth. The decorative painting was executed by the artist Ludwig Mössel. The amphitheatre-like auditorium offers excellent viewing.

A statue of Richard Wagner (1913) by Waderé stands on grass next to the Prinzregententheater.

Location
Prinzregenten-platz

U-Bahn
U4 (Prinzregen-tenplatz)

Bus
53, 54 (Prinz-regentenplatz)

Viewing
By arrangement only

Richard Wagner Monument

Promenadeplatz/Kardinal-Faulhaber-Strasse   41/42 54

Once Munich's salt market, Promenadeplatz, a long green space between the Frauenkirche and Dreifaltigkeitkirche (see entries), is today embel-lished with statues of the Prince Elector Max Emanuel, the composers Christoph Willibald Gluck and Orlando di Lasso and the Bavarian historian Lorenz von Westenrieder. The first two are by Friedrich Brugger (1848, 1861), the last two by Max von Widnmann (1849, 1854).

Location
North of the Frauenkirche

Tram
19

Turn-of-the-century architecture of the Prince Regent Theatre

Bayerischer Hof, Kleine Komödie	Bounding the square on the north side are the elegant Hotel Bayerische Hof (in part the former Palais Montgelas) and the Kleine Komödie, a popular theatre.
Palais Montgelas	The palace, in mature Neo-Classical style, was built by Herigoyen for Count Maximilian Joseph von Montgelas, who is regarded as the creator of modern Bavaria (having preserved the independence of Bavaria between the two great powers, Austria and France, and established a central administration). In 1971–72 the palace was almost completely rebuilt and taken over by the Bayerischer Hof Hotel. Some rooms have survived in their original form.
Gunetzrhainer-Haus	Gunetzrhainer-Haus, on the south side of the square, was built in 1730 for his own use by the then Court Architect.
*Palais Holnstein (Archbishop's Palace)	Outstanding among several fine buildings in Kardinal-Faulhaber-Strasse is the Archbishop's Palace (No. 7), an imposing Baroque mansion built by Cuvilliés the Elder in 1733–37 for Countess Holnstein, mistress of the Elector Karl Albrecht. It has a beautifully articulated façade, with a central balcony over the doorway, arched windows protected by grilles and circular windows on the ground floor. The stucco ornament (ascribed to J. B. Zimmermann) is less noteworthy than the Early Rococo architecture of the façade.
Palais Porcia	The Baroque palace at Kardinal-Faulhaber-Strasse No. 12, now the premises of the Bayerische Vereinsbank, was built by Enrico Zuccali in 1693 for Count Fugger. Together with Montgelas-Palais and the Archbishop's Palace it gives this part of the city its distinctive character. It was the first building in Munich modelled on the Italian palaces of the Baroque period. In 1731 the Elector Karl Albrecht presented the palace to his mistress Countess Moravitzka, later Princess Porcia, and in 1736 François Cuvilliés remodelled it in Rococo style.

This Late Gothic brick church with its tall steeple was built by Lukas Rottaler in 1493–94. Originally the cemetery church of the parish of Unserer Lieben Frau (Our Lady), it is now the church of Munich's Greek Orthodox community. The churchyard, which was closed in 1789, contains the graves of Orlando di Lasso and François Cuvilliés. There are remains of Gothic frescoes in the Ridler Memorial Chapel on the north side of the church.

Salvatorkirche
(St Salvator's
Church)

See entry

Dreifaltigkeits-
kirche

Ramersdorf

43–46 50–52

From the Middle Ages up to recent times, Ramersdorf's Kirche Mariä Himmelfahrt (Church of the Assumption) has earned this former village south-east of the city centre a reputation as one of the principal places of pilgrimage in Bavaria. Having earlier this century become a suburb of Munich, it is now the south-eastern gateway to the Bavarian capital, lying on the very busy A8 Autobahn from Salzburg, Innsbruck and the Brenner Pass.

Location
3km/2 miles
south-east of
the city centre

U-Bahn
U1, U2 (Karl-
Preis-Platz)

Although surrounded by densely populated residential areas, the small nucleus of the former village is still easily identified.
Around Bernauer Strasse, to the south-west of Ramersdorf's old village centre, there is an interesting model development of small one- and two-family and terraced houses with little south-facing gardens. It was built for the Deutsche Siedlungsausstellung, an urban building exhibition held in 1934

Bus
45, 95, 96

* Mariä Himmelfahrt (Ramersdorfer Kircherl)

45 51

Mariä Himmelfahrt, better known as "Ramersdorfer Kircherl" (Ramersdorf Little Church), is one of the oldest churches in Bavaria, and stands on the site of an even earlier 11th c. predecessor. The present Late Gothic church was built in 1399 to house a relic of the Cross which had been presented to Ludwig the Bavarian. The church was remodelled in the High Baroque style in 1675 and a dome added to the Gothic tower in 1792.
The image of the enthroned Madonna on the high altar, to which the church owes its fame, probably dates from about 1470.

Location
Aribonenstr. 9

U-Bahn
U1, U2, (Karl-
Preis-Platz)

The Late Gothic furnishings include:
North wall of the nave: winged altar with a high relief of the Crucifixion by Grasser (1483). Nave: panel picture of the Virgin of Mercy ascribed to Jan Polack (1503); paintings of SS Sylvester, Wolfgang, Barbara, Elizabeth, Catherine and Margaret. Chancel: large and impressive votive tablets dating from the 17th and 18th c.

Regierung von Oberbayern (Upper Bavaria Government Building)

42 54

This monumental building, more than 170m/560ft long, in Maximilian-strasse (see entry), was built between 1856 and 1864 for the Upper Bavarian government. The architect responsible, Friedrich Bürklein, embellished his design with arcades, projections, low towers and a number of novel features. The building was badly damaged in the Second World War, only the original façade surviving. The rest was reconstructed in a new form after the war.
Facing the Regierung stands the Völkerkundemuseum (see entry).

Location
Maximilianstr.
39

Tram
19

121

Residenz

Location
Max-Joseph-
Platz 3

U-Bahn
U3, U4, U5, U6
(Odeonsplatz)

Tram 19

Bus 53

Opening times
Tue.–Sat.
10am–4.30pm
Sun. 10am–1pm

Entrance fee

Often referred to as "the ventrical of Bavaria", the Residenz, situated on the north-east edge of the Old Town, was for centuries the seat of the Dukes, then the Electors, and from 1806 to 1918, the Kings of Bavaria. An extensive complex of buildings laid out around seven courts, it comprises three principal sections: the Königsbau, fronting onto Max-Joseph-Platz; the Alte Residenz, facing Residenzstrasse; and the Festsaalbau (Banqueting Hall wing) which overlooks the Hofgarten. The buildings and their furnishings form a magnificent unified whole, the result of stylistic evolution from the Late Renaissance through the Baroque and Rococo to Neo-Classicism. At each stage in the process the finest artists of the day were employed to produce furniture, paintings, tapestries, porcelain and gold- and silver-work. Although much was lost for ever in the bombing, four decades of intensive renovation have seen the majority of the rooms restored to their former splendour.

History of
the buildings

The site on which the Residenz stands was originally occupied by the Neuveste (New Fortress), a moated castle begun in 1385 as a replacement for the Alte Veste on which the medieval city had started to encroach. Located in the north-west corner of the circle of city walls, the Neuveste was initially enlarged around a courtyard between 1470 and 1500, and fortified with a moat. Further enlargement took place in the 16th c. In 1750 however, the old castle burned down (the foundations of its towers and casemates still survive, buried beneath the Apothekenhof). In the 16th c. Albrecht V (1550–79) built the Antiquarium (7), which still exists, and Wilhelm V (1579–97) added the range of buildings adjoining it to the west (by the Grottenhof). In 1611–19 Maximilian I (1597–1651) commissioned what is now called the Alte Residenz, a masterpiece of the late Renaissance and testimony to the growing power of Bavaria. Most of the buildings designed by Zuccali and Effner and constructed during the reign of Max II Emanuel (1679–1726) were destroyed by fire in 1729.
The rooms of the Residenz were richly decorated in the Rococo style in the reign of Karl Albrecht (1726–45). Under his successor Max III Joseph (1745–77), the royal apartments were furnished and the Residenztheater was built. Ludwig I (1825–48) finally brought the evolution of the palace to a splendid conclusion by adding the Neo-Classical Königsbau, the Festsaalbau and the Court Church.

Exterior

The principal features of the exterior reflect two different phases of building. The Neo-Classical façade of the Königsbau on the south side of the complex (Max-Joseph-Platz), which mirrors in style the Renaissance palaces of Florence, and the façade of the Festsaalbau on the north side (Hofgartenstrasse), were both built in the early 19th c. The handsome west front was built at the beginning of the 17th c., with trompe-l'œil painting in tones of grey and blue to give the effect of architectural form and decoration. The two doorways, framed in red marble like triumphal arches, are surmounted by coats of arms and figures of the Virtues and guarded by bronze lions. In a niche in the centre of the façade is a bronze figure (by Hans Krumpper, 1616) of Patrona Bavariae (Patroness of Bavaria) – the Virgin as Queen of Heaven with the Infant Jesus on a crescent moon.
Three of the seven courtyards (Kaiserhof, Kapellenhof, Brunnenhof) have trompe-l'œil painting like that on the west front. The narrow Kapellenhof (Chapel Court) was originally an old lane, the Jägergassl, which was incorporated into the Residenz. The largest of the seven courtyards, the Apothekenhof (Pharmacy Court), is without decoration. (For the Grotten-hof and Königsbauhof, see below under Residenzmuseum.)
The most handsome of the courtyards is the eight-sided Brunnenhof (Fountain Court) flanking the Antiquarium, which was built in 1610. In the

The Residenz, in the Brunnenhof ▶

Residenz

GROUND FLOOR

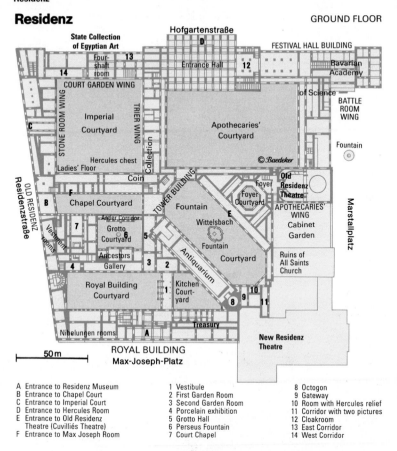

A Entrance to Residenz Museum
B Entrance to Chapel Court
C Entrance to Imperial Court
D Entrance to Hercules Room
E Entrance to Old Residenz
  Theatre (Cuvilliés Theatre)
F Entrance to Max Joseph Room

1 Vestibule
2 First Garden Room
3 Second Garden Room
4 Porcelain exhibition
5 Grotto Hall
6 Perseus Fountain
7 Court Chapel

8 Octogon
9 Gateway
10 Room with Hercules relief
11 Corridor with two pictures
12 Cloakroom
13 East Corridor
14 West Corridor

centre of the courtyard stands the large Wittelsbacher-Brunnen (Wittelsbach Fountain, 1611–23), erected in honour of Duke Otto von Wittelsbach. The bronze figure of the Duke is by Hans Krumpper (1610–20); the reclining river gods (representing the Danube, the Isar, the Lech and the Inn), the standing figures of gods and goddesses (Ceres, Vulcan, Neptune, Juno) and the grotesque fishes, monsters and frogs are by Hubert Gerhard and his pupils (c. 1600).

**Residenzmuseum

Among the most interesting rooms are:

Vestibül

The Vestibule in the Grüne Galerie (Green Gallery) range: built in 1733 by François Cuvilliés the Elder.

The Gallery of Ancestors in the former Gartensaal (Garden Room): probably by Joseph Effner (1726–30), the walls being adorned with 121 portraits of Bavarian rulers, mainly Wittelsbachs and their ancestors.

The Porcelain Room: designed by François Cuvilliés the Elder (1730–33); Nymphenburg, Frankenthal, Sèvres, Vienna, Meissen and Würzburg porcelain in cabinets around the walls. — Porzellankabinett

The Grotto Court: a Mannerist grotto constructed from tufa, crystals and shells (1581–86), with a bronze figure of Mercury (probably by Giovanni da Bologna) and the Perseus Fountain by Hubert Gerhard (c. 1590). — Grottenhof

The Antiquarium: the first part of the present Residenz to be built (by Edkl, 1569–71), a hall 69m/226ft long with a barrel-vaulted roof and side vaults over the windows. Along the walls are antique busts and statues collected by Duke Albrecht V. Allegorical paintings on the vaulting by Peter Candid. In the window recesses are more than a hundred views of Bavaria towns and castles by Hans Donauer. — Antiquarium

Battle Rooms: formerly antechambers to Ludwig I's apartments. Paintings of scenes from the Napoleonic Wars (1805–14) by Peter Hess, Wilhelm von Kobell, Albrecht Adam, Karl von Heideck and Dietrich Monten, which once adorned the officers' banqueting hall in the Festsaalbau, have now replaced the original murals (by Ludwig von Schwanthaler and Schnorr von Carolsfeld) illustrating the legend of the Argonauts and the poems of Hesiod and Homer, which sadly were completely destroyed. — Schlachtensäle

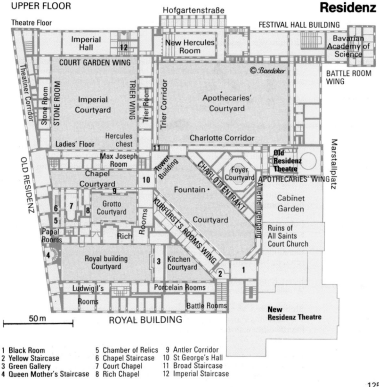

UPPER FLOOR

Residenz

1 Black Room
2 Yellow Staircase
3 Green Gallery
4 Queen Mother's Staircase
5 Chamber of Relics
6 Chapel Staircase
7 Court Chapel
8 Rich Chapel
9 Antler Corridor
10 St George's Hall
11 Broad Staircase
12 Imperial Staircase

Residenz

Porzellan-kammern
The Porcelain Rooms (19th c. porcelain): mainly from the Nymphenburg and Berlin factories and French potteries.

Oriental Porcelain Collection
Since 1920 the Rückwärtige Kurfürstenzimmern (Rear Royal Apartments) have housed a superb collection of oriental porcelain. The artistic perfection achieved by the Chinese porcelain in particular is noteworthy. – The walls are adorned with 17th c. Polish tapestries presented to the House of Wittelsbach as part of a dowry.

Allerheiligengang
All Saints' Corridor (so called because it gave access to the Court Church of All Saints, the Allerheiligkirche, now ruined): cycle of landscape frescoes on Italian travel (1830–33), originally painted by Carl Rottmann for the arcades of the Hofgarten.

Charlottenzimmer
Charlotte Rooms: named after Maximilian I's daughter, whose apartments they were from 1814 to 1816; typical examples of early 19th c. interior decoration.

Reiche Zimmer
Rich Apartments: a series of rooms round the Grottenhof; sumptuous Rococo interiors by Joseph Effner and François Cuvilliés the Elder (1726–37). The stucco decoration by Johann Bapist Zimmermann was reinstated in 1956–60.

Grüne Galerie
The Green Galerie: richly furnished with valuable paintings from the 16th–18th c.

Parade-schlafzimmer
The State Bedroom: a magnificent room designed by François Cuvilliés the Elder in 1730; stucco ceiling, originally by Johann Baptist Zimmermann, restored in the 1950s; carvings by Wenzeslaus Miroffsky. Some of the furniture was made in Paris.

Spiegel-kabinett
Little Hall of Mirrors: also by François Cuvilliés the Elder; stucco ceiling by Johann Baptist Zimmermann and carvings by Wenzeslaus Miroffsky (largely restored after the devastation of the Second World War).

Miniaturen kabinett
Miniature Room: 129 portrait miniatures by German, French, Dutch and Flemish painters of the 16th–18th c. set in the walls.

Nibelungen-säle
Nibelung Rooms: large frescoes of scenes from the "Nibelungenlied", by Schnorr von Carolsfeld, Olivier and Hauschild (19th c.).

Porzellan-kammern
The Porcelain Rooms around the Grottenhof: 18th c. European porcelain – Meissen, Frankenthal, Nymphenburg, Sèvres, Vienna, Ludwigsburg, Berlin, Höchst, Wedgwood, Kassel and Fulda.

Hofkapelle
The Court Chapel: dating from the beginning of the 17th c. and rebuilt after the Second World War.

Reliquien-kammer
Reliquary Room: sacred relics preserved by Maximilian I and his successors. Also a collection of valuable goldsmiths' work from the 16th–18th c.

Reiche Kapelle
Rich Chapel: Maximilian I's private audience chamber, sumptuously decorated by Hans Krumpper.

Silberkammern
Silver Rooms: 17th and 18th c. silver, mainly German and French; the Wittelsbach table silver (3500 items).

Steinzimmer
Stone Rooms: so called on account of the stucco-marble decoration (1612–17) reflecting Maximilian I's conception of the world; sumptuous furnishings (sculpture, furniture, 17th c. tapestries) and collections of majolica and weaponry (1770–90).

Wohnräume König Ludwig I
King Ludwig I's Apartments (upper floor of the Königsbau): designed by Leo von Klenze. Open to the public again after extensive rebuilding, the

Gallery of Ancestors

ceilings, floors and wall decoration are faithful reproductions of the originals. Most of the furniture and other items of furnishing survived the Second World War. Materials used for the upholstery, curtains and baldachines were copied from rediscovered remnants of the original fabrics.

*Schatzkammer (Treasury)

The treasures assembled by the Dukes and Electors over the centuries make this one of the largest, most important and most valuable collections of its kind. The Treasury was founded by Duke Albrecht V (1550–79) with the "house jewels" of the Wittelsbachs, the ownership of which could not be transferred to another family. In the reign of Karl Theodor further treasures came from Heidelberg, Düsseldorf and Mannheim. The latest items in the collection are the insignia of the kingdom of Bavaria established in 1806.

Opening times
Tue.–Sun.
10am–4.30pm

Entrance fee

Arrangement of the rooms:

Early and late Middle Ages: the Emperor Charles the Bald's prayer-book (*c.* 860), crown of the Empress Kunigunde, reliquary of the True Cross which belonged to the Emperor Henry II, a cross which belonged to Queen Gisela (all *c.* 1000), English Queen's crown (*c.* 1370).

Room 1

Late Gothic and Early Renaissance: ostrich-egg ciborium (*c.* 1440), Rappoltstein Goblet (*c.* 1540).

Room II

Statuette of St George (Munich, *c.* 1599).

Room III

Religious art of the Renaissance and Baroque periods: domestic altar of Albrecht V (*c.* 1560), domestic altar (southern Germany, *c.* 1580), Augsburg Crucifix (by G. Petel, *c.* 1630).

Room IV

Insignia and orders of the Bavarian kings, including insignia of the Emperor Charles VII,·ceremonial sword, and ruby jewellery which belonged to Queen Therese.

Room V

Room VIII — High and Late Renaissance: gold and amber work including fine goblets and ornamental vessels.

Room IX — Baroque and Rococo: gold work, tableware, toiletries.

Room X — Non-European art and craftwork, including ivories from Ceylon, Turkish daggers and Chinese porcelain.

**Altes Residenztheater (Cuvilliéstheater)

Entrance
in the
Brunnenhof

Opening times
Mon.–Sat.
2–5pm, Sun.,
and holidays
10am–5pm

Entrance fee

The Altes Residenztheater, also known as the Cuvilliéstheater, is located on the east side of the Residenz. Built by François Cuvilliés in 1750–55 it is the finest Rococo theatre with tiered boxes in Germany. Nowadays used for selected performances, it is well worth visiting. The magnificent carved woodwork of the auditorium, with its four tiers of boxes, Elector's box and proscenium boxes, was safely stored away during the Second World War, thus allowing the theatre to be reconstructed anew in the Apothekenpavilion in 1958.

Architecturally the arrangement of the theatre, which has its entrance in the Brunnenhof and a delightful foyer, is highly successful. The rare elegance and rich hues of the intimate Rococo interior make this a unique setting for Late Baroque operas. It was here in 1781 that Mozart's "Idomeneo" was given its first performance.

Festsaalbau

Location
South side of
the Hofgarten

Access to the Festsaalbau (Banqueting Hall wing), the interior of which suffered severe bomb damage in the Second World War, is from the Hofgarten. During rebuilding in 1952–53 the former Throne Room behind

Bavarian royal insignia

Cuvilliés Theatre (Old Residence Theatre)

the portico was turned into a banqueting and concert hall with seating for 1270. At the same time it was rechristened the Neuer Herkulessaal after the Antwerp tapestries illustrating the myth of Hercules (by M. de Bos; c. 1565 to 1579) which now hang there. Since the Second World War the east wing of the Festsaalbau has been the home of the Bavarian Academy of Sciences, whose old building in Neuhauser Strasse was destroyed in 1944. On the ground floor to the west of the Festsaalbau are a suite of exhibition rooms housing the State Egyptian Collection.

The State Coin Collection is accommodated in part of the building between the Kaiserhof and the Kapellenhof.

*Staatliche Münzsammlung

Established by Duke Albrecht V in 1570, the State Coin Collection has been housed in the Residenz since 1960. one of the largest collections of coins in the world, it embraces all aspects of numismatics, also the history of money and of medallions.

One section is devoted to cut stones (gems and cameos), another to outstanding examples of the medallion-maker's art from the Renaissance to the present day, mainly from Germany and Italy.

A selection of coins, etc. from ancient, medieval and modern times illustrates the history of coinage in Europe and elsewhere.

Entrance
Residenzstr. 1

Opening times
Tue.–Sun.
10am–5pm

Entrance fee

---

*Sankt Maria in Thalkirchen (St Mary's Church in Thalkirchen)   39 50

The site of Sankt Maria in Thalkirchen was already occupied in the 13th c. by a Late Romanesque church, of which the tower and east wall of the nave can still be seen. The present church was constructed in several phases

Location
Thalkirchen,
Fraunbergplatz 1

U-Bahn
U3 (Thalkirchen)

Bus
57

from about 1400. It was remodelled in the Baroque style at the end of the 17th c., and in 1907–08 a Neo-Baroque extension was added (west side) by Gabriel von Seidl.

The late 17th c. altar was refashioned in 1759 by Ignaz Günther whose workshop was also responsible for the figures of the Angels of the Annunciation, St Joachim and St Anne.

The image on the high altar of the Madonna enthroned, to which miraculous powers are traditionally ascribed, is part of a Gothic retable dating from about 1482. It was probably made in Munich rather than Ulm (by Erhart).

The late 17th c. pulpit has exceptionally fine sculptures by Heiland. Opposite are a Mater Dolorosa and a Crucifixion.

Also noteworthy are the ceiling painting of the "Adoration of the Magi" by Schleibner (1917) and the Neo-Baroque altar of St Anthony by Büchsenmann (1911), both in the extension on the west side.

****Sankt Michael** (St Michael's Church)   41 54

Location
Neuhauser Str.
52

U-Bahn
U4, U5 (Karlsplatz/Stachus),
U3, U6
(Marienplatz)

S-Bahn
S1–S7 (Karlsplatz/Stachus,
Marienplatz)

Sankt Michael, the largest Renaissance church north of the Alps, was built by Duke Wilhelm the Pious between 1583 and 1597 as a spiritual centre of inspiration for the Counter-Reformation. It was erected in two stages. In the first stage (1583–88) the church was built and given a barrel-vaulted roof by an unknown architect (the vault being the largest in the world apart from that of St Peter's in Rome). There were grave doubts about the stability of the vaulting; but in fact it was the tower that collapsed, in 1590, destroying the choir. Thereupon, in a second phase of construction lasting until 1597, Friedrich Sustris built on to the undamaged nave a new choir and a transept not envisaged in the original plan. Having suffered severe damage during the Second World War the church was rebuilt in 1946–48. Further costly restoration took place between 1980 and 1983, the stucco-work being beautifully reinstated.

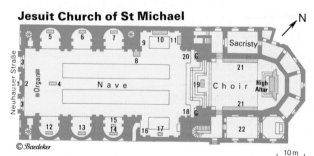

Jesuit Church of St Michael

© Baedeker

10 m

1 St Michael (1588)
2 Christ child (Porta Clausa)
3 Stained glass (c. 1590)
4 Consecration basin angel (1596)
5 Altar of St Ursula
6 Altar of St Andrew
7 Chapel of the English Greeting (Maria Haar Chapel)
8 Pulpit (1697)
9 Round picture, Japanese martyrs
10 Tomb of Eugène Beauharnais, Duke of Luxembourg (d. 1824; B. Thorvaldsen, 1830)
11 Altar of the Name of Jesus
12 The sorrowing Madonna

13 Altar of St Sebastian
14 Altar of St Peter and St Paul
15 Shrine of the Blessed Doctors Cosmos and Damian (Bremen, 1400)
16 Bronze memorial slab of William V
17 Bronze cross (Giovanni da Bologna, 1595)
18 Altar of St Francis Xavier
19 High Altar
20 Altar of St Ignatius
21 Choirstalls (1593)
22 Holy Cross Chapel (1592, with above it the Ducal oratorium)

G Stairs to the Vault of the Princes

Façade of St Michael's Church

With the Alte Akademie (see entry) and the former Augustinian church now occupied by the Hunting and Fishing Museum, Sankt Michael forms an impressive ensemble. Its façade is a masterpiece of proportion. Divided horizontally by three bold cornices, a strong sense of unity is nevertheless preserved by the windows, doorways and niches, all of which are round-headed.

Façade

The figures on the façade proclaim the political programme of the Counter-Reformation. In the ground-floor niche the Archangel Michael (a magnificent figure by Hubert Gerhard, 1588) is shown fighting evil in the world, while in the smaller niches on the upper levels are stone figures (by unknown sculptors) of the kings and dukes who spread Christianity in Bavaria.

Interior

The aisleless nave with its high barrel-vaulted roof is of impressive spatial effect. The dominant feature is the triumphal arch at the entrance to the choir, the pattern of which is continued in the arches of the transepts, side chapels and galleries.

The furnishing of the interior with altars and figures is dictated by a rigorous programme of atonement and purification. A striking feature is the tall three-storey high altar, a joint work by Friedrich Sustris, Wendel Dietrich and Christoph Schwarz; the altarpiece "St Michael fighting the Devil" (1587) is by Schwarz. The four bronze reliefs by Gerhard (c. 1595) were intended for the tomb which Duke William V planned to have erected for himself beneath the triumphal arch, but which was never executed. In the side chapels are fine pictures by Peter Candid, Hans von Aachen and Antonio Viviani, and a precious reliquary of SS Cosmas and Damian (c. 1400, Bremem).

Royal Crypt

Buried in the Fürstengruft (Royal Crypt; open: May–Oct., Mon.–Fri. 10am–1pm and 3–4.30pm) underneath the choir are 41 members of the House of Wittelsbach, among them Duke Wilhelm V, the church's patron, the Elector Maximilian I and King Ludwig II.

Jesuit Crypt

Under the Kreuzkapelle is an old Jesuit crypt.

---

*Sankt Michael in Berg am Laim (St Michael's Church in Berg am Laim)　46 52

Location
Berg am Laim,
Clemens-August-
Str. 9

U-Bahn
U2, U5 (Michaeli-
bad)

Tram
19

Bus
92, 93, 137

Sankt Michael in Berg am Laim is among the most perfectly preserved Rococo churches in Bavaria as well as the loveliest church in the eastern part of Munich. It was built by Johann Michael Fischer in 1738–58 for Archbishop Clemens August of Cologne, son of the Elector Maximilian Emanuel, who held the nearby castle of Berg am Laim. This former Court Church, which was served by a Brotherhood of St Michael, has been since 1913 the parish church of Baumkirchen ward.

The handsome façade, with its twin towers providing a strong vertical accent, was designed as the terminal feature of a street which was never built. The central section is flanked by double columns. Over the main doorway is a shallow niche containing a figure of St Michael (1911) which appears unduly small for its setting.

The interior of the church is dominated by the large round-headed arches between the different sections. The rectangular central space is articulated by pilasters and columns and the corners are rounded off by niches. The beautiful ceiling paintings (episodes from the life of St Michael) are by Johann Baptist Zimmermann, the high altar and the altars in the central area by Johann Baptist Straub. The gilded figures on either side of the tabernacle are attributed to Ignaz Günther.

---

*Schackgalerie (Schack Gallery)　42 55

Location
Prinzregenten-
str. 9

Tram
20

Bus
53

Ground floor

The Schackgalerie occupies a building designed in 1907 by the architect Max Littman for the Prussian legation. The Gallery houses a notable collection illustrating the development of German painting in the 19th c. Its founder, Count Adolf Freidrich von Schack (1815–94), was a generous patron of the arts, purchasing and commissioning works by many 19th c. German painters including Schwind, Spitzweg, Lenbach and Böcklin. The collection, which von Schack bequeathed to the German Emperor, now forms part of the Bavarian State collection.

It is divided into three sections.

Opening times: Wed.–Mon. 9.15am–4.30pm. Entrance fee (Sun. and holidays free).

Room I: Paintings of the Early Romantic school by Johann Georg von Dillis ("View of the Quirinal", etc.), Leo von Klenze, Joseph Anton Koch and others.

Room II: Carl Rottmann.

Schack Gallery

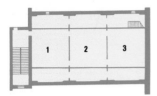

SECOND FLOOR

1 Munich landscape painters
2 German landscape painters
   in Italy
3 Later German historic
   painters

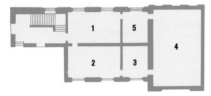

FIRST FLOOR

1, 2 Böcklin
3 Lenbach
4 Feuerbach
5 Kopien,
  Marées

GROUND FLOOR

1 Early
  Romanticism
2 Rottmann
3 Führich,
  Steinle
4, 5 Schwind
6 Neureuther
7 Spitzweg
  Schleich
8, 9 Landscape
  painters

© Baedeker

Room III: Joseph von Führich, Edward Jacob von Steinle.
Rooms IV and V: Moritz von Schwind ("In the Forest", "Early Morning", "Rübezahl", etc.).
Room VI: Eugen Napoleon Neureuther.
Room VII: Eduard Schleich ("Lake Starnberg"), Carl Spitzweg ("A Hypochondriac").
Rooms VIII and IX: Late Romantic landscape painting.

Lenbach copies

Stairs

Rooms I and II: Arnold Böcklin ("Pan frightens a Shepherd", "House by the Sea").
Room III: Franz von Lenbach ("Shepherd Boy", "Self-Portrait", "The Alhambra in Granada", etc.).
Room IV: Anselm Feuerbach ("Portrait of a Roman Lady", "Children making Music, watched by a Nymph", "Paola and Francesca", etc.).
Room V: Hans von Marées, copies.

First floor

Room I: Munich landscape painters.
Room II: German landscape painters in Italy.
Room III: Late German historical painters.

Second floor

Schäftlarn (Abbey)

Kloster Schäftlarn was founded in about 760 by Benedictine monks who settled on the higher ground here on the western edge of the often flooded

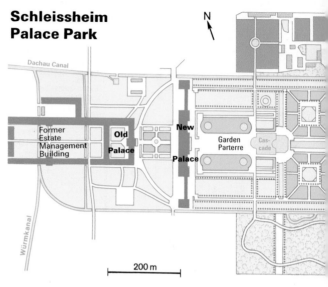

Schleissheim Palace Park

N

Dachau Canal

Former Estate Management Building

Old Palace

New Palace

Garden Parterre

Cascade

Würmkanal

200 m

Location
25km/16 miles
south of the
city centre

S-Bahn
S7 (Ebenhausen-
Schäftlarn)

Bus 961

Isar valley. However the abbey soon passed to the Bishop of Freising. In the 10th c. Schäftlarn was occupied by an order of canons and in 1140 was assigned to the Premonstratensians.

Subsequently the property fell into a state of decay. In 1527 the greater part of the Late Gothic monastery burned down, its replacement, completed in 1594, being granted abbey status at the end of the 16th c. At the beginning of the 18th c. a new abbey building was erected. Having been secularised in 1803, in 1866 Ludwig I of Bavaria gave the property to the Benedictines and in 1910 it became an abbey once more.

Schleissheim (Palace and Park)

Location
12km/7½ miles
north of Munich
city centre

S-Bahn
S1 (Ober-
schleissheim)

Schleissheim (485m/1592ft), on the eastern edge of the Dachauer Moos (Dachau Fen), is famous for its three handsome palaces. After abdicating early in favour of his son the Elector Maximilian I, Duke Wilhelm V (reigned 1579–97) retired to Schleissheim to devote himself to religious contemplation. Here he purchased isolated farmhouses, erected hermitages and chapels and, in 1598–1600, built himself a modest country house. This was completed by Maximilian between 1617 and 1623 and is known as the Alte Schloss (Old Palace).

Altes Schloss

Opening times
Tue.–Sun.
10am–5pm

Entrance fee

The Altes Schloss is an unpretentious country manor with two corner turrets and a flight of steps leading up to the entrance. Badly damaged by fire in 1944, the exterior was restored after the war (work completed 1972). At the rear is a courtyard with old trees, from which a gatehouse gives access to the domestic offices of Wilhelm V's original house.

An exhibition "Das Evangelium in den Wohnungen der Völker" (The Gospel in the Homes of the People; Gertrud Weinhold Collection) can be seen inside the Altes Schloss.

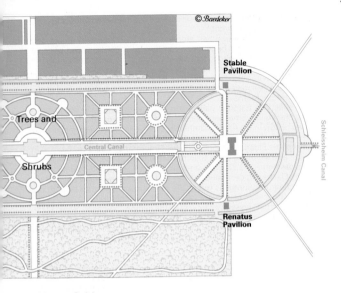

© *Baedeker*

Stable
Pavilion

Trees and

Central Canal

Shrubs

Schleissheim Canal

Renatus
Pavilion

*Neues Schloss

The 330m/1083ft-long Neues Schloss (New Palace) comprises a main
building with taller, triple-articulated central section, linked by arcades to
lateral pavilions either side. In style it reflects the transition from Italian to
French taste and is at present painted white and grey with window frames
and other decorative elements picked out in yellow.

Opening times
Tue.–Sun.
10am–12.30pm
and 1.30–4pm

Entrance fee

Following his victory over the Turks in 1688 the Elector Max Emanuel, then
at the height of his power, resolved to mark the fact by constructing one of
the largest buildings of his time. A start was made under Enrico Zuccali in
1701–04 with the shell of the Neues Schloss, intended to be part of a great
palace laid out four-square around a central courtyard (with the Altes
Schloss forming the west wing). Max Emanual was forced to abandon this
ambitious plan however. From 1719 work continued on a more modest
scale under Joseph Effner, ceasing altogether in 1727. Almost a century
later Ludwig I commissioned Leo von Klenze to alter Effner's façade, giving
it strict articulation. The palace was badly damaged during the last war, but
since the summer of 1972 all the rooms have again been open.

The particular charm of the beautifully designed and decorated interior (by
Effner and others, 1720–26), lies in its successful mingling of Italian Late
Baroque and Early Rococo. The murals and stucco-work are full of motifs
from the Turkish wars.

The fine carving on the main doors on both fronts was the work of Ignaz
Günther (1736).

The following rooms are especially fine:
Entrance hall, with eight red Lake Teger marble columns and *trompe-l'œil*
paintings by Nikolaus Stuber in the low domes framed in stucco ornament.
Garden Room, with grisaille paintings by Stuber and stucco-work (sea-
monsters) by Guiseppi Volpini.
Staircase Hall, designed by Effner, with green Brixen marble columns and
Corinthian pilasters; fresco in dome "Vulkan's Forge" by C. D. Asam,

stucco ornament (Turkish trophies) above the windows and doors by J. B. Zimmermann and C. Dubut.

Great Hall, rising through two storeys; stucco ornament by Dubut and Zimmermann and two huge battle pictures by J. Beich; ceiling-painting "Aeneas and Turnus fighting for Princess Lavinia" by Jacopo Amigoni. The chessboard floor is of Lake Teger marble.

Hall of Victories, which takes its name from nine battle pictures by Beich; the Régence decoration of this former dining-room makes it one of the finest Baroque rooms.

Great Gallery: a Baroque gallery 61m/200ft long, originally designed to house Maximilian Emanuel's collection of pictures from the Netherlands. These are now in the Alte Pinakothek (see entry) and have been replaced by other Dutch, Flemish, German and Italian works by, among others, Brueghel the Elder, Honthorst, Teniers, Tintoretto and Veronese.

To right and left of the Great Gallery, overlooking the garden, are magnificent staterooms, the Elector's embellished with white and gold panelling and the Electress's decorated in silver and blue. Noteworthy even in these extraordinarily sumptuous rooms are the Brussels tapestries by J. d. Vos (1724) with scenes of military campaigns; also the ceiling fresco in the dining-room of Odysseus's captivity by the nymph Calypso (C. Wink, 1772), and the Scagliola wall-covering in the Kammerkapelle. The rooms beneath on the ground floor, formerly the apartments of the Prince and Princess Electors, now house a gallery of European Baroque painting.

The Maximilianskapelle was the work of Joseph Effner. Extending upwards through each of the storeys, it has a fine ceiling fresco by C. D. Asam. The box seating behind the windows on the east side was for members of the Court.

New Schleissheim Palace (Neues Schloss)

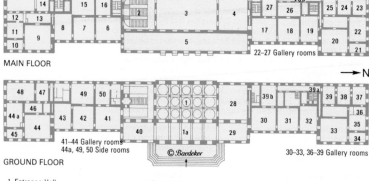

MAIN FLOOR

→ N

GROUND FLOOR

41–44 Gallery rooms
44a, 49, 50 Side rooms

22–27 Gallery rooms

30–33, 36–39 Gallery rooms

© Baedeker

1 Entrance Hall
1a Sala terrena
2 Stairwell
3 Great Hall
4 Hall of Victories
5 Grotto Gallery
6 Prince's antechamber
7 Prince's audience chamber
8 Prince's state bedroom
9 Prince's living-room
10 Red chamber (hunting room)

11 Dutch paintings
12 Oratorium
13 Oratorium with altar
14 Balcony of the Great Hall
15 Room with model of palace
16 Documentation room
17 Princess's antechamber
18 Princess's audience chamber
19 Princess's state bedroom
20 Princess's living-room

21 Upper chapel
28 Dining hall
29 North antechamber (billiard or music room)
34 Stucco exhibition
35 Wood-turning room
40 South antechamber
45 Blue Room
46 Sacristy
47 Anteroom of the Great (Maximilian's chapel)

*Park

Schleissheim Park was laid out in 1720 to plans by D. Girard, its dimensions (1250 by 350m/1370 by 380yd) having been set considerably earlier, in 1684, by the construction of Schloss Lustheim – as a "point de vue" – and the two lateral canals. Together with the parks at Herrenhausen in Hannover and Veitshöchheim near Würzburg, Schleissheim is one of the few Baroque gardens in Germany to have survived in its original state. In front of the Neues Schloss lies a parterre (renewed in about 1830), with two fountains and a cascade (1724); beyond this are two square gardens enclosed by hedges and beyond these again, in the centre of the park, is a circular garden. A canal runs the whole length down the middle of the park, dividing at its farther end to form a ring around Lustheim. Beautiful avenues of limes border the garden on either side. The statuary unfortunately has disappeared.

Schloss Lustheim

Older than the Neues Schloss, this small yellow and white palace at the far end of the park was built in 1684–88 by Enrico Zuccali on the occasion of the marriage of the Elector Max Emanuel to Maria Antonia, daughter of Leopold I, Emperor of Austria. Built in the style of an Italian garden casino, it stands on a circular island ringed by a canal, the intention undoubtedly being to recreate Cythera, legendary island of love and happiness. On the north side of the palace stand what were once stables for the Electoral couple's horses, to the south the former Renatius Chapel, also by Zuccali. These two buildings were apparently linked at one time by semi-circular arcades with an orangery in the middle, but today there is only a hedge. The ground floor of the palace is laid out with a main hall extending up through the floor above, and twelve smaller rooms. The hall is noteworthy for its fine ceiling painting by F. Rosa, G. Turbillo and J. A. Gumpp cele-

Opening times
Tue.–Sun.
10am–12.30pm
and 1.30–4pm

Entrance fee

Schleissheim New Palace: the garden front

Lustheim Palace

brating Diana, Goddess of Hunting, and also its six large paintings of Maximilian's Court at the hunt.

**Ernst Schneider Collection of Meissen Porcelain in Schloss Lustheim

Ten ground floor rooms and four rooms on the lower ground floor today house Ernst Schneider's superb collection of Meissen porcelain, installed here in 1971. Displayed in 56 cabinets are Johann Friedrich Böttger's first experiments with stoneware and more than 1800 other exhibits arranged chronologically and thematically, ranging in date from 1710, when the Meissen manufactory was established, to the Seven Years' War (1756–63). The magnificent collection, accumulated by Schneider over a period of 50 years, is surpassed only by that in Dresden's Zwinger.

Among the finest of the items are the large Augustus Rex vases, the Elephant Candelabra (1735), the wildlife pieces by the great master J. J. Kändler (1706–75), particularly his gaily coloured birds, examples of the massive dinner services which were supplied to the Courts of Europe, painted by J. G. Höroldt (1696–1775), pieces from the "Möllendorf" service designed by Friedrich the Great, and Count Brühl's famous "Swan Service".

Schwabing

Location
North of the city centre

U-Bahn
U3, U6 (Universität, Giselastr., Münchner Freiheit)

The name "Swapinga" first appears in the records in 782, long before the foundation of Munich. At the beginning of the 19th c. Schwabing was still a mere village with little more than 500 inhabitants, but it began to develop after the construction of Ludwigstrasse (see entry), which linked it with Munich. In 1887 it acquired its municipal charter, but only four years later, in 1891, was incorporated into Munich.

Its fame as the artists' quarter of Munich began at the turn of the century, when painters, writers and poets, musicians and actors settled here, leading the *vie de bohème* in studios, artists' bars and the English Garden. The good citizens of Munich tended to regard them as layabouts, though many artists and writers who were by no means layabouts also lived in Schwabing, including Joachim Ringelnetz, Franz Wedekind and Thomas Mann. Unfortunately Schwabing is now steadily losing its distinctive character. Few of the artists' old haunts remain, the street scene today owing more to boutiques, galleries, beer bars, ice-cream parlours and kebab and pizza stalls. Schwabing has become an "in" place to live and the professional classes – doctors and dentists, lawyers and business people – have moved into the buildings dating from the Gründerzeit. Rents have consequently rocketed to astronomical heights and houses change hands for record sums.

Numerous fine examples of Munich Jugendstil (Art Nouveau) still survive in Schwabing, some of them painstakingly restored. Among the most notable are the Pacelli-Palais (Georgenstr. 8), built by Josef Hölzle in 1881, the Palais Bissing (Georgenstr. 10) designed by E. R. Fiechter, the Romeis buildings in Schackstrasse (Nos. 1, 2 and 4), the houses by Henry Helbig and Ernst Haiger in Ainmillerstrasse (No. 22) and Römerstrasse (No. 11), and the house built by Johann Lang at Belgradstr. 22/24.
There are also beautiful Jugendstil houses in Franz-Joseph-Strasse, Kaiserstrasse and Isabellastrasse.

*Jugendstil buildings

See entry

Leopoldstrasse

*Siegestor

42 56

This triumphal arch, modelled on the Arch of Constantine in Rome, was built by Friedrich von Gärtner in 1843–52 as the terminal point of Ludwigstrasse (see entry). It commemorates the valour of the Bavarian Army, being the counterpart therefore to the Feldherrnhalle at the south end of Ludwidgstrasse which was built to honour Bavaria's military leaders.
The Siegestor was badly damaged during the Second World War and was not fully restored. Its new inscription (1958) reads: "Dedicated to victory, destroyed by war, calling for peace". The arch is topped by a figure of Bavaria in a chariot drawn by lions.

Location
North end of
Ludwigstr.

U-Bahn
U3, U6
(Universität)

Sendlinger Tor (Sendling Gate)

41 54

Construction of the Sendlinger Tor, at the end of Sendlinger Platz, took place in the 14th c., which also saw the building of the Karlstor (see Karlsplatz) and the Isartor (see entry). Only the two flanking towers of the original gate survive.
The fountain in the square in front of the gate was replaced in 1972.
The west side of Sendlinger Torplatz is dominated by Matthäuskirche (see entry).

Location
South-west of
the city centre

*Silbersalon (Silver Salon)

41 54

These rooms on the first floor of the Altes Hackerhaus are the sole surviving example of an interior from an upper class Munich home in the late 19th c. (around 1885). The magnificent period-piece was uncovered during restoration work in 1982, and afterwards renovated. The luxurious décor was originally commissioned by Mathias Pschorr jun., whose family had owned the property since 1794. The principal rooms were furnished in accordance with the style of the time, the salon in Neo-Rococo, newly returned to fashion after being revived in the furnishing of Schloss Linderhof (1874–78) for King Ludwig II. The same two Munich firms of Radspieler

Location
Sendlinger Str.
75 (entrance in
Hackenstr.)

S-Bahn
S1–S7
(Marienplatz)

The Sendling Gate, at the south-west edge of the Old Town

in the Silver Drawing Room (Silbersalon)

and Pössenbacher employed at Schloss Linderhof were engaged to decorate the Silbersalon.

The model for the salon was the "silver" décor of François Cuvilliés' Amalienburg (see also Nymphenburg).

The Silbersalon is a branch of the Münchner Stadtmuseum (see entry).

Open: Sat. 1–5pm (tour at about 2.30pm), Sun. 10am–5pm.

U-Bahn
U3, U6
(Marienplatz);
U1, U2, U3, U6
(Sendlinger Tor)

---

*Staatliche Antikensammlungen (State Collection of Antiquities)   41 55

The building which since 1967 has been the home of the Staatliche Antikensammlungen was designed by Georg Friedrich Ziebland and built in the Late Neo-Classical style in 1838–48. It originally housed an "Exhibition of Art and Industry" which was moved to the Glaspalast in the Alter Botanische Garten in 1854. The building was expressly conceived as the counterpart of the Glyptothek (see entry) which stands opposite; hence the figure of Bavaria, patroness of Bavarian art and industry, adorns the centre of the pediment, the position occupied in the case of the Glyptothek by the figure of Athene, patroness of the Greek arts, the ideal to which Bavarian art aspired.

Between 1898 and 1916 the Galerie der Münchner Secession (a group of avant garde artists founded in 1892) occupied the building, and in 1919 it became the Neue Staatsgalerie (now in the west wing of the Haus der Kunst, see Staatsgalerie moderner Kunst). After being severely damaged in the last war (1943), it was restored in the 1960s, the architect being Johannes Ludwig. The collection comprises a magnificent array of vases, together with bronzes, pottery, terracottas and small sculptures.

Location
Königsplatz 1

U-Bahn
U2 (Königsplatz)

Tram 18
(Karolinenplatz)

Bus 53
(Schellingstr.)

Opening times
Tue., Thur–Sun.
10am–4.30pm,
Wed. noon–
8.30pm

Tour with commentary on tape

Cretan-Mycenaean, early Greek and early Attic pottery (14th–8th c. B.C.); Hans von Schoen Collection of Greek earthenware vessels, terracottas and bronzes. The famous Helicon Lekythos (case D).

Room I

Archaic Attic vases, early Greek vases from Athens, Corinth, Sparta and Ionia; Greek pottery from the 8th to 7th c. B.C., eastern Greek clay sarcophagus.

Room II

Beautiful Dionysian bowl (case 12).

(Central area): Late archaic and Early Classical Attic vases, Panathenaic prize amphorae; Greek pottery of the 6th and 5th c. B.C. including the amphora of Andodices (case 6).

Room III

Classical Attic vases, Greek pottery from the 5th c. B.C.

Room IV

Late Classical vase, Greek pottery of the 5th to 2th c. B.C.; James Loeb collection, with Greek earthenware vessels, terracottas and bronzes.

Room V

Bronze articles, bronze kettles (presented by James Loeb), small bronzes, earthenware vessels and sculptures from Etruria; Italian ceremonial vessels.

Upper floor with staircase (over the central area)

Greek landscapes by Carl Rottmann (1797–1850).

Corridor: earthenware vessels from Bœotia (8th–6th c. B.C.) and Cyprus (10th–6th c. B.C.).

Basement

Etruscan gold jewellery, ancient silver.

Room VII

Greek bronze-work, ancient glass. Roman reticulated glass (case 2); Greek bronze, the "Maiden of Beröa".

Room VIII

Greek and Roman terracottas and bronzes. Spartan upright mirror (case 1).

Room IX

Greek and Roman gold jewellery and gold jewellery from the James Loeb Collection; superbly worked gold funerary garland from Armento (case 2, wall)

Room X

Staatliche Graphische Sammlung (State Graphic Collection)   41 55

Since 1949 the State Graphic Collection has been housed in one of the former "Führerbauten" situated just off Königsplatz (see entry). The building, designed by Paul Ludwig Troost, was erected in 1933–35.

Location
Meiserstr. 10

U-Bahn
U2 (Königsplatz)

Tram
18
(Karolinenplatz)

Opening times
Mon.–Fri.
10am–1pm and
2–4.30pm

The collection, one of the most important of its kind in Central Europe, comprises more than 300,000 sheets of drawings and graphics, ranging in date from the 15th c. to the present day. Among the German artists whose works are displayed are Altdorfer, Dürer and Eisheimer, among the Italians Fra Bartolomeo, and among the Dutch and Flemish Rembrandt. The collection is particularly rich in material from the Baroque period in southern Germany (the Asam brothers, Ignaz Günther) and in 19th c. work (von Klenze, Kobell, Schwind, Marée and Busch). The Expressionist and post-Second World War periods are also well represented. A study room and library (some 24,000 volumes on graphics-related topics) may be used by visitors. The Staatliche Graphische Sammlung holds temporary exhibitions in the Neue Pinakothek (see entry).

*Staatliche Sammlung Ägyptischer Kunst
(State Collection of Egyptian Art)   42 54

Entrance
Hofgartenstr. 1
(Residenz)

S-Bahn
S1–S7
(Marienplatz)

U-Bahn
U3, U4, U5, U6
(Odeonsplatz)

Tram
19 (National-
theater)

Opening times
Tue.–Sun.
9.30am–4pm,
Tue. also 7–9pm

Entrance fee
(Sun. and
holidays free)

The State Collection of Egyptian Art is housed on the ground floor of the Residenz (see entry), on either side of the passage leading to the Kaiserhof. One of the oldest museums of its kind, it grew out of the collections assembled by Duke Albrecht V and King Ludwig I. During the 20th c. it acquired much additional material from donations. The present museum also contains the Egyptian antiquities formerly held by the Glyptothek (see entry).

The collection covers the whole range of ancient Egyptian history – the Pre-dynastic period (4500–3000 B.C.), the Period of Unification (about 3000 B.C.), the Old Kingdom (5th and 6th Dynasties, 2660–2160 B.C.), Middle Kingdom (11th–13th Dynasties, 2040–1160 B.C.) and New Kingdom (18th–20th Dynasties, 1550–1080 B.C.), the Late period (25th–30th Dynasties), the Graeco-Roman period (700 B.C. to the end of the 3rd c. A.D.) and the Coptic period (4th–9th c. A.D.).

Items on display include sculptures and reliefs, weapons, jewellery and ornaments, cult objects, domestic and other implements, sarcophagi, papyri and textiles.

Among those of particular interest are:

A limestone statue of a seated female figure from the earliest temple precinct at Abydos (Period of Unification).

A thin-walled goblet of green slate (Period of Unification).

A granite group of Dersenet and his family, false doors from the Tomb of Meni, and slaughtering scenes from the Tomb of Ni-auch-nesent at Sakkara (Old Kingdom).

A copper figure of a naked man and a cult image (bronze and gold) of the crocodile god Sobek (Middle Kingdom).

A limestone lion's head, the head of a sphinx (Amenophis II), squatting figure of a high priest of Amun, and a hoard of weapons from Sichem (New Kingdom).

A bronze figure of Osiris and the gold treasure of Queen Amani-sha-heto from a pyramid at Meroe in the Sudan (Late period).

A glass figure of a youth (intarsia work) and painted pottery (Coptic art).

*Staatsbibliothek (State Library)   42 55

Location
Ludwigstr. 16

U-Bahn
U3, U6
(Universität,
Odeonsplatz)

The Bavarian State Library is Germany's largest library with some 5.1 million volumes and more than 32,000 periodicals. The library has several sections of particular note: the science, manuscript and incunabula departments, the music collection, the oriental and Far Eastern department, the comprehensive East European collection and, last but by no means least, the large map collection of more than 800 atlases and 250,000 maps.

The long range of buildings, with seven wings laid out around two court-yards, was built by Friedrich von Gärtner in 1834–39 within the plan for the development of Ludwigstrasse (see entry).

The style is modelled on that of the Early Renaissance palaces of Italy. The strong emphasis on the horizontal articulation of the façade contributes to the continuity and monumental effect of the street.

On the steps leading up to the entrance are statues of Thucydides, Homer, Aristotle and Hippocrates, all by Ludwig Schwanthaler.

Opening times
General reading room: Mon.–Fri. 9am–8pm
Sat. 9am–5pm
special collections: Mon.–Fri. 9am–5pm

Steps

Staatsgalerie moderner Kunst im Haus der Kunst
(State Gallery of Modern Art in the Haus der Kunst)

42 55

Immediately on coming to power Adolf Hitler ordered the construction of a "Haus der Deutschen Kunst" (House of German Art, known today as the "Haus der Kunst") in Prinzregentenstrasse at the southern edge of the English Garden. Designed by Paul Ludwig Troost, the 160m/525ft-long, 60m/197ft-wide building with its row of Doric columns running the length of the front, was opened to the accompaniment of a large procession and much ceremony in 1937. To heighten the effect of the monumental building Hitler widened Von-der-Tann-Strasse (the continuation of Prinzregentenstrasse), demolishing the famous Jugendstil (Art Nouveau) façade of August Endell's studio "Elvira". The entire south side of the street was taken down and Prinz-Carl-Palais, the Neo-Classical style of which influenced Troost's design, was given a new north front.

Location
Prinzregenten-str. 1

U-Bahn
U3, U4, U5, U6
(Odeonsplatz)

Tram
20

Bus
53

Staatsgalerie moderner Kunst

The State Gallery of Modern Art has been temporarily housed in the western half of the building since 1946, something of an irony since many of the works on display were considered "degenerate" during the Third Reich. Originally moved from the Neue Pinakothek in 1919 owing to lack of space, the collection includes both modern classical and contemporary works. About half of the 450 items on display are by German artists, among them Klee, Schlemmer, Nolde, Baselitz and Kiefer. The Gallery also possesses a considerable collection of works by modern Italian artists, the basis of which was a substantial gift from Marino & Marina Marini. France, Spain and the USA are among other countries represented.

Opening times
Tue.–Sun.
9,15am–4.30pm,
Thur. also
7–9pm

Entrance fee
(Sun. and holidays free)

Staatskanzlei, Haus der Bayerischen Geschichte
(Chancellory, House of Bavarian History)

42 54/55

When completed the large complex of buildings at present under construction on the east side of the Hofgarten will house the new Chancellory and House of Bavarian History. Highly controversial – at least during its planning stage – the development is set around the domed shell of the Bavarian Army Museum which was erected in 1906 and destroyed during the last war.
The greater part of this Bavarian "Kremlin", approximately 200m/650ft long and over 11,000sq.m/13,000sq.yd in area, will be occupied by 300 plus employees of the State government.
The aim of the "Haus der Bayerischen Geschichte" is to nurture the already considerable public interest in Bavarian history, through the medium of words and pictures and a well-thought out selection of exhibits.

At the northern end of the gleaming new complex are some Renaissance arcades which survived the wartime bombing, the lower dating from the

Location
East side of the Hofgarten

U-Bahn
U3, U4, U5, U6
(Odeonsplatz)

Renaissance arcades

time of Duke Albrecht V (16th c.), the upper being added by the Elector Maximilian I in around 1615. Threatened with demolition to make way for the new project, they were eventually reprieved.

Pump-house

Also on the site is a pump-house designed by Leo von Klenze complete with its machinery, an early 19th c. monument to the dawn of the technological age.

Staatssammlung für Allgemeine und Angewandte Geologie
(General and Applied Geology Collection)

41 55

Location
Luisenstr. 37

U-Bahn
U2 (Königsplatz)

Opening times
Mon.–Fri.
8am–6pm

Located in the substantial complex of buildings in Luisenstrasse belonging to the Technical University, the General and Applied Geology Collection boasts informative exhibitions on the twin themes of "Erdkruste im Wandel" (The Changing Crust of the Earth) and "Bodenschätze der Erde" (The Earth's Mineral Resources). Also of considerable interest are two display cases explaining the structure and rock formations of the eastern Alps (northern limestone Alps, central Alps and southern Alps) and a third devoted to the geology of carbon deposits (fossil fuels).

Pieces of rock can be examined under a magnifying glass, so revealing their complex structures and constituent minerals.

*Staatssammlung für Paläontologie und Historische Geologie
(State Palaeontology and Geology Collection)

41 55

Location
Richard-Wagner-
Str. 10

U-Bahn
U2 (Königsplatz)

Opening times
Mon.–Thur.
8am–4pm,
Fri. 8am–2pm,
1st Sun in the
month 10am–4pm

The State Palaeontology and Geology Collection occupies a hybrid and somewhat monumental building designed by Leonard Romeis, originally for a school of commercial art.

The palaeontological section has an extensive display of animal and other fossils from crucial epochs in the Earth's history. The particular strength of the collection lies in the material from the Swabian and Franconian Jura (e.g. ichthyosaurs from the Holzmaden Lias, pterosaurs from around Eichstätt in the upper Jura). Other highlights include the skull of a triceratops from Wyoming and the skeleton (cast) of a giant elephant which perished in the Mühldorf/Inn area sometime in the Late Tertiary. Also worth seeing are the fossils of Ice Age fauna and the special display devoted to the Nördlingen Reis meteorite crater.

*Stuck-Villa

43 54

Location
Prinzregenten
str. 60

U-Bahn
U4 (Prinzregen-
tenplatz)

Tram
18

Opening times
daily 10am–5pm,
Thur. till 9pm

In 1897–98 Munich's "prince of painters" Franz von Stuck (1863–1928) designed for himself, in co-operation with the Munich firm of Heilmann & Littmann, a splendid house which, in both its architecture and furnishings, mingles Jugendstil (Art Nouveau) with elements of the Late Neo-Classical style.

The same exquisite blend was preserved when the house was enlarged in 1913–14 by the addition of a studio annexe. In the front garden, in front of the portico, stands Stuck's superb "Bronze Amazon", considered by many to be his finest sculpture.

The facade of the upper storey is embellished with reliefs, as also is the entrance hall (including a copy of the Medusa Rondanini, the original of which is in the Glyptothek, see entry).

The walls of the elegant ground floor living rooms were decorated by the painter himself, evidently influenced by the frescoes at Pompeii. Many of his paintings are on display, among them a version of "The Guardian of Paradise" and "Sin", a work much discussed in Stuck's own time.

Other rooms in the house no longer have their original furnishings and are used for temporary exhibitions.
In 1992 work began on establishing a permanent exhibition of Munich Jugendstil on the first floor.

Theatermuseum (German Theatre Museum) 42 55

The Theatre Museum, founded in 1910 in the house of the actress Clara Ziegler (1844–1909), a member of the Court Company, is now accommodated in the Churfürstlichen Galerie (Old Electoral Gallery), which was built by Lespelliez in 1780–81.

Location
Galeriestr. 4
(Hofgarten-arkaden)

The collection of documents relating to the history of world theatre includes plans of theatres, pictures, sketches of stage sets and costume designs. There are also role portraits of actors and actresses, photographs of scenes, theatre masks and stage props.

U-Bahn
U3, U4, U5, U6
(Odeonsplatz)

The museum archive preserves several thousand manuscripts, production scripts, programmes, letters, revues and sound recordings, while the specialist library of some 80,000 items contains more manuscripts, librettos, scores, theatre journals and important works of secondary literature.

Opening times
Tue. 10am–noon
Thur. 2–4pm

The museum also runs a unique service – Münchner Spielplan, or Munich Repertoire – providing information on all performances currently being staged at Munich theatres (photographs, programmes, texts, librettos). Open: Tue.–Fri. 10am–4pm. Tel. 22 24 49.

Information service

**Theatinerkirche (Theatine Church of St Cajetan) 42 54

The Theatinerkirche, dedicated to St Cajetan, founder of the Theatine Order, stands just to the west of the Feldherrnhalle. A basilica in the style of the Italian High Baroque, it is one of Munich's finest churches, and together with the Frauenkirche and Peterskirche (see entries) one of the city's most prominent landmarks.

Location
Brienner Str./
Theatinerstr.

U-Bahn
U3, U4, U5 U6
(Odeonsplatz)

The church was founded by the Elector Ferdinand Maria and his wife Henrietta Adelaide in thanksgiving for the birth of Max Emanuel, the son and heir they had long desired. After its consecration the church, which also served as a Court Church, was assigned to the Theatine Order. Since 1954 it has been served by Dominicans.

The church (Latin cross plan, domed) was designed by the Italian architect Agostino Barelli, who also directed the first stage of its building (1663–69). His successor Enrico Zuccali completed the 71m/233ft-high dome, decorated the interior and built the twin towers which had not been provided for in Barelli's plan; this second building phase was completed by 1690. The façade was completed only in 1765–68, in the reign of Max III Joseph, being designed in the style of the Late Rococo period by François Cuvilliés and his son.

The façade with its twin towers is clearly articulated both vertically and horizontally. The marble statues in the niches (SS Ferdinand, Adelheid, Maximilian and Cajetan) are by Roman Boos. The towers have serpentine ornament just below their domed tops while the massive central dome is capped by a lantern with a lion weather-vane.

Façade

The interior is dominated by the tall round-headed arches of the barrel vaulting and the dome over the crossing. The whole interior surface is washed in white, with rich stucco ornament by Giovanni Antonio Viscardi. Among the most notable features are:
The high altar, with a picture, "The Virgin enthroned with Angels" (1646), by Caspar de Crayer, a pupil of Rubens.
The Altar of the Virgin (right transept), with a "Holy Kinship" by Cignani (1676) and an "Annunciation" by Desmarées (on altar-table).

Interior

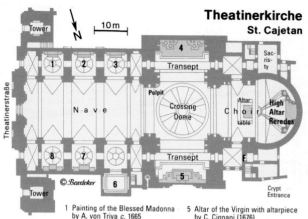

Theatinerkirche
St. Cajetan

1 Painting of the Blessed Madonna by A. von Triva *c.* 1665
2 "Descent from the Cross" by Tintoretto
3 "St Andrew" by K. Loth (1677)
4 St Cajetan Altar with altarpiece by J. von Sandrart (1671)
5 Altar of the Virgin with altarpiece by C. Cignani (1676)
6 Burial chapel of King Maximilian II (1864)
7 "Guardian Angel" by A. Zanchi (17th c.)
8 Altar of St Cecilia with altarpiece by P. Liberi and Triva (17th c.)

The Altar of St Cajetan (left transept), with a painting by Sandrart, "Intercession of St Cajetan during the Plague in Naples".
The magnificent black pulpit by Andreas Faistenberger (1685–90).

Ducal Burial Vault (closed in winter)	In the Ducal Burial Vault under the high altar are the tombs of members of the House of Wittelsbach, including Ferdinand Maria, Max Emanuel, Karl VII Albrecht (Holy Roman Emperor and Elector of Bavaria), Max III Joseph and Carl Theodor, Kings Maximilian I and Otto of Greece, the Prince Regent Luitpold and Crown Prince Ruprecht.
Salvatorkirche	See Promenadeplatz/Kardinal-Faulhaber-Strasse

Theatinerstrasse
42 54

Location Northern part of the Old Town Preysing-Palais	The Preysing-Palais, Munich's first Rococo palace, was built by Joseph Effner in 1723–28 for Count Maximilian von Preysing, Master of the Electoral Hunt. The Feldherrnhalle (see entry) was built against its north wall in 1841–44.

During the Second World War the palace was so badly damaged that the outer walls, with the exception of the Residenzstrasse façade, had to be pulled down and rebuilt (1958–75).
The interior, including the banqueting hall and chapel, had already been destroyed in the 19th c. and is today traversed by shopping arcades. The beautiful grand staircase with its caryatides has, however, survived.

*Hypo-Bank Art Gallery	A shrine to contemporary art amidst the temples of mammon, the Hypo-Bank Gallery at Theatinerstrasse No. 15 is one of Munich's more unusual attractions. Large numbers of visitors are frequently drawn to its temporary exhibitions, which usually highlight particular artists, periods or affinities in art. Open: daily 10am–6pm, Thur. 10am–9pm. – Information: tel. 22 44 12.

Theatinerstrasse

Preysing Palace

** **Tierpark Hellabrunn** (Hellabrunn Zoo)   40 49/50

Spread over some 36ha/89 acres at Hellabrunn, Munich's zoo is one of the most popular attractions in Bavaria. When it was laid out in 1928 it was the world's first geographically organised zoo. Grouped according to the different parts of the globe from which they come, more than 4000 of the world's most interesting animals are held in open enclosures reproducing as far as possible conditions in the wild. Landscape and architecture harmonise to a degree rarely achieved. Species which normally share habitats are kept together wherever possible (e.g. chamois and marmots).

Such popular features as the Elephant House (now a listed building), the enormous 5000sq.m/6000sq.yd covered free-flight aviary, the polarium and the ape houses, which are among the highlights of the zoo, have been enlarged and improved in the last few years at considerable expense.

Hellabrunn Zoo is situated on a lower terrace of the Isar, now a designated nature conservation area. In the case of enclosures recently refurbished, railings have been kept to a minimum. Delightful footpaths, children's playgrounds, eating and picnic places, contribute to making the zoo a recreational oasis.

Hellabrunn enjoys an international reputation for its success both in resurrecting the extinct aurochs and grey wild horse (by selective breeding from primitive domestic breeds), and in safeguarding rare species threatened with extinction. These include Przewalski's horse, bison, musk-ox, ibex, king penguins, gorillas, orang-utans, chimpanzees, gibbons, Siberian tigers, Persian leopards, tapirs, Indian rhinos and Mhorr gazelles (the latter are already extinct in the wild).

Location
Tierparkstr. 30

U-Bahn
U3
(Thalkirchen)

Bus
31, 52, 57

Opening times
Apr.–Sept.:
daily 8am–6pm
Oct.–Mar.
daily 9am–5pm

Entrance fee

Site

Rare species

Tierpark Hellabrunn

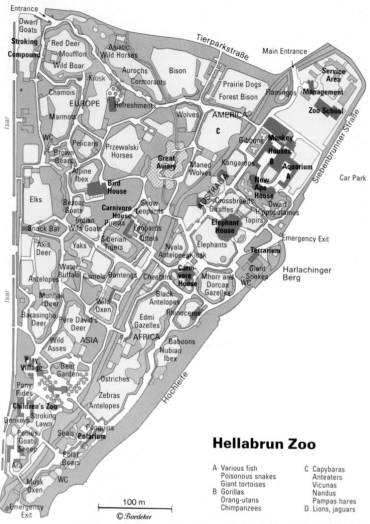

Hellabrun Zoo

A Various fish
  Poisonous snakes
  Giant tortoises
B Gorillas
  Orang-utans
  Chimpanzees

C Capybaras
  Anteaters
  Vicunas
  Nandus
  Pampas hares
D Lions, jaguars

100 m

© Baedeker

Feeding times

Lions: Apr.–Sept. 4.30pm, Oct.–Mar. 3.30pm (daily except Tue. and Fri.). – Tigers: Apr.–Sept. 3pm, Oct.–Mar. 2pm (daily except Tue. and Fri.). – Apes: daily 10am, 2 and 4pm. – Seals: daily (except Fri.) 11.30am and 2.30pm. – Polar bears: daily (except Tue. and Fri.) 4pm. – Penguins: daily 11am and 3pm. – Aquarium: Wed. and Sun. 3pm.

N.B.

Visitors are forbidden to feed the animals, except those in the Children's Zoo and the fallow deer (only with food from special dispensing machines). Foods such as bread and sugar can cause serious illness or even death, so the ban on feeding must be scrupulously observed.

Üblackerhäusl

During the period of rapid expansion in the 18th and 19th c., modest single-storey dwellings were erected for the city's poorer inhabitants. Houses such as the "Üblackerhäusl", a day labourer's home, were once very typical of the Haidhausen district.

Faithfully restored and furnished from the ample resources of the Münchner Stadtmuseum (see entry), of which it is a branch, the Üblackerhäusl is also used for temporary exhibitions.

Opening times: Tue., Thur., Sun. 10am–noon, Wed., Fri. 6–7pm (closed during Bavarian school holidays).

Location
Preysingstr. 58

S-Bahn
S1–S7 (Rosenheimer Platz)

Tram
18 (Gasteig)

Opening times

Universität, Aula (University, Great Hall)

The Great Hall, beautifully restored a few years ago, is the loveliest feature of the Ludwig-Maximilian-Universität. Built in 1909 it was designed by German Bestelmeyer, a highly respected architect in his day, to replace a much smaller building by Friedrich von Gärtner. The mosaics depicting the sun god Helios, and the medallions by the artist Wilhelm Koeppen, a pupil of Franz von Stuck, are exceptional.

In front of the arcading on the north side stand two tall granite monoliths bearing figures of Prometheus and Hercules by Ulfert Janssen – note the motto "Nil sine magno vita labore dedit mortalibus" (Life grants nothing to the mortal without great effort).

Location
Geschwister-Scholl-Platz 1

U-Bahn
U3, U6 (Universität)

University buildings in Geschwister-Scholl-Platz

Viktualienmarkt (Food Market)   42 54

Location
South end of the
Old Town

S-Bahn
S1–S7
(Marienplatz)

U-Bahn
U3, U6
(Marienplatz)

The provision market which has been held in this square since 1807 is a very characteristic feature of Munich life. In addition to numerous stalls selling fruit, vegetables, dairy produce, eggs, poultry, bread and cakes, there are also meat and fish halls. Particularly lively on Saturday mornings the Viktualienmarkt, of course, has a beer garden – much frequented, especially in the warmer months – and a gaily decorated maypole, a permanent fixture which adds further colour to the scene.

The market boasts several fountains with statues of celebrated Munich figures still remembered with affection – the legendary comic actor Karl Valentin (see Famous People), the actress Liesl Karlstadt (1892–1960) who played opposite him for many years, the folk-singer Weiss Ferdl (1883–1949), Elise Aulinger (1891–1965), Roider Jakl (1906–75) and Ida Schumacher (1895–1956).

*Völkerkundemuseum (State Museum of Ethnology)   42 54

Location
Maximilianstr.
42

Tram 19, 20

Opening times
Tue.–Sun.
9.30am–4.30pm

Entrance fee

The State Museum of Ethnology occupies an imposing building in Maximilianstrasse designed by E. Riedel and completed in 1865. With its extensive collection of art and artefacts from all over the world it ranks as one of the principal museums of its kind in Europe.

Having begun as a collection of curios assembled in the 16th c. by the Dukes and Electors of Bavaria, the museum started to develop in its present form during the reign of Ludwig II, when all the items of non-European origin were placed together in a separate gallery of their own.

East Asia, West and Central Africa and South America (especially Peru) are particularly well represented in the museum.

Provision market: fresh vegetables . . .

. . . and a beer-garden

The collections

Near East: weapons and booty from the Turkish Wars.
Far East: lacquerware, Buddhist art, Preetorius Collection with some outstanding works of art, mainly from China and Japan.

South and Central America: Peru (grave goods, textiles, vessels, masks, figures and jewellery), Mexico (various items).
North America: craftwork and cult objects of the North-west Coastal Indians and the peoples of Alaska (including furs, implements, masks and paintings).

West Africa: masks, carvings, weapons.
Benin and Upper Guinea: ivory carvings, bronzes; East Africa: silver from Abyssinia; Southern Africa: body jewellery.

At the present time the museum is undergoing refurbishment and only temporary exhibitions are being held.

Volksbad (Müllersches Volksbad, Müller's Public Baths)   43 53

The Müllersches Volksbad, still rightly considered one of the most splendid swimming pools in Germany, is remarkable for the magnificence of its architecture and the lavishness of its décor. Designed by Karl Hocheder and constructed between 1897 and 1901, the building has something of a Moorish quality, at the same time echoing a Roman thermes. Elements of South German Baroque and Jugendstil (Art Nouveau) are also evident.
The baths were built through the generosity of Karl Müller, a Munich engineer, who bequeathed to the city five houses with a value of 1.8 million gold marks on condition that the money be used to construct an attractive swimming pool for the citizens of Munich. For this Müller was later ennobled by the Prince Regent Luitpold.
In its day the most modern baths in Europe, Müller's was completely renovated a few years ago. In addition to a gentlemen's pool (with barrel vaulting) and a ladies' pool (with domed vaulting), it has individual baths, showers and sweat-baths. At one time there was even a "Zamperlbad" (doggy bath) in the basement!

Location
Rosenheimer
Str. 1

S-Bahn
S1–S7 (Isartor,
Rosenheimer
Platz)

Tram
18, 20

Entrance fee

Mon. 10am–5pm, Tue. 8am–7.30pm, Wed. (warm water day) 6.45am–7.30pm, Thur. 8am–7.30pm, Fri. (warm water day) 8am–8.45pm, Sat. 8am–5.30pm, Sun. (closed July and Aug.) 8.30am–noon.

Opening times

See entry

Gasteig

---

*Westpark   36–39 52/53

Westpark, laid out for the 4th International Garden Show (IGA 83), lies some 3km/2 miles south-west of the main railway station. Beautifully designed and planted, it has an area of 72,000sq.m/178 acres and extends for about 2km/1¼ miles from east to west, divided into an eastern and western half by Garmischer Strasse.

Location
Between Westend
and Laim

U-Bahn
U6 (Westpark)

The park has extensive lawns on which to relax, and ponds stocked with carp, goldfish and turtles. Scent from the flower-beds and rose bushes fills the air. Other features include an attractive lily pond, several playgrounds and football pitches, a narrow-guage railway, outdoor chess, a Kneipp treatment centre, a lakeside theatre (open-air concerts), two beer gardens and two cafés.

Recreation
area

The delightful ensemble commonly known as Klein-Asien (Little Asia) consists of a Chinese garden, a Japanese garden, a Thai Sala and a pagoda (constructed by 200 Nepalese craftsmen).

Little Asia

Wittelsbacherplatz

Children's play areas	The park is particularly appealing to children on account of its several well-designed play areas equipped with a variety of apparatus, paddling pools, etc. There is even a specially constructed stream with miniature barrages.
Playground for disabled children	One of the playgrounds is designed specifically for disabled youngsters.
Bayerwaldhaus	At Bayerwaldhaus there is a well-stocked medicinal plant and herb garden.
Mollsee	Situated in the eastern section of the park, the little Mollsee attracts model boat enthusiasts with their radio-controlled craft.
Rudi-Sedlmayer-Halle	Also in the eastern part of the park is the large Rudi Sedlmayer Sports Hall, a frequent venue for pop and rock concerts as well as sporting events.
ADAC head office	At the eastern end of the park stand the ultra-modern headquarters of the German motoring organisation ADAC (Allgemeine Deutsche Automobil-Club).

Wittelsbacherplatz

Location
Northern edge of the city centre

U-Bahn
U3, U4, U5, U6
(Odeonsplatz)

The architectural unity of the rectangular Wittelsbacherplatz with its ensemble of Neo-Classical buildings, bears all the hallmarks of its designer Leo von Klenze. The square is bounded on the north side by the Alfons-Palais, built in 1825 as a home for von Klenze himself but later acquired by Prince Ludwig Ferdinand von Wittelsbach. Renovated in the 1960s, the palace is today the head office of the Siemens Corporation. On the west side stands the Neo-Classical Palais Arco-Zinneberg (1820), which was badly damaged in the last war. Since restored it is now given over to

Wittelsbacherplatz, with the Maximilian Monument and Siemens' headquarters

business premises, chiefly boutiques and suchlike. The famous Odeon (see Odeonsplatz), present home of the Bavarian Ministry of the Interior, bounds the square on the north-east side.
An equestrian statue of the Elector Maximilian I, unveiled in 1839, adorns the centre of the square. Modelled by Bertel Thorvaldsen, it was cast in bronze by Johann Baptist Stiglmaier.

Zentrum für aussergewöhnliche Museen (ZAM)
(Centre for Unusual Museums)

42 54

This most curious of museums houses seven unusual collections all assembled by the lawyer Manfred Klauda, in addition to which it also mounts special exhibitions on unusual themes.
One section is devoted to Sissy, the Empress Elisabeth of Austria (see Famous People); the life-size wax likeness (from the Tussaud workshop) is dressed in Sissy's own clothes. Also on view is a four-poster bed which the Empress slept in.
The Chamber Pot Museum boasts more than 2000 potties, many of which once graced the most aristocratic houses of Europe (Bismarck's among others). The earliest is some 2000 years old and came from Syria. One of the highlights is the Bourdalou Collection of the type of pot used by high society ladies in the 18th and 19th c.
The lock collection consists of numerous padlocks, some up to 2000 years old, used to secure all kinds of possession from treasure chests to pillories and chastity belts.

Location
Westenrieder-
str. 26

S-Bahn
S1–S7 (Isartor)

U-Bahn
U3, U6 (Marien-
platz)

Opening times
Daily 10am–6pm

Entrance fee

More than 1000 exhibits illustrating the 300-year-old history of the humble corkscrew.

Corkscrew
collection

The Pedal Car Museum features over 100 of these scaled-down vehicles, manufactured for children from the late 19th c. onwards. Among them are versions of some famous real-life marques such as Auto Union, Bugatti and Mercedes.

Pedal Car
Museum

The Easter Bunny Museum is dedicated to the egg-producing rabbit which has been a principal character in traditional Easter celebrations for at least 300 years.

Easter Bunny
Museum

Zentrum für die Geschichte der Luft- und Raumfahrt
(Centre for the History of Air and Space Travel)

Land which used to belong to the Oberschleissheim aircraft repair works has recently been turned into the Centre for the History of Air and Space Travel, a branch of the Deutsches Museum (see entry), enabling the latter's extensive aircraft collection to be displayed to great effect.
Developments in aircraft construction are traced with the aid of a selection of vintage machines. The multiplicity of uses, civil and military, served by flying devices of various kinds, is also illustrated with particular clarity.

Location
Oberschleissheim

S-Bahn
S1 (Ober-
schleissheim)

*Zirkus Krone (Krone Circus)

40 55

Munich is the home of the world-famous Zirkus Krone, permanently based here since 1919. Bombed out during a blitz in 1944, a new building in the shape of a big top with seating for more than 2500 was completed in 1962. Brilliant artistry and outstanding animal acts are guaranteed throughout

Location
Marsstr. 43

Zirkus Krone

S-Bahn
S1–S7
(Hackerbrücke)

the circus season (December to March), the annual "Stars in der Manege" (Stars in the Ring; beginning of December) and the first performance of the winter programme (Christmas Day) being exceptional.

From April to October when the circus takes to the road, pop concerts, sports meetings and political events are staged.

In front of the Zirkus Krone building stands a bronze statue commemorating Charlie (actually José Andreo) Rivel (1896–1983), the clown who was loved the world over.

The Old City Hall, seen from Marienplatz ▶

Taster flying course (2 hrs theory, ½-hr flight): information from Munich Flying Club (Fliegerclub München, Säulenstrasse 8, D(W)-8025 Unterhaching; tel. 6 11 50 93)

Antiques

Munich has over 300 antique shops covering the whole range of different periods and specialisations, from elegant upmarket establishments to humble junkshops. As in most cities the antiques trade tends to be concentrated in particular streets. In Schwabing these are Amalienstrasse, Türkenstrasse, Barerstrasse, Kürfustenstrasse and Hohenzollernstrasse, while in the city centre they are Ottostrasse, Lenbachplatz, Promenadenstrasse, Promenadenplatz, Theatinerstrasse, Residenzstrasse, and Westenrieder Strasse.

German Art and Antiques Fair, held annually in late autumn in Haus der Kunst.

Antique fairs and markets

Fairs run by art and antique dealers three times a year in the Deutsches Museum.

Occasional antique markets, with a colourful variety of items for sale, in various beer cellars.

Auer Dult (see Events, Markets): stalls selling antiques, folk art, junk and collectables.

Banks

See Currency

Beer gardens, beer cellars and brew pubs

Munich's beer gardens are large open-air places where on afternoons, evenings and weekends during the warmer months you can sit at tables under the chestnut trees, drinking beer out of one-litre tankards (masskrüge) accompanied by "Brotzeit" snacks of pretzels, horseradish, bread and cheese or sausage, etc. which either you can bring in with you or buy from the appropriate stand nearby.

The older beer gardens near the cellars where the breweries keep their beer are called beer cellars, or simply cellars, though no-one actually sits in the cellar. Many beer gardens also have rooms indoors for their customers in the winter.

Every year during Lent strong dark beers with names ending in "ator" are served. Despite their high alcohol content they taste deceptively light so take care not to drink too much without realising it.

The following list gives some of Munich's best-known beer gardens, beer cellars and brew pubs.

Aumeister, M 45, Sondermeierstrasse 1, Englischer Garten

Beer gardens

Biergarten by the Chinese Tower, M 22, Englischer Garten
Flaucher, M 70, Isarauen 1
Grüntal, M 81, Grüntal 15
Hirschgarten, M 19, Hirschgartenallee 1
Iberl Garten, M 71, Wilh.-Leibl Strasse 22
Menterschwaige, M 90, Harthauser Strasse 70
Seehaus, Kleinhesseloher See
St Emmerams Mühle, M 81, St. Emmeram 41
Waldwirtschaft Grosshesselohe, D-8023 Grosshesselohe
Zic-Zac, M 80, Roenheimer Strasse 240

Bistros

Beer cellars, brew pubs	Alter Ofen, M 40, Zieblandstrasse 41; tel. 52 75 27
	Augustiner, M 2, Neuhaser Strasse 16; tel. 5 51 99–257
	Augustinerkeller, M 2, Arnulfstrasse 52; tel. 59 43 93
	Bärenwirt, M 19, Winthirplatz 1; tel. 16 36 16
	Donisl (Wirtshaus zur AltenHauptwache), Weinstrasse 1; tel. 22 01 84
	Hackerkeller, M 2, Therienhöhe 4; tel. 50 70 04
	Haxnbauer am Platzl, Münzstrasse 8; tel. 22 19 22
	*Hofbräuhaus am Platzl, M 2, Platzl 9; tel. 22 16 76
	Hofbräukeller, M 80, Inner Wiener Strasse 19; tel. 48 94 89
	Krabler Garten, M 2, Thalkirchnerstrasse 2; tel. 2 60 85 17
	Leopold, M 40, Leopoldstrasse 50; tel. 39 94 33
	Löwenbräukeller, M 2, Nymphenburger Strasse 2; tel. 52 60 21
	Mathäser Weissbierkeller, M 2, Bayerstrasse 1; tel. 59 54 31
	Platzl, M 2, Platzl 1; tel. 2 37 03–0
	Salvatorkeller am Nockherberg, M 90, Hochstrasse 77; tel. 48 32 74
	Schelling Saloon, M 40, Schellingstrasse 54; tel. 2 72 07 88
	Spatenhaus-Bräustuben, M 2, Residenzstrasse 12
	Spatenhof, M 2, Neuhauser Strasse 26; tel. 26 40 10
	Thomasbräu, M 2, Kapuzinerplatz 5
	Trararium, M 19, Elvirastrasse 19; tel. 18 67 18
	Weihenstephan, M 21, Fürstenrieder Strasse 22
	Weisses Bräuhaus, M 2, Tal 10
	Wirtshaus am Hart (beer garden), M 45, Sudetendeutsche Strasse 40
	Zoozie's, M 5, Wittelsbacherstrasse 15; tel. 2 01 00 59
	Zum Franziskaner, M 2, Perustrasse 8; tel. 23 18 12–0
	Zum Pschorr-Bräu, M 2, Neuhauser Strasse 11; tel. 2 60 30 01
	Outside Munich:
Andechs	Andechser Klosterbräu
Aying	Brauereigasthof Aying
Erding	Erdinger Weissbräu
Oberschleissheim	Berglwirtshaus
	Schlosswirtschaft Schleissheim
Freising	Bräustüberl Weihenstephan
	Waldgaststätte Plantage
Haag a.d. Amper	Schlossallee
Dachau	Zieglerbräu

Bistros

Sigrid Bantl, Fauenplatz 10
Garibaldi, Schellingstrasse 60
*Käfer, Schumannstrasse 1
Schwarzwälder Eck, Hartmannstrasse 8
Windrose, Rosenbuschstrasse 2

Business hours

Department stores	The city centre department stores and their branches elsewhere are open Mon.–Fri. 9am–6.30pm and 8.30–2pm on Saturdays except for the first Saturday in the month when they stay open until 6pm. Late-night shopping is on Thursdays when they stay open until 8.30pm.

Other shops set their own opening times – from between 7 and 9am to about 6 or 6.30pm. Outside the city centre some close during the lunch hour. Again, late-night shopping is on Thursdays until 8.30. Some of the smaller butchers and bakers close on Monday afternoons. | Other shops

It is up to individual shops whether they stay open later on the first Saturday in the month, but as a general rule those in the city centre remain open while those elsewhere do not.

Shops close on national public holidays and those observed in Bavaria (see Public Holidays). On Shrove Tuesday, at the end of Fasching, they shut at about midday. | Public holidays

Central Station has a number of shops, including a chemist, baker, food, flower and book stores, on the lower ground floor which open up between 6 and 8am and close been 9 and 11pm. | Shopping after hours

See Currency | Banks

See Post | Post offices

Cafés and Ice-cream Parlours (selection)

Cafés

Alte Börse, Maffeistrasse 3 | City centre
Annast Hofgarten, Odeonsplatz 18
Bodo's Backstube, Herzog-Wilhelm-Strasse 29
* Feldherrnhalle, Theatinerstrasse 38
Galerie-Café Freiraum, Pestalozzistrasse 8
* Glockenspiel, Marienplatz 28
Hag (Rottenhöfer), Residenzstrasse 26
Höflinger, Schleissheimer Strasse 85
Kleines Wiener Kaffeehaus, Kreuzstrasse 3A
* Kreutzkamm (originally of Dresden), Maffeistrasse 4
Kustermann, Lindwurmstrasse 36
* Luitpold, Brienner Strasse 11
Maxburg, Maxburgstrasse 4
Mövenpick, Künstlerhaus on Lenbachplatz
Peterhof, Marienplatz 22
Reber, Herzogspitalstrasse 9
* Rischart, Marienplatz 18
Wiener Platz, Innere Wiener Strasse 48

Extrablatt, Leopoldstrasse 7 | Schwabing
Monopteros, Königinstrasse 43
Münchner Freiheit, M 40, Münchener Freiheit 20

Wiener Buffet Café, Rosenkavalierplatz 15 | Bogenhausen

Schlosscafé in the Palm House | Nymphenburg

Die Melodie, Rosenheimer Strasse 12 | Haidhausen

Ice-cream Parlours

Adamello, M 80, Preysingstrasse 29
Adria, M 40, Türkenstrasse 59
Baskin & Robbins, M 40, Marktstrasse 17
Café Schmidt, M 2, Ledererstrasse 23
Häägen Dazs, M 40, Leopoldstrasse 43
Italia, M 5, Ehrengutstrasse 23

Münchner Freiheit, M 40, Münchner Freiheit 20
Mövenpick, M 2, Lenbachplatz
Scarletti, M 5, Reichenbachstrasse 11
Soravia, M 80, Max-Weber-Platz 3
Venezia, M 40, Leopoldstrasse 31

Camping

Information	German Camping Club (Deutscher Campingclub), M 40, Mandlstrasse 28; tel. 33 40 21
	Details on how to get to campsites can also be found in the "Where to Stay" section of the Tourist Office's "Young People's Guide to Munich".

The campsites listed below are only those in Munich or its immediate vicinity. There are many others further afield which are easy to get to from the city such as the ones on Ammersee and Starnberger See.

Ampersee	On the A8 autobahn (Olching exit): 40 touring spaces; tel. (0 81 42) 1 27 86
Langwieder See	Eschenrieder Strasse 119 (on the A8 autobahn to Stuttgart). 300 touring spaces, open April 1 to October 15; tel. 8 14 15 66
Obermenzing	M 60, Lochhausener Strasse 59 (at the beginning of the A8 autobahn to Stuttgart). 300 touring spaces, open March 15 to end October; tel. 8 11 22 35
Thalkirchen	M 70, Zentralländstrasse 49 (near Hellabrunn Zoo). 700 touring spaces, open mid-March to end October; tel. 7 23 17 07
Nordwest	M 50 (Moosach), Dachauer Strasse 571: 300 tourist spaces; tel. 1 50 69 36

Chemists

Munich's chemists operate an emergency service so that there is always a chemist on duty at night and on Sundays and public holidays. The addresses and telephone numbers of the chemists on duty in the various parts of the city for the following week are listed in the Munich supplement of the Friday edition of the Süddeutsche Zeitung

Chemist on duty	Tel. 59 44 75. The address of the nearest chemist on duty is posted up at every chemist's shop.

Cinemas

"Kinophon"	Cinema information line: tel. 1 16 04
What's On phonelines	City Centre, A–K: tel. 1 15 11 City Centre, L–Z: tel. 1 15 12 Isar right bank: tel. 1 15 13 North-west: tel. 1 15 14 South-west: tel. 1 15 15
Cinemas (a selection) fda = full disabled access lda = limited disabled access	ABC, M 40, Herzogstrasse 1; tel. 33 23 00, fda Arri, M 40, Türkenstrasse 91; tel. 38 19 04 50 Atlantik-Palast, M 2, Schwanthalerstrasse 2; tel. 55 56 70 Cadillac, Rosenkavalierplatz 12; tel. 91 20 00 Cinema (foreign-language), M 2, Nymphenburger Strasse 31; tel. 55 52 55, fda

City, M 2, Sonnenstrasse 12; tel. 59 19 83, lda
Eldorado, M 2, Sonnenstrasse 7; tel. 55 71 74, lda
Elisenhof, Prielmayerstrasse 3 (on Central Station); tel. 55 75 40
Fantasia, M 2, Schwanthalerstrasse 3; tel. 55 57 54
Filmzentrum Schwabing, M 40, Leopoldstrasse 35; tel. 39 51 40
Gloria-Filmpalast, M 2, Karlsplatz 5; tel. 59 37 21, fda
Leopold, M 40, Leopoldstrasse 80; tel. 33 10 50 lda
Lupe 2, M 40, Ungererstrasse 19, in the Fuchsbau; tel. 34 76 51, fda
Marmorhaus, M 40, Leopoldstrasse 35; tel. 34 40 46, lda
Mathäser-Filmpalast, M 2, Bayerstrasse 5; tel. 59 53 63
Maxim, M 19, Landshuter Allee 33; tel. 16 87 21, fda
Museum-Lichtspiele, M 80, Lilienstrasse 2 (Ludwigsbrücke); tel. 48 24 03
Neue Arena, M 5, Hans-Sachs-Strasse 7; tel. 2 60 32 65, fda
Neues Rex, M 21, Agricolastrasse 16; tel. 56 25 00
Neues Rottmann, M 2, Rottmannstrasse 15; tel. 52 16 83, lda
Odyssee, M 2, Schwanthalerstrasse 3; tel. 55 57 54
Rio, M 80, Rosenheimer Platz 46; tel. 48 69 79, fda
Sendlinger Tor, M 2, Sendlinger Torplatz 11; tel. 55 46 36, lda
Sonnen-Filmtheater, M 2, Schwanthalerstrasse 2; tel. 55 56 70, fda
Stachus-Kino-Center, M 2, Sonnenstrasse 6; tel. 59 42 75
Theater am Karlstor, M 2, Neuhauser Strasse 34; tel. 55 42 00, fda
Theatiner-Filmkunst, M 2, Theatinerstrasse 32; tel. 22 31 83
Tivoli, M 2, Neuhauser Strasse 3; tel. 26 43 26, lda
Türkendolch, M 40, Türkenstrasse 74; tel. 2 71 88 44, lda

Conferences

Munich has about 250 venues which together provide conference facilities
capable of seating 40,000 people.

Olympiahalle (11,000 capacity)
Messegelände Congress Centre (3319 capacity)
European Patent Office (hall for 460, plus 28 rooms for between 15 and 130
persons)
Deutsches Museum conference hall (2500 seating capacity)
Kulturzentrum Gasteig (up to 2500 capacity)
Arabella conference centre (11 halls and meeting rooms)

Conference and meeting venues

The following well-known hotels can take conferences with up to 1200
participants: Arabella, Bayerischer Hof, Hilton, Sheraton, Vier
Jahreszeiten.

Hotel conference facilities

Conference infoline: tel. 23 91–81

Conference information

Cultural Institutes (international societies)

Amerikahaus, M 2, Karolinenplatz 3; tel. 59 53 67
British Council, M 80, Rosenheimer Strasse 116B (house 93); tel. 40 18 32
English-Speaking Union, POB 80 10 66; tel. 68 31 80
German-Canadian Society, c/o F. D. Müller; tel. 42 15 84
German-English Society, POB 34 01 47; tel. 2 80 20 77
Goethe Institute, M 90, Balanstrasse 57; tel. 4 18 68–0
Munich Caledonians, c/o Greinerberg 14; tel. 723 72 66
Munich Scottish Association, c/o B. Bradford; tel. 8 94 82 79

Currency

Banking hours

Banking hours are usually between 8.30am and 3.45pm, with late-night opening on Thursdays until 5.30pm. Some banking premises close in the lunch hour.

Changing money

All banks will change foreign notes during normal banking hours.

Money-changing automats

There are money-changing automats at several places in the city. These include the main station, the air terminal and the one at the branch of the Stadsparkasse in the Tal near Marienplatz. These also change banknotes only.

DVKB late-opening exchange counters

The Deutschen Verkehrs Kredit Bank (DVKB) also has a number of counters which stay open till late. The one in the main station is open from 6am until 11.30pm and the three at the airport are open from 7 or 7.30am until 8.30 or 10pm.

Eurocheque stopline

If Eurocheques or Eurochequecards become lost, stolen or mislaid this should be reported immediately so that they can be stopped. The 24-hour number to ring is: Frankfurt am Main (069) 74 09 87.

Customs Regulations

From January 1st 1993 new regulations came into operation. In theory there are no limits to the amounts of goods imported from one EU country to another, *provided they have been purchased tax paid in an EU country, are for personal use and are not intended for resale*. However the customs authorities have issued a list of maximum amounts considered reasonable for persons over 17 years of age, of alcoholic drinks, tobacco goods, perfume, etc. These are:

spirits or strong liqueurs over 22% volume – 10 litres; fortified wines (port, sherry, etc.) – 20 litres; table wine – 90 litres (of which not more than 60 litres may be sparkling wine); beer – 110 litres; cigarettes – 800 or cigarillos 400 or cigars 200 or pipe tobacco 1kg. Personal use includes gifts, but if a passenger is receiving any payment in return for buying alcohol and tobacco (such as help with travelling expenses) the transaction will be dutiable and the duty must be paid to the Customs authorities.

For those coming direct from a country outside the EU or who have arrived from another EU country without having passed through customs control with all their baggage, the allowances for goods obtained anywhere outside the EU are:

Spirits – 1 litre or fortified wine – 2 litres or table wine – 3 litres plus a further 2 litres of table wine. Perfume – 60cc; toilet water – 250cc. 200 cigarettes or 100 cigarillos or 50 cigars or 250gr of tobacco. All other goods, including gifts, £36 worth. "Duty-free" goods are still available at major airports, on aircraft and ferries; amounts are virtually the same as those above and are controlled by the carriers concerned. The duty-free allowances are scheduled to be phased out by 1996.

Cycling

The city of Munich has gone to great lengths to improve the lot of the cyclist, building many new well-signed cycle-paths, as well as extra overpasses and cycle subways, replacing car parking with cycle parks and putting up barriers to keep cyclists away from motorists. Cycles are available from a large number of the local transport authority (MVV) stations and can also be taken on S-Bahn and U-Bahn trains within certain limitations (see Public Transport).

Allgemeiner Deustcher Fahrrad Club (ADFC, German Cycling Club), Stein-strasse 17; tel. 4 80 10 01: open Tue.–Fri. 4–7pm, Sat. 10am–1pm.

ADFC

The local authority publishes a map of the city for cyclists (Münchner Radlstadtplan), available from the Tourist Office as well as cycle shops and book stores, showing all the routes open to cyclists and offering suggestions for touring the city and its surroundings by cycle.

City map
for cyclists

Diplomatic Representation

Consulates in Munich:

Tal 29/III; tel. 22 26 61

Canada

Mauerkircherstrasse 1a; tel. 98 57 23

Eire

Sendlinger-Tor-Platz 5; tel. 2 31 16 30

South Africa

Bürkleinstrasse 10; tel. 21 10 90

United Kingdom

Königinstrasse 5; tel. 2 88 80

United States

Electricity

Current is supplied in Germany at 220–250 volts 50 cycles AC; sockets are of the usual continental type. Visitors from Great Britain, Ireland, the United States or Canada require an adaptor for use with electric razors, etc.

Emergency Services

Tel. 110

Police

Tel. 112

Fire

Tel. 1 92 22

Ambulance

Tel. 55 86 61

Medical
emergency

Tel. 59 44 75

Duty Chemist

Tel. 76 37 37

Women's
crisis line

Tel. 41 40 22 11

Poisons helpline

Tel. 1 92 13

Vehicle insurers
helpline

See also Useful Telephone Numbers

Events

The Munich Tourist Office publishes a full calendar of events in the official monthly programme which is available from its offices, newsagents and bookstores. Events listings are also given in the Munich supplement of the Friday edition of the Süddeutsche Zeitung.

Programme
of events

Events

The "Schäfflertanz", a traditional dance performed every seven years

German-American Folk Festival ("Kleine Wies'n") at Perlacher Forst.	July
Munich Opera Festival.	
Bell'Arte (music in the open air in the Brunnenhof of the Residenz.	
Tournament of Knights at Schloss Kaltenberg (near Ammersee; S-Bahn 4 to Geltendorf).	
End of the month: Holzhausener Music Festival (on Lake Starnberger).	
Palace concerts at Schleissheimer Schloss and Schloss Dachau.	July/August
Late July/early August (around what used to be the festival of St Jacob): Jakobidult in the Au district.	
Dachau Folk Festival and Fair.	August
Keferloh Horse Fair (22km/14 miles east of Munich).	September
Freisinger Folk Festival and Fair.	
Erding Autumn Festival ("Miniwies'n").	
Oktoberfest: ceremonial entry on the first day of the Mayor and the host breweries; colourful procession in national dress and costumes on the first Sunday.	Mid-September –1st Sunday in October
St Leonard's Ride (procession, with blessing of horses) at Bad Tölz and other venues.	November
Christkindlmarkt and other Christmas markets on the Marienplatz and in front of the Frauenkirche.	December
Auer Dult is a traditional market held three times a year on the square in front of the Mariahilfkirche in the Au district. See Markets.	Auer Dult

Excursions

The easiest way to get to many of the attractions around Munich is by the Underground and rapid transit trains and buses operated by the city's transport authority, the MVV (see Public Transport). 34 of its suburban stations are designated "Wanderbahnhöfe" and serve as starting points for the 111 walks and trails of varying lengths in and around the outskirts of the city. These are well-signed and make an ideal way of getting to know the many interesting features of the local countryside.

By MVV trains
and buses

Olching (S 3)
Dachau (Altomünster), Röhrmoos (S 2)
Oberschlaissheim, Freising (S 1)
Kieferngarten (U 6)
Unterföhring, Ismaning (S 3)
Poing, Markt Scwaben, Ottenhofen, Erding (S 6)
Eglharting, Kirchseeon, Ebersberg (S 5)
Aying, Kreuzstrasse (S 1)
Deisenhofen, Holzkirchen (S 2)
Icking, Wolfratshausen (S 7)
Planegg, Mühlthal, Starnberg, Tutzing (S 6)
Harthaus, Wessling, Herrshing am Ammersee (S 5)
Fürstenfeldbruch, Schöngeising, Grafrath, Geltendorf (S 4)

MVV
Wanderhbahnhöfe

One excursion well worth making is a trip on German Rail's Glass Train which runs on various routes taking in the highlights of Upper Bavaria. Probably the best views from its observation cars are to be had on the cleverly engineered line included in the "Karwendel" tour into the Tirol via Garmisch-Partenkirchen and Mittenwald.

Glass train

Coach tour operators:
Panorama Tours, M 2, Arnulfstrasse 8; tel. 59 15 04
Official Bavarian Travel Bureau (Bayerisches Reisebüro), M 19, Landshuter Allee 38; tel. 12 04–0

By coach

Autobus Oberbayern, M 45, Heidemannstrasse 220; tel. 3 23 04–0
Isaria-Reisen, M 2, Neuhauser Strasse 47; tel. 2 37 23–0
Collection and dropping-off point:
Elisenstrasse, Neptunbrunnen (near Karlsplatz/Stachus)

The most popular coach tours from Munich are to Herrsching am Ammer-see with Andechs Monastery, Chiemsee, Schliersee, Spitzingsee, Tegern-see, Berchtesgaden and Königsee, Garmisch-Partenkirchen and the Zugspitze, Oberammergau, Linderhof Castle, Neuschwanstein Castle, Ettal Monastery, Salzburg and Innsbruck.

| Sightseeing programme | See entry |

Fasching

Munich throws itself with great enthusiasm into its celebration of the Shrovetide carnival of Fasching. This extends for the period from Epiphany (January 6) to Shrove Tuesday, and is marked by "Fasching balls" on each weekend during the carnival season, culminating in the "Gaudi Wurm" on the final Sunday when everyone processes in carnival costume through the streets of the city centre.
On Shrove Tuesday, the last night of the carnival, many places in Munich are the scene of final gatherings to see out the end of Fasching.

Carnival
hotspots

Lonely Hearts Ball, Klenzestrasse 71
Deutsches Theater, Schwanthalerstrasse 13
Hacker Keller, Theresienhöhe 4
Heide-Vollm, Planegg, Bahnhofstrasse 51
Hofbräuhaus, on the Platzl
Hofbräu Keller, Innere Wiener Strasse
Hotel Bayerischer Hof, Promenadeplatz
Löwenbräukeller, Nymphenburger Strasse 2
Mathäser, Bayerstrasse 5
Max Emanuel Brauerei, Adalbertstrasse 33
Pschorr Keller, Theresienhöhe 7
Salvator Keller, Hochstrasse 77
Schwabingerbräu, Leopoldstrasse 82

Food and Drink

Although Bavarian food has a reputation for being rather stodgy and lacking in imagination, with too much emphasis on cabbage and dumplings, it does include a whole range of appetising dishes and delicacies which no visitor should miss, especially since it also features several specialities from elsewhere such as Swabia and the Tirol. Meat figures prominently on every menu, with vegetables being of less importance, and much use is made of thyme, bay leaves and nutmeg for flavouring. Cakes and pastries are also firm favourites.

Brotzeit

"Brotzeit", literally "bread time", is a snack meal which will vary according to how hungry and thirsty you are at the time, but is likely to include some of the following popular specialities.

Leberkäs'
(meat loaf)

Bavarian "Leberkäs" (literally "liver cheese") is a meat loaf of roast beef, pork and bacon, but hardly any liver, often in a crispy coating, spiced with marjoram, nutmeg and onions.

Bavarian snacks

Radi is horseradish in thin slices or spirals and salted to make it "weep".

Radi
(horseradish)

Garlic bread – a slice of bread spread with butter or cream cheese and sprinkled with finely chopped garlic – is gaining in popularity as a quick snack.

Garlic bread

Munich's famous "Queen of Sausages" is the white sausage, or "Weisswurst", which was first invented here in 1857 in the "Zum ewigen Licht" tavern. A veal and bacon sausage in a white skin, weisswurst is seasoned with salt and pepper, onions, lemon and parsley, and should be eaten with sweet Bavarian mustard and pretzels, but not after noon – tradition has it that the white sausage must never hear the clock strike midday. Leave the skin; the meat should be scooped out, not cut and sliced. And any request for ketchup or even a cup of coffee to go with it will be greeted with scorn and derision.

Weisswürste

Cheese (Camembert or Gervais) with chopped onions, paprika, caraway seed, yolk of egg, butter, pepper and salt.

Obatzda

Soups

The following two soups enjoy great popularity in Bavaria.

Meat broth with dumplings made from flour, liver, breadcrumbs, milt, onions, garlic, marjoram, salt and pepper.

Leberknödelsuppe

Broth with long semolina dumplings.

Griessnockerl-suppe

Meat

Here are some of Bavaria's many tasty meat dishes.

Beef cooked in meat stock and sliced. Often served with horseradish.

Tellerfleisch

167

Food and Drink

Tafelspitz	An Austrian dish in origin, steamed loin of beef, usually eaten with horseradish.
Tiroler Geröstel	Boiled meat diced and fried up with egg and potatoes.
Kalbsschäuferl	Steamed slices of shoulder of lamb.
Kalbsvögerl	Steamed roll of veal, stuffed with bacon and gherkins.
Kalbshaxe, Schweinshaxe	Among Munich's best-known specialities, these are knuckle of veal or pork which have been skinned, washed, seasoned with salt and pepper, then fried or grilled. Served with cabbage and dumplings.
Kaiserfleisch	Known elsewhere as "Kassler Rippenspeer". Pork spare rib, smoked, roasted and boiled.
G'selcht's	A term for meat that has been smoked.
Fleischpflanzl	Fried meat rissoles, known in Northern Germany as "Frikadellen" or "Bouletten", and eaten with potato salad.
Lüngerl	Lights, cut into thin strips, cooked in a sauce and served with bread dumplings.
Beuscherl	Calf's lights, with the heart and milt.
Krautwickerl	Steamed rolled white cabbage leaves with a meat stuffing.
Backhendl	Grilled or oven-roast chicken.
Wammerl	Streaky fat belly of pork.
Schweinsbraten	Leg or fillet of pork, usually served with bread dumplings and occasionally cabbage.

Sausage

Some of the other sausages found in Munich besides "weisswurst".

Schweinswürstl	Pork sausages eaten with mustard and sauerkraut.
G'schwollne	Veal sausages, fried in butter, and also known as "Wollwürste".
Dicke	A small spicy beef and pork sausage, also known as "Regensburger".
Milzwurst	Made from calf's sweetbread and milt, cut into slices, coated with breadcrumbs and fried.
Leoni	The Bavarian name for "Lyoner" sausages, made from beef, pork and veal with pistachio nuts.
Weisswurst	See under Brotzeit

Garnishes

Semmelknödel	Dumplings made from stale bread, onions, egg and parsley. Particularly popular with Schweinsbraten, Lüngerl (see under Meat) and "Schwammerl" (mushrooms).
Sauerkraut	Shredded white cabbage, salted and cooked until juicy with bacon and juniper berries.
Reiberdatschi	Bavarian name for potato fritters.

Confectionery

Anyone with a sweet tooth will be in their element in Munich which has a reputation for rich and fattening cakes and pastries.

Sweet yeast dumplings cooked in milk and sugar, usually accompanied by a vanilla sauce.	Dampfnudeln
Oven-baked yeast dumplings.	Rohrnudeln
Doughnuts.	Schmalznudeln
Round yeast cakes, thinner in the middle.	Aus'zog'ne
Apple fritters.	Apfelkücherl, Apfelrad
Jam doughnuts.	Krapfen
Succulent plum cake made with yeast dough, baked in large cake-tins and sold in slices.	Zwetschgndatschi
Layers of filo pastry rolled round fillings of apple, curd cheese (quark), etc.	Strudel

Beer

Munich may have a rather indifferent reputation for its food, but its beer is quite another matter. Down through the centuries this has earned itself worldwide acclaim founded on the concern for quality exercised by its famous brewers to meet the demands of its most discerning critic, the Munich beerdrinker. The city's six great breweries – Augustinerbräu, Hacker-Pschorr, Hofbräu, Löwenbräu, Paulaner-Thomas and Spaten-Franziskaner Brauerei – were founded as such in the 19th c. but can trace their origins back to the Middle Ages. The beers on offer range from strong ales to light lagers, with traditional special brews at certain times of the year.

Galleries

Munich Tourist Office operates a "What's On" line for the city's museums and galleries: tel. 23 91 62.

Besides the galleries housing major collections listed elsewhere in the A–Z section Munich has many other public and commercial galleries. Their addresses can be found in the Yellow Pages edition of the telephone directory under such headings as Antiquitäten, Antiquariate, Bilder, Galerien and Kunsthandlungen.

What's On phoneline

Getting to Munich

Most visitors from overseas will choose to travel to Munich by air. The city is one of the main centres for air travel in this part of Europe and many of the major international airlines operate scheduled and charter flights to its new Franz-Josef-Strauss Airport. For details of how to get to and from the airport see Air Travel.

By air

Munich has good rail connections with the rest of Germany and all other major European cities. One particularly speedy and comfortable way to travel is German Rail's InterCity Express (ICE) which only takes 7½ hours to get to Munich from Hamburg via Hannover, Frankfurt and Stuttgart.

By rail

Ostbahnhof, Munich's east station (see Rail Stations), takes regular motorail services carrying cars and passengers from other German stations (Berlin, Bremen, Cologne, Düsseldorf, Hagen, Hamburg, Hannover, Münster) and from Narbonne and Paris in France, Budapest (Hungary), Thessaloniki and Athens (Greece), Istanbul (Turkey) and Rimini (Italy).

Motorail

Hotels

The roads and motorways for getting to Munich are the A9/E45 from the north (Frankfurt am Main or Berlin), the B12/E522 from the east (Passau), the A8/E52 from the south-east (Salzburg), the A95/E533 from the south (Innsbruck, Mittenwald, Garmisch-Partenkirchen), the A96/E54 from the south-west (Switzerland/Lake Constance), and the A8/E52 from the west (Karlsruhe, Stuttgart, Ulm, Augsburg).

Hotels (a selection)

Room availability line

24-hour service; tel. 1 94 12

(no rest.) = no restaurant, breakfast only

City centre

Admiral (no rest.), Kohlstrasse 9, 32 r.; tel. 22 66 41
Alexandra, Amalienstrasse 20, 50 r.; tel. 28 40 01
Alfa (no rest.), Hirtenstrasse 20/22, 70 r.; tel. 59 84 61
Alpen-Hotel, Adolf-Kopling-Strasse 14, 60 r.; tel. 55 45 85
Altano (Best Western), Arnulfstrasse 12, 140 r.; tel. 55 18 80
Amba (no rest.; Minotel), Arnulfstrasse 20, 74 r.; tel. 59 29 21
Apollo (no rest.), Mittererstrasse 7, 72 r.; tel. 53 95 31
Arcade, Dachauer Strasse 21, 200 r.; tel. 55 19 30
Ariston (no rest.), Unsöldstrasse 10, 60 r.; tel. 22 26 91
Arabella Central, Schwanthalerstrasse 111, 102 r.; tel. 51 08 30
Arosa, Hotterstrasse 2/4, 65 r.; tel. 26 70 87
Atrium (Best Western), Landwehrstrasse 59, 160 r.; tel. 51 41 90
Austrotel, Arnulfstrasse 2, 172 r.; tel. 5 38 60
Bavaria, Gollierstrasse 9, 52 r.; tel. 50 10 78
*Bayerischer Hof with Palais Montgelas, Promenadeplatz 2/6, 440 r.; tel. 2 12 00
Blauer Bock, Sebastiansplatz 9, 60 r.; tel. 23 17 80
Bosch (no rest.), Amalienstrasse 25, 80 r.; tel. 28 10 61
Brack (no rest.), Lindwurmstrasse 153, 52 r.; tel. 77 10 52
Bristol, Pettenkoferstrasse 2, 56 r.; tel. 59 51 51
Brunnenhof (no rest.), Schillerstrasse 36, 60 r.; tel. 55 49 21
Budapest, Schwantalerstrasse 36, 100 r.; tel. 5 51 11–0
City, Schillerstrasse 3a, 65 r.; tel. 55 80 91
Concorde (no rest.), Herrnstrasse 38, 72 r.; tel. 22 45 15
Condor, Zweigstrasse 6, 65 r.; tel. 59 85 31
Daniel, Sonnenstrasse 5, 74 r.; tel. 55 49 45
Dietl, Goethestrasse 11, 40 r.; tel. 59 28 47
Domus, St-Anna-Strasse 31, 45 r.; tel. 22 17 04
Drei Löwen (Best Western), Schillerstrasse 8, 130 r.; tel. 55 10 40
Eden-Hotel Wolff, Arnulfstrasse 4/8, 210 r.; tel. 55 11 50
Einhorn, Paul-Heyse-Strasse 10, 112 r.; tel. 53 98 20
Erzgiesserei Europe, Erzgiessereistrasse 15, 105 r.; tel. 18 60 55
Europäischer Hof, Bayerstrasse 31, 120 r.; tel. 55 15 10
Excelsior, Schützenstrasse 11, 112 r.; tel. 55 13 70
Germania (Best Western), Schwanthalerstrasse 28, 100 r.; tel. 5 16 80
*Grand Hotel Continental, Max-Joseph-Strasse 5, 150 r.; tel. 55 15 70
Herzog, Häberlstrasse 9, 70 r.; tel. 53 04 95
*Hilton City, Rosenheimer Strasse 15, 483 r.; tel. 48 04–0
*Hilton Park, on Tucherpark 7, 481 r.; tel. 38 45–0
Hungar-Hotel, Paul-Heyse-Strasse 24, 158 r.; tel. 51 49 00
Intercity-Hotel, in the main station, 200 r.; tel. 55 85 71
King's Hotel, Dachauer Strasse 13, 85 r.; tel. 55 18 70
*Königshof, Karlsplatz 25, 105 r.; tel. 55 13 60
Maria, Schwanthalerstrasse 112, 70 r.; tel. 50 30 23
Mark (no rest.), Senefelderstrasse 12, 90 r.; tel. 59 28 01
Meier, Schützenstrasse 12, 56 r.; tel. 59 56 23
Metropol, Bayerstrasse 43, 220 r.; tel. 53 07 64
Platzl, Platzl 1, 170 r.; tel. 2 37 03–0
Präsident, Lindwurmstrasse 13, 70 r.; tel. 26 30 11

*Rafael, Neuturmstrasse 1, 75 r.; tel. 29 09 80
Regent, Seidlstrasse 2, 224 r.; tel. 55 15 90
Reinbold, Adolf-Kopling-Strasse 11, 60 r.; tel. 59 79 45
Schweiz-Gebhardt, Goethestrasse 26, 60 r.; tel. 53 95 85
Senator, Martin-Greif-Strasse 11, 30 r.; tel. 53 04 68
Senefelder, Senefelderstrasse 4, 70 r.; tel. 55 15 40
Stachus, Bayerstrasse 7, 60 r.; tel. 59 28 81
Torbräu, Tal 37, 85 r.; tel. 22 50 16
Trustee Parkhotel, Parkstr. 31, 36 r.; tel. 51 99 50
*Vier Jahreszeiten (Kempinski), Maximilianstrasse 17, 340 r.; tel. 23 03 90,
with Walterspiel Restaurant
Wallis, Schwanthalerstrasse 8, 53 r.; tel. 59 16 64

Arabella Olympiapark, Helene-Meyer-Ring 12, 105 r.; tel. 3 51 60 71	Schwabing
Holiday Inn München, Leopoldstrasse 194, 360 r.; tel. 38 17 90	
Ibis, Ungererstrasse 139, 138 r.; tel. 36 08 30	
International, Hohenzollernstrasse 5, 70 r.; tel. 33 30 43	
International Garden, Hohenzollernstrasse 9, 75 r.; tel. 39 80 01	
König Ludwig (Best Western), Hohenzollernstrasse 3, 45 r.; tel. 33 59 95	
Leopold, Leopoldstrasse 119, 60 r.; tel. 36 70 61	
Marriott, Berliner Strasse 93, 350 r.; tel. 36 00 20	
Mercure, Leopoldstrasse 120, 66 r.; tel. 39 05 50	
Nikolai, Maria-Josepha-Strasse 4, 63 r.; tel. 39 70 56	
*Ramada Parkhotel, Th.-Dombart-Strasse 4, 260 r.; tel. 36 09 90	
Residence, Artur-Kutscher-Platz 4, 192 r.; tel. 40 16 69	
Tourotel, Domagkstrasse 26, 230 r.; tel. 36 00 10	
Vitalis, Kathi-Kobus-Strasse 22/24, 100 r.; tel. 12 00 80	
Weinfurtner's Garden Hotel, Leopoldstrasse 132, 190 r.; tel. 36 80 04	
*Arabella Bogenhausen, Arabellastrasse 5, 540 r.; tel. 9 23 20	Bogenhausen
Queens Hotel, Effnerstrasse 99, 152 r.; tel. 92 79 80	
Palace, Trogerstrasse 21, 72 r.; tel. 4 70 50 91	
Prinzregent, Ismaninger Strasse 42, 66 r.; tel. 41 60 50	
*Sheraton, Arabellastrasse 6, 625 r.; tel. 9 26 40	
Wetterstein, Grünwalder Strasse 16, 60 r.; tel. 6 97 00 25	Giesing
*Preysing, Preysingstrasse 1, 72 r.; tel. 48 10 11	Haidhausen
Penta Hotel, Hochstrasse 3, 580 r.; tel. 4 48 55 55	
K + K Hotel am Harras (Best Western), Albert-Rosshaupter-Strasse 4-6, 117 r.; tel. 77 00 51	Harras
Rivoli, Albert-Rosshaupter-Strasse 18, 60 r.; tel. 77 00 41	
Transmar Park Hotel, Zschokkestrasse 55, 70 r.; tel. 57 93 60	Laim
Deutsche Eiche, by the station, 20 r.; tel. 8 14 15 57	Lochhausen
Ambassador Parkhotel, M 90, Plinganserstrasse 102, 42 r.; tel. 72 48 90	Mittersendling
Königin Elisabeth, Leonrodstrasse 79, 70 r.; tel. 12 68 60	Neuhausen
Novotel, Rudolf-Vogel-Bogen 3, 254 r.; tel. 63 80 00	Neuperlach
Orbis, Karl-Marx-Ring 87, 185 r.; tel. 6 32 70	
Mayerhof (no rest.), Dachauer Strasse 421, 70 r.; tel. 1 41 30 41	Nymphenburg
Nymphenburg, Nymphenburger Strasse 141, 44 r.; tel. 18 10 86	
*Holiday Inn München-Süd, Kistlerhofstrasse 142, 320 r.; tel. 78 00 20	Obersendling
Martinshof, Martin-Empl-Ring 8, 15 r.; tel. 92 20 80	Riem
Carmen, Hansastrasse 146, 62 r.; tel. 7 60 10 99	Untersendling
Arabella Westpark, Garmischer Strasse 2, 256 r.; tel. 5 19 60	Westpark

Information

Munich City Tourist Office	Munich City Tourist Office (Fremdenverkehrsamt der Landeshauptstad München) runs Munich's tourist information centres and also publishes a number of useful maps and leaflets including its official monthly programme and "Young People's Guide to Munich". These can be obtained from the following addresses. Accommodation can also be arranged but this has to be done either by mail in advance or in person at one of the tourist information centres.

Central office, postal address: 8000 Munich 1; telex 524 801, fax 23 91–313, tel. (089) 23 91–1 (information, leaflets, details of accommodation booking service).

Tourist information centres:
Hauptbahnhof (main station, south exit on Bayerstrasse); tel. 23 91–2 56, 23 91–2 57. Open: Mon.–Sat. 8am–10pm, Sun. 11am–7pm.

Munich Airport, central building; tel. 97 59 28 15 (no room bookings by phone or flight information). Open: Mon.–Sat. 8.30am–10pm, Sun. and holidays 1–9pm.

Rindermarkt/Pettenbeckstrasse; tel. 23 91–2 72. Open Mon.–Fri. 9.30am–6pm.

Room information	On-screen information in the Main Station and at the Messegelände.
Tourist office infolines	Museums and galleries: tel. 23 91–62. Palaces and other attractions: tel. 23 91–72. Conferences, trade fairs, exhibitions: tel. 23 91–81.
Municipal Information office	Presse- und Informationsamt der Landeshauptstadt München, M 1, Rathaus, Marienplatz, room 241; tel. 2 33–9 26 00. Open: Mon.–Thur. 8am–4pm, Fri. 8am–2pm.
City information	Stadtinformation, M 2, Stachus shopping floor; tel. 2 33–82 42, 55 44 59. Open: Mon. 11am–6pm, Tue.–Thu. 8.30am–6pm, Fri. 8.30am–noon.
Information for young people	Youth Information Centre, M 2, Paul-Heyse-Strasse 22; tel. 51 41 06 60. Open: Mon.–Fri. noon–6pm, Thu. noon–8pm.
Alpine information	Deutscher Alpenverein, M 22, Praterinsel 5; tel. 29 49 40.
Flight infoline	Tel. 97 52 13 13.
Train infoline	Tel. 1 94 19 (DB/German Rail).
Munich Public Transport (MVV)	Munich Transport (MVV, Münchner Verkehrs- und Tarifverbund) M 22, Thierschstrasse 2; tel. 2 38 03–0. S-Bahn information: tel. 55 75 75. Also EFA interactive screens at Hauptbahnhof and Munich Airport.
Information for women	Treibhaus Women's Centre, M 2, Güllstrasse 38; 7 25 42 71 (café, advice, therapy, library) Women's Cultural Centre, M 80, Richard-Strauss-Strasse 21; tel. 4 70 52 12. Open: Tue., Wed., Fri. 2–5pm, Thu. 6–10pm (meeting point, courses, gallery, café) Women only café, M 2, Güllstrasse 3; tel. 7 25 51 12. Open: Tue. 6–9pm. Frauenhaus München, day and night help for women; tel. 3 54 83–0. Lillemor's Frauenbuchladen (women's bookshop), M 40, Arcisstrasse 57; tel. 2 72 12 05. Open: Mon.–Fri. 10am–6pm, Sat.10am–2pm. Babysitter service: tel. 22 92 91 (all languages). Lady cabs: Angelika's Hexenbesen; tel. 7 55 85 37. Women's crisis line (help and counselling for women victims of sexual violence): tel. 76 37 37.

Insurance

Visitors are strongly advised to ensure that they have adequate holiday insurance including loss or damage to luggage, loss of currency and jewellery.

Under European Union regulations British and Irish visitors to Munich are entitled to medical care under the German social insurance scheme on the same basis as German citizens. Before leaving home they should apply to their local social security office for form E 111 and the accompanying leaflet on "How to get medical treatment in other European Community countries".
These arrangements may not cover the full cost of medical treatment, and it is advisable, therefore, even for EU citizens, to take out short-term health insurance. Visitors from non-EU countries should certainly do so.

Medical
insurance

Visitors travelling by car should ensure that their insurance is comprehensive and covers use of the vehicle in Europe.

Vehicles

See also Travel Documents

Language

German, like English, is a Germanic language, and the pronunciation of German usually comes more easily to English-speakers than does a Romance language like French. Much of the basic vocabulary, too, will be familiar to those whose native language is English, though they may have more difficulty with more complex terms incorporating native Germanic roots rather than the Latin roots so common in English. The grammar is not difficult, but has retained a much more elaborate system of conjugations and declensions than English.
Standard German (*Hochdeutsch*) is spoken throughout the country, although many Germans speak a strong local dialect as well.

The consonants are for the most part pronounced broadly as in English, but the following points should be noted: *b, d* and *g* at the end of a syllable are pronounced like *p, t* and *k* (in some parts of Germany like the Scottish *ch* in "loch"); *c* (rare) and *z* are pronounced *ts; j* is pronounced like consonantal *y; qu* is somewhere between English *qu* and *kv; s* at the beginning of a syllable is pronounced *z; v* is pronounced *f;* and *w* is pronounced *v.* The double letter *ch* is pronounced like *ch* in "loch" after *a, o* and *u;* after *ä, e, i* and *ü* it is somewhere between that sound and *sh. Sch* is pronounced *sh,* and *th* (rare) *t.*
The vowels are pronounced without the diphthongisation normal in English; before a single consonant they are normally long, before a double consonant short. Note the following: short *a* is like the flat *a* of northern English; *e* may be either closed (roughly as in "pay"), open (roughly as in "pen") or a short unaccented sound like the *e* in "begin" or "father"; *ä* is like an open *e; u* is like *oo* in "good" (short) or "food" (long); *ö* is like the French *eu,* a little like the vowel in "fur"; *ü,* like the French *u,* can be approximated by pronouncing *ee* with rounded lips.
Diphthongs: *ai* and *ei* similar to *i* in "high"; *au* as in "how"; *eu* and *äu* like *oy; ie* like *ee.*

Pronunciation

173

Numbers

0	null
1	eins
2	zwei
3	drei
4	vier
5	fünf
6	sechs
7	sieben
8	acht
9	neun
10	zehn
11	elf
12	zwölf
13	dreizehn
14	vierzehn
15	fünfzehn
16	sechzehn
17	siebzehn
18	achtzehn
19	neunzehn
20	zwanzig
21	einunzzwanzig
22	zweiundzwanzig
30	dreissig
40	vierzig
50	fünfzig
60	sechzig
70	siebzig
80	achtzig
90	neunzig
100	hundert
101	hundert und eins
153	hundert dreiundfünfzig
200	zweihundert
300	dreihundert
1000	tausend
1001	tausend und eins
1021	tausend einundzwanzig
2000	zweitausend
1,000,000	eine Million

Ordinals

1st	erste
2nd	zweite
3rd	dritte
4th	vierte
5th	fünfte
6th	sechste
7th	siebte
8th	achte
9th	neunte
10th	zehnte
11th	elfte
20th	zwanzigste
100th	hundertste

Fractions

half	Hälfte
third	Drittel
quarter	Viertel
three-quarters	drei Viertel

Useful Expressions

Good morning	Guten Morgen
Good day	Guten Tag
Good evening	Guten Abend
Good night	Gute Nacht
Goodbye	Auf Wiedersehen
Do you speak English?	Sprechen Sie Englisch?
I do not understand	Ich verstehe nicht
Yes	Ja
No	Nein
Please	Bitte
Thank you (very much)	Danke (sehr)

The usual response to "Danke" is "Bitte" ("Not at all", "Don't mention it")

Yesterday	Gestern
Today	Heute
Tomorrow	Morgen
Help!	Hilfe!
Have you a single room?	Haben Sie ein Einzelzimmer?
. . . a double room?	. . . ein Doppelzimmer?
. . . with twin beds?	. . . mit zwei Einzelbetten?
. . . with private bath?	... mit Bad?
What does it cost?	Was kostet das?
Please wake me at six	Wollen Sie mich bitte um sechs Uhr wecken?
Where is the lavatory?	Wo ist die Toilette?
Where is the bathroom?	Wo ist das Badezimmer?
Where is the chemist's?	Wo ist die Apotheke?
Where is the post office?	Wo ist das Postamt?
Where is there a doctor?	Wo gibt es einen Arzt?
Where is there a dentist?	Wo gibt es einen Zahnarzt?
Is this the way to the station?	Ist dies der Weg zum Bahnhof?

Months, Days of the Week and Festivals

January	Januar	Months
February	Februar	
March	März	
April	April	
May	Mai	
June	Juni	
July	Juli	
August	August	
September	September	
October	Oktober	
November	November	
December	Dezember	
Sunday	Sonntag	Days of the week
Monday	Montag	
Tuesday	Dienstag	
Wednesday	Mittwoch	
Thursday	Donnerstag	

Friday	Freitag
Saturday	Samstag, Sonnabend
Day	Tag
Public holiday	Feiertag

Festivals

New Year	Neujahr
Easter	Ostern
Ascension	Christi Himmelfahrt
Whitsun	Pfingsten
Corpus Christi	Fronleichnam
Assumption	Mariä Himmelfahrt
All Saints	Allerheiligen
Christmas	Weihnachten
New Year's Eve	Silvester

Road and Traffic Signs

Abstand halten!	Keep your distance
Achtung!	Caution
Baustelle	Road works
Durchfahrt verboten	No thoroughfare
Einbahnstrasse	One-way street
Einordnen	Get into line
Gefahr	Danger
Halt!	Halt
Kurve	Bend
Langsam	Slow
Rollsplit	Loose stones
Stadtmitte	Town centre
Stop	Stop
Strasse gesperrt	Road closed
Vorsicht!	Caution
Zoll	Customs

Rail and Air Travel

Aircraft	Flugzeug
Airport	Flughafen
All aboard!	Einsteigen!
Baggage	Gepäck
Baggage check	Gepäckschein
Bus station	Autobushof
Bus stop	Haltestelle
Departure	Abfahrt (*train, bus*), Abflug (*aircraft*)
Flight	Flug
Halt (*railway*)	Haltestelle
Information	Auskunft
Lavatory	Toilette(n)
Line (*railway*)	Gleis
Luggage	Gepäck
Luggage trolley	Kofferkuli
Non-smoking	Nichtraucher
Platform	Bahnsteig
Porter	Gepäckträger
Restaurant car	Speisewagen
Sleeping car	Schlafwagen; Liegewagen (*couchettes*)
Smoking	Raucher
Station	Bahnhof
Stewardess	Stewardess

Ticket	Fahrkarte
Ticket collector	Schaffner
Ticket window	Schalter
Timetable	Fahrplan; Flugplan (*air*)
Train	Zug
Waiting room	Wartesaal
Window seat	Fensterplatz

At the Post Office

Address	Adresse
Express	Eilboten
Letter	Brief
Parcel	Paket
Post-box	Briefkasten
Postcard	Postkarte
Poste restante	Postlagernd
Postman	Briefträger
Post office	Postamt
Registered	Einschreiben
Small packet	Päckchen
Stamp	Briefmarke
Telegram	Telegramm
Telephone	Telefon
Telex	Fernschreiben

Topographical Terms

Allee	avenue, walk
Amt	office
Anlage	gardens, park
Auskunft	Information
Aussicht	view
Ausstellung	exhibition
Autobushof	bus station
Bahn	railway; lane (*in road*)
Bahnhof	railway station
Bau	building
Berg	hill, mountain
Bezirk	region (*an administrative subdivision of a* Land)
Bibliothek	library
Börse	(stock) exchange
Brücke	bridge
Brunnen	fountain
Bundes-	Federal
Burg	(fortified) castle
Denkmal	monument, memorial
Dom	cathedral
Dorf	village
Eingang	entrance
Einkaufszentrum	shopping centre
Eisenbahn	railway
Fernmeldeturm	telecommunications tower
Fernsehturm	television tower
Feste, Festung	fortress, citadel
Flughafen	airport

Fluss	river
Forst	forest
Freilichtmuseum	open-air museum
Fremdenverkehrsverein	tourist information office
Friedhof	cemetery
Garten	garden
Gasse	lane, street
Gau	region
Gebäude	building
Gebirge	(range of) hills, mountains
Gelände	tract of land, grounds
Gemeinde	commune (*the smallest local government unit*)
Gericht	(law) court
Grab	tomb, grave
Graben	ditch, moat
Gut	estate, country house, farm
Hafen	harbour, port
Halde	hillside
Halle	hall
Hallenbad	indoor swimming pool
Hauptbahnhof	main railway station
Hauptpost (amt)	head post office
Hauptstrasse	main street
Haus	house
Heim	home
Heimatmuseum	local or regional museum
Hochhaus	multi-storey building, tower block
Hochschule	higher educational establishment, university
Hof	courtyard; farm; (royal) court
Höhe	hill, eminence
Hospital	hospital, hospice
Hügel	hill
Hütte	hut; iron and steelworks, glassworks
Insel	island
Jugendherberge	youth hostel
Kammer	chamber, room
Kapelle	chapel
Keller	cellar
Kino	cinema
Kirche	church
Kloster	monastery, convent, religious house
Krankenhaus	hospital
Kreis	district (*an administrative subdivision of a* Bezirk)
Kurhaus	spa establishment
Kurort	spa, health resort
Land	land; specifically, one of the *Länder* or provinces of the Federal Republic
Landkreis	rural district
Laube	arcade, loggia
Markt (platz)	market (square)
Marstall	court stables
Mauer	wall

Meer	sea
Messe	trade fair
Münster	minster, monastic church
Nord	north
Ober-	upper
Oper	opera (house)
Ost	east
Palais, Palast	palace
Pfad	path, trail
Pfalz	(royal) palace, stronghold
Pfarrkirche	parish church
Pforte	doorway
Platz	square
Post (amt)	post office
Rasthaus, Raststätte	"rest-house" in motorway service area
Rathaus	town hall
Ratskeller	cellar (restaurant) of town hall
Reisebüro	travel agency
Rennbahn	race-track
Residenz	residence, seat of a ruling prince; princely capital
Ruine	ruin
Rundfunk	radio
S-Bahn, Stadtbahn	urban railway, tramway
Saal	hall, room
Säule	column
Schatzkammer	treasury
Schauspielhaus	theatre
Schloss (*plural* Schlösser)	castle, palace, country house (*usually designed for show rather then defence*)
Schnellweg	expressway
Schule	school
See	lake; sea
Spielbank	casino
Spital	hospital
Staats-, staatlich	state, national
Stadt	town, city
städtisch	municipal
Stätte	place, spot
Steig	path
Steige	staircase; steep ascent
Stein	stone
Sternwarte	observatory
Stiege	staircase
Stift	religious house; chapter, college; foundation
Stiftskirche	collegiate church; monastic church
Strasse	street, road
Strassenbahn	tramway
Süd	south
Tal	valley
Theater	theatre
Tiergarten, Tierpark	zoo, animal park

Lost property

Tonhalle	concert-hall
Tor	gate (way)
U-Bahn	underground railway
Unter-	lower
Verkehr	traffic, transport
Verkehrsamt, -büro, -verein	tourist information office
Veste	fortress, citadel
Viertel	quarter, district
Vorort, Vorstadt	suburb, outer district
Wald	wood, forest
Wall	rampart
Wallfahrt	pilgrimage
Wand	wall
Wasser	water
Weg	way, road
Weinstube	wine-bar, -house
West	west
Wildpark	game park, wild-life park
Zimmer	room
Zitadelle	citadel

Lost property

Municipal lost property office	M 2, Ruppertstrasse 19; tel. 2 33–1. U-Bahn: Poccistrasse Open: Mon.–Fri. 8.30am–noon, Tue. 2–5.30pm Lost property found on the street and in city public transport.
DB/German Rail lost property office (Main Station)	Hauptbahnhof, Bahnhofsplatz 2 (opposite platform 26); tel. 1 28–66 94 U- and S-Bahn: Main Station Open: Mon.–Fri.8am–noon, 12.30–3.30pm. Lost property found on DB trains and around the Main Station, Holzkirchner and Starnberger Stations.
S-Bahn lost property office (East Station)	Ostbahnhof (window 8); tel. 1 28–8 44 09. S-Bahn: Ostbahnhof. Open: Mon.–Fri. 8am–5.45pm, Sat. 8–11.45am. Lost property found on the S-Bahn.
Postal services lost property	Post Office 3, Arnulfstrasse 195, room 103; tel. 12 62–5 52 U- and S-Bahn: Hauptbahnhof. Open: Mon.–Fri. 8–9 and 9.25–11.15am, Mon. and Tue. 12.15–3.15pm, Thur. 12.15–2.45pm, Fri. 12.15–2.15pm. Lost property found on post office premises, including telephone kiosks.

Markets

Food and produce	Munich's most famous market for food and produce is the Viktualienmarkt in the city centre (see A–Z, Viktualienmarkt). Other regular produce markets are to be found in Haidhausen (Wiener Platz), Pasing (Bäckerstrasse), Schwabing (Elizabethplatz) and Sendling ("Grüner Markt", Implerstrasse 11).
Flea markets	Flea markets are held at irregular intervals, usually at weekends, at many places around the city. The best known venues are at Theresienwiese, Mariahilfplatz and Münchner Freiheit, together with Berliner Strasse in the north of Schwabing and an area at the Olympic site. See the daily press for dates and times.
Christkindlmarkt	Munich's pre-Christmas Christkindlmarkt, which takes place every year and lasts for three to four weeks, carries on a tradition dating back to the

14th c. when records first appeared of the "Nikolausmarkt". Concentrated around the Marienplatz and extending into Fingerstrasse and Weinstrasse it is open daily between 9am and 7pm.

Christkindl markets also take place on Grossen Freiheit in Schwabing, Weissenburger Platz in Haidhausen and by the Pfarrkirche in Pasing.

Other Christmas markets

Auer Dult is a traditional market and funfair held three times a year on the square of the Mariahilfkirche in the Au district. The Maidult in May is followed by the Jakobidult in July and the Kirchweihdult in October. As well as all the fun of the fair, complete with Ferris wheel and roundabouts, there is also a vast market with stalls selling a whole range of wares from antiques to junk.

Auer Dult

Motoring

As in most of Continental Europe the rule of the road is drive on the right, pass on the left. The speed limit in built-up areas is 50kph/31mph but goes down in some places to 30kph/18mph. On other roads the speed limit is 100kph/62mph except for motorways (autobahn) and dual carriageways where unless indicated there are no speed restrictions. Use of seat belts is compulsory. See also Insurance, Travel Documents.

Driving in Germany

Freimann (Nürnberg autobahn); tel. 32 54 17
Ramersdorf (Salzburg autobahn); tel. 67 27 55
Obermenzing (Stuttgart autobahn); tel. 8 11 24 12

Road routing stations

ADAC (Allgemeiner Deutscher Automobil-Club)
Ridlerstrasse 35; tel. 51 95–0, information line tel. 50 50 61

Motoring organisations

AvD (Automobilclub von Deutschland)
Seeriederstrasse 25; tel. 4 70 81 41/Wotanstrasse 70; tel. 1 78 30 64
(Mon.–Fri. 9am–noon, 2–5pm), information line tel. (069) 6 60 63 00

DTC (Deutscher Touring Automobil Club)
Amalienburgstrasse 23; tel. 89 11 33–0, information line 8 11 10 48

ACE: tel. 5 30 90 69 or 1 92 16
ADAC: tel. 1 92 11 or 01 802 22 22 22
AvD: tel. 30 45 69 (Lübben)
DTC: tel. 8 11 12 12

Breakdown services

Car rental is included in a number of fly-drive packages, and DB/German Rail operates a rail and road car-rental scheme. There are also car-hire desks at Munich Airport. The rental companies in town include the following:

Car rental

Avis: M 2, Nymphenburger Strasse 61; tel. 12 60 00–20
Hertz: M 19, Nymphenburger Strasse 81; tel. 1 29 50 01
interRent/Europcar: M 2, Hirtenstrasse 14 (at the Main Station); tel. 55 71 45
Sixt/Budget: M 22, Seitzstrasse 9/11; tel. 22 33 33

Practically the only places to park for the city centre during the day are the surface parks on the Theresienwiese or the multi-storey car parks. These and all other car parks are shown on the map accompanying this guide. Since Munich has such an excellent public transport system, covering all the city sights, the best way to travel is to leave the car at one of the many park-and-ride sites (P+R-Plätze) and take to the MVV's trains, trams and buses.

Car parking

Multi-storey car parks which are supervised and well-lit:
Gasteig underground garage, M 80, Rosenheimer Strasse 5; tel. 48 49 56, Open: 8am–midnight. St-Jakobs-Platz multi-storey, M 2, Oberanger 35/37; tel. 26 66 96. Open: 24 hours.

Reserved parking for women

An old model railway and accessories . . .

Museums

Opening times	Most of Munich's museums are open Tuesdays to Sundays between 9.15am and 5pm. Many of them close on Mondays and public holidays.
Admission	Museums and galleries usually charge admission but some of them are free on Sundays and holidays.
Museums pass	The 8-day Museums Pass (Verbund-Eintrittskarte), issued by the Bavarian authorities and costing DM 20, gives admission to over 20 museums, galleries and other collections in the Munich area. These include the Residenz Treasure, Nymphenburg Palace and both Pinakotheks.
Temporary exhibitions	Information about temporary exhibitions can be found in the local press and in the official monthly programme published by Munich Tourist Office. There is also a museums and galleries information line: tel. 23 91–62.
Museum workshop	Museum workshop (Museumswerkstatt) is a scheme run by experts whereby visitors can learn at first hand about the background to treasures in the Munich collections.

Most museums are featured in the A–Z section (for page number see Index). Other museums are:

Architecture Museum of the Technical University
M 2, Arcisstrasse 21 (entrance Luisenstrasse). Open: Mon.–Fri. by appointment; tel. 21 05–24 93.
Germany's largest collection of architectural drawings.

Bayerischen Rückversicherung AG's collections and exhibitions
M 22, Sederangerstrasse 4/6. Open: Mon.–Fri. 7.30am–6.30pm; tel. 38 44–2 34.
Collection of 20th c. graphics; modern art and design "on the move".

. . . and the dolls' collection in the Toy Museum (Old Town Hall)

Doll Museum (Puppenmuseum)
M 45, Gondershauser Strasse 37. Open: Mon. and Thu. 11am–5pm, Sun.
11am–1pm.

Firearms (Feuerwehr) Museum
M 2, Blumenstrasse 34. Open: Sat. 9am–4pm.

Historical Museum of Sewing Machines and Irons
M 2, Heimeranstrasse 68/70, on the premises of J. Strobel & Söhne
Open: sewing machines Mon.–Fri. 10am–4pm, irons by appointment only.

Kunstraum München (contemporary art)
M 40, Viktor-Scheffel-Strasse 20. Open: Tue.–Fri. 2–6pm, Sat. 11am–1pm.

Kunstverein München (contemporary art)
M 22, Galeriestrasse 4 (Hofgarten arcade). Open: Tue.–Sun. 10am–6pm.

Künstlerwerkstatt (artists' workshop)
M 80, Lothringer Strasse 13 (factory). Open: daily 2–6pm.
Contemporary experimental art.

Meter Museum (Zählermuseum, exhibition by city public utilities)
M 40, Franzstrasse 9. Open: Wed. 9am–noon.

Museum for casts of classical sculpture (sculpture casts, archaeological
photographic archive)
M 2, Meiserstrasse 10. Open: Mon.–Fri. by appointment; tel. 55 91–01.

Natural History Museum (Tiermuseum)
M 82, Bajuwarenstrasse 104. Open: Mon.–Fri. 10am–6pm, Sat., Sun., holidays 10am–4pm; collection of stuffed animals.

Olaf-Gulbransson Museum
Tegernsee. Open: Tue.–Sun. 2–6pm.

Siemens Museum
Praunerstrasse 10. Open: Mon.–Fri. 9am–4pm, Sat., Sun. 10am–2pm.

State Anthropological Collection
M 2, Karolinenplatz 2A. Viewing by prior appointment only; tel. 59 52 51.
Anthropological material and finds including those from the Klausen cave
in Altmühltal and the Ofnet cave at Nördlingen.

State Botanical Collection
M 19, Menzinger Strasse 67. Viewing by prior appointment only;
tel. 17 92–1.

State Geology Collection
M 2, Luisenstrasse 37. Open: Mon.–Fri. 8am–6pm.

State Zoological Collection
M 60, Münchhausenstrasse 21. Open only to specialists and by prior
appointment; tel. 8 10 7–0.

Music

Besides being a mecca for theatre and the visual arts Munich is also one of
Europe's leading cities for its music, hosting such major events in the
international music calendar as its Opera Festival and the season of summer concerts in Nymphenburg Palace.

It is home to the orchestras of the Bavarian State Opera and the Gärtnerplatz Theatre as well as the Munich Philharmonic, Bavarian Radio Symphony Orchestra, Munich Chamber Orchestra, Graunke Symphony
Orchestra and many smaller ensembles, usually specialising in the music
of a particular period. Other internationally famous groupings and soloists
also give regular guest performances in programmes ranging from classical music to jazz and pop.

Opera, ballet

Bayerische Staatsoper (Bavarian State Opera), National Theatre, M 22,
Max-Joseph-Platz 2; tel. 22 13 16
Altes Residenztheater (Cuvilliés Theatre), M 2, Residenzstrasse 1;
tel. 22 57 54
Staatstheater am Gärtnerplatz (Gärtnerplatz Theatre), M 5, Gärtnerplatz 3;
tel. 2 01 67 67
Prinzregententheater, M 80, Prinzregentenplatz 12; tel. 22 57 54
Deutsches Theater, M 2, Schwanthalerstrasse 13; tel. 59 34 27
Kultuzentrum Gasteig, Carl Orff Hall, M 80, Rosenheimer Strasse 5;
tel. 4 80 98–0

Palace concerts

Residenz, Brunnenhof, Herkulessaal, Kaisersaal, M 2; tel. 22 57 54
Neues Schloss Schleissheim, D(W)–8042, Oberschleissheim; tel. 3 15 02 12
Schloss Nymphenburg, M 19; tel. 17 90 8–0
Schloss Blutenburg, M 60; tel. 93 99 33
Schloss Dachau, D(W)-8060 Dachau; tel. 2 72 45 39

Church music

Frauenkirche, M 2, Frauenplat 1
St Bonifaz, M 2, Karlstrasse 34
St Kajetan (Theatinerkirche), M 22, Theatinerstrasse 22
St Lukas, M 2, Mariannenplatz
St Markus, M 2, Gabelsberger Strasse 6
St Michael, M 2, Neuhauser Strasse 52
Klosterkirche Fürstenfeldbruck
Klosterkirche Schäftlarn

Concert venues
(selection)

Bavarian Radio concert hall, M 2, Rundfunkplatz 1; tel. 59 00–23 25
Freies Musikzentrum, M 80, Ismaningerstrasse 29; tel. 4 70 63 14
Kulturzentrum Gasteig, M 80, Rosenheimer Strasse 5; tel. 4 80 98–0
Music College concert hall, M 2, Arcisstrasse 12
Stuck-Villa, M 80, Prinzregentenstrasse 60; tel. 4 70 70 86

Sophiensaal, M 2, Sophienstrasse 6; tel. 59 95–1
University Aula, M 22, Geschwister-Scholl-Platz 1

Allotria, M 40, Türkenstrasse 33; tel. 28 58 58
Domicile, M 40, Leopoldstrasse 19; tel. 39 94 51
"Zum Isartal" tavern, M 70, Brudermühlstrasse 2; tel. 77 50 01
Kaffee Giesing, M 90, Bergstrasse 5; tel. 6 92 05 79
Waldwirthschaft Grosshesselohe, 8023 Grosshesselohe, Georg-Kalb-Strasse 3; tel. 79 50 88 (summer only)
Grünes Eck, M 90, St-Martin-Strasse 7; tel. 69 40 51
Manege, M 80, Steinseestrasse 2; tel. 49 72 10
Technical University Mensa, M 2, Arcisstrasse 17
Nachtcafé, M 2, Maximiliansplatz 5; tel. 59 59 00
Oklahoma-Country Saloon, M 70, Schäftlarnstrasse 156; tel. 7 23 43 27
Olympiahalle, M 40, Spiridon-Louis-Ring 7; tel. 3 06 13–1
Pasinger Fabrik, M 60, August-Exter-Strasse 1; tel. 8 34 14 81
Schwabinger Podium, M 40, Leopoldstrasse 17; tel. 39 40 81
Theatre in the Leopoldstrasse, M 40, Leopoldstrasse 17; tel. 39 40 81
Theaterfabrik Unterföhring, Föhringer Allee 23; tel. 9 50 56 66
Theatron, M 40, in Olympiapark, Spiridon-Louis-Ring; tel. 3 06 13–1
Unterfahrt, M 80, Kirchenstrasse 96; tel. 4 48 27 94
Gaststätte Waldheim, M 70, Zöllerstrasse 1; tel. 7 14 62 88
Zirkus-Krone-Bau, M 2, Marstrasse 43; tel. 53 51 58

Jazz, rock
and pop
(selection)

What's On line: tel. 115 17
Also in the local press (see Newspapers) and the official monthly programme published by Munich Tourist Office.

Programme
of events

Newspapers

Munich's daily broadsheet of national standing is the "Süddeutsche Zeitung", first published in 1945 and successor to the "Münchner Neuesten Nachrichten", founded in 1848.
The popular tabloids are the "Münchner Abendzeitung", "tz", and the Munich edition of "Bild-Zeitung".
Leading British and American newspapers and magazines can be bought from newsagents in the city centre, big hotels, Hauptbahnhof and Munich Airport.

Night Life

It would be difficult to find anywhere to compare with Munich for its night life, which tends to centre on Schwabing (M 40). In fact the city has so many nightspots of all kinds that those which follow are just a selection.

"In" places

Babalu, M 40, Leopoldstrasse 19
Backstage, M 70, Graubündner Strasse 100
Climax, M 22, Sternstrasse 20
Club Shalom, M 40, Leopoldstrasse 113
Far Out, M 2, by the Kosttor
Hamlet Light, M 40, Leopoldstrasse 194
Magrathea-Halle, M 60, Berduxstrasse 30
Metropolis, near the main station, in the Mathäser-Festsaal-Gebäude, entrance in Zweigstrasse
Nachtwerk, M 21, Landsberger Strasse 185
Park-Café, M 2, Sophienstrasse 7

Night Life

Pulverturm, M 45, Schleissheimer Strasse 393
Vertigo Soundbar, M 40, Leopoldstrasse 23
Wirtshaus im Schlachthof, M 2, Zenettistrasse 9

Bars

Hotel bars

Bayerischer Hof, hotel bar and night club, Promenadeplatz 2–6
Hilton München, piano bar, Tucherpark 7
Hotel Regent, night club, Seidlstrasse 2, at the main station
Sheraton, Vibraphon night club, Bogenhausen, Arabellastrasse 6
Vier Jahreszeiten, hotel bar, Maximilianstrasse 17

Other well-known
bars and clubs

Americanos, M 2, Thalkirchener Strasse 71
Babalu, M 40, Leopoldstrasse 19
*Harry's New York Bar, Falkenturmstrasse 9
Havana Club, M 22, Herrnstrasse 30
Iwan, M 2, Josephspitalstrasse 15
Juleps, Breisacher Strasse 18
Mammasita's, M 80, Schumannstrasse 9
Maximum, Maximilianstrasse 38
Nachtcafé, M 2, Maximiliansplatz 5
Odeon, Brienner Strasse 10
Pappasito's, Schraudolphstrasse 44
Paris Bar, M 80, Gravelottestrasse 7
Peppermint Park, Lilienstrasse 58
*Schumann's, M 22, Maximilianstrasse 36
Vinothek, L.R., M 80
Wunderbar, M 2, Hochbrückenstrasse 3

Discos

With over 70 discos Munich has something for everyone, from hard rock to karaoke.
Allee-Café, Nymphenburger Strasse 145
Aquarius, Leopoldstrasse 134
Crash, M 2, Lindwurmstrasse 88 (heavy metal and hard rock)
Gaslight, M 40, Ainmillerstrasse (Latino disco)
Jackie O., M 81, Rosenkavalierplatz 12
Liberty, M 80, Rosenheimer Strasse 30
Maximilian's, Maximiliansplatz 16
Oly, Helene-Mayer-Ring, Olympic village
P 1, M 2, Prinzregentenstrasse 1 (in Haus der Kunst)
Sugar Shack, Herzogspitalstrasse 6

Jazz Clubs

Allotria, Schwabing, Türkenstrasse 3; tel. 28 58 58
Blue Note, München-Nord, Moosacher Strasse 24; tel. 3 51 05 20
Jenny's Place, Schwabing, Georgenstrasse 50 (entrance on Nordenstrasse); tel. 2 71 93 54
Nachtcafé, Maximiliansplatz 5
Unterfahrt, Kirchenstrasse 96, near Ostbahnhof; tel. 4 48 27 94

Hot meals after midnight

Kapuziner, Kapuzinerstrasse 6 (until 1.30am)
Regenten-Schenke, Bogenhausen, Prinzregentenstrasse 11 (until 3am)
Waikiki, Neureutherstrasse 39 (until 2am)
Warsteiner Wildschütz, Hildegardstrasse 2 (until 2am)
Waschkuchl, Luisenstrasse 25 (until 4am)

Opening Times

See Business Hours

Post

German letter boxes are yellow with a black posthorn on the front. Stamps can be bought from vending machines, also yellow, and some newsagents and other shops.

Postamt (post office) 32
M 2, Bahnhofplatz 1 (opposite main station); tel. 54 54–27 32/33. Open: Mon.–Fri. 6am–10pm, Sat., Sun. and holidays 7am–10pm.
Public fax and telex, and postal savings bank service, cashing of cheques and money-changing also at night. This is the post office where all postal matter addressed "poste restante 80074 Munich" can be collected. Write-read telephone for the deaf. No acceptance of parcels or consignments of valuables.

Chief post offices

Postamt 31
M 2, Bahnhofplatz 2 (in the main station); tel. 55 22 62–0/10.
Open: Mon.–Fri. 8am–7pm, Sat. 8am–2pm, closed Sun. and holidays.

Postamt 1
M 2, Residenzstrasse 2 (near Marienplatz); tel. 29 03 87–10.
Open: Mon.–Fri. 8am–6pm, early counter 7–8am, late counter 6–6.30pm, Sat. 8am–1pm (parcels not taken after noon), early counter 7–8am.
Money-changing, fax, express mail service.

Postamt 85356
Munich Airport, central building; tel. (089) 970 14 60/61.
Open: Mon.–Fri. 8am–8pm, Sat. 8am–6pm, Sun., holidays 10am–6pm.

Most other city post offices are open Mon.–Fri. 8am–noon, 3–6pm, Sat. 8am–noon.

Public holidays

Bavaria has more public holidays than anywhere else in Germany. Consequently Munich celebrates public holidays on New Year's Day (January 1), Epiphany (January 6), Good Friday, Easter Day and Easter Monday, Labour Day (May 1), Ascension Day, Whit Sunday and Whit Monday, Corpus Christi, Assumption Day (August 15), Day of National Unity (October 3), All Saints Day (November 1), Day of Prayer and Repentence, and Christmas (December 25 and 26).

Public Transport

Munich's public transport authority, the MVV, operates the city's underground (U-Bahn, 6 lines), rapid transit rail (S-Bahn, 8 lines), trams and buses, and the same ticket can be used for all of them.

MVV (Münchner Verkehrs- und Tarifverbund)

MVV, M 22, Thierschstrasse 2; tel. 23 80 30
S-Bahn: Hauptbahnhof (main station), platform 26; tel. 55 75 75
For easy reference use the map of the S-Bahn and U-Bahn in this part of the guide. The tourist information centres also supply free maps and information. The timetable for all the MVV services is updated twice a year and can be obtained from bookstores and newsagents.

Information

Munich Integrated Public Transport System

MVV - HA 1 / Stand : Juni 1991

U and S Rail Network

MVV

U6 Kieferngarten
Freimann
Studentenstadt
Alte Heide
Nordfriedhof
Dietlindenstraße
Münchener Freiheit
Giselastraße
Universität
Odeonsplatz Lehel Max-Weber-Platz
...splatz Isartor Rosenheimer Platz
(...achus)

Marienplatz
Kolumbus- Untersberg-
platz straße
...dlinger Fraunhofer- Silberhorn- Giesing Karl-Preis-
straße straße Platz
Goetheplatz
Fasangarten Perlach
Fasanenpark
Unterhaching
Mon.–Fri. rush hours Taufkirchen-U.
S27
Furth
Deisenhofen
Sauerlach
Otterfing
S2 Holzkirchen

U4 Arabellapark
Richard-Strauss-Str.
Böhmerwaldplatz
Prinzregentenplatz
S4
S7 Leuchtenbergring
Ostbahnhof Berg am Laim
St Martinstraße
U1 Innsbrucker Ring
Michaelibad
Quiddestraße
Neuperlach Zentrum
Therese-Giehse-Allee
Neuperlach Süd
Neubiberg
U2 Ottobrunn
U5 Hohenbrunn
Wächterhof
Höhenkirchen-Siegertsbrunn
Dürrnhaar
Aying
Peiß
Großhelfendorf
Kreuzstraße **S1**

S3 Flughafen München II Terminal
Flughafen Besucherpark
Hallbergmoos
Ismaning
Unterföhring
Johanneskirchen
Englschalking
Daglfing

S6
Erding
Altenerding
Aufhausen
St Kolomann
Ottenhofen
Markt Schwaben
Poing
im Bau
Grub
Heimstetten
Feldkirchen
Riem
Trudering
Gronsdorf
Haar
Vaterstetten
Baldham
Zorneding
Eglharting
Kirchseeon
Grafing Bahnhof
Grafing Stadt
Ebersberg
S5

Free Parking for MVV passengers
S-Bahn Interchange Stations

189

Public Transport

Ticket zones

For ticketing purposes Munich and the surrounding area is divided into five concentric ticket zones, as shown on the map at every stop. The price of a ticket depends on the number of zones in the journey. Tickets can be bought as single tickets or as strips. These strips are blue for adults and red for children. All tickets have to be cancelled at the start of the journey in the blue cancelling machines on train platforms and in trams and buses. Adults should cancel two strips per zone, with five zones, i.e. 10 strips, the maximum for a journey, and children one strip for up to two zones and two strips for any distance of three zones or beyond. The inner area of Munich, the pale blue metropolitan area, counts as one zone, thus every trip inside the metropolitan area requires two blue strips for adults and one red strip for children. The maximum time for a journey, from when the ticket is cancelled, is up to two hours within one zone, up to three hours for three zones and up to four hours above four zones. Free transfers are possible provided the journey continues in the same direction.

Tickets

Single tickets (Einzelfahrkarte) can be bought for a journey covering any number of zones. Strip tickets (Streifenkarte) – blue for adults, red for children – are cheaper. Both kinds of tickets can be bought from MVV vending machines on S-Bahn and U-Bahn platforms and on trams and buses, as well as at MVV sales points such as newsagents, etc. These display a white K on a green background. Adults can use one blue strip for a short journey so long this does not exceed four stops, of which only two may be may be covered by S-Bahn and U-Bahn. Changes are possible but the trip may not last more than an hour. Any suburban bus trip within a single district can count as a short journey.

Children

Children under the age of five can travel free if accompanied. There are two fare stages – up to two zones and from three zones – for children between five and 15. There is a single ticket for each stage. Children can also use the cheaper red strip ticket, with one strip required for two zones and two strips over three zones.

Day Ticket

Day tickets are good value for visitors and locals alike. There are different prices for children and adults and different flat-rates for travel within the inner metropolitan zone and for the whole network. Day tickets for five cover a whole day's travel (from 9am weekdays and all day on holidays and at weekends) for up to five people, only two of whom may be aged over 18, and a dog! There is no starting time for singles. A day ticket (24-Stunden-Karte) is valid from the time it is first cancelled until 4am the following morning and can be used during that time anywhere on the MVV system as often as required.

Tourist tickets

Tourist tickets can be issued for a specific period, and are valid for the whole of that time and until 4am the following morning.

Group and Conference tickets

Group tickets are available for groups of over five persons, with every tenth person in larger groups entitled to free travel, although the group has to stay together during the journey.
Conference tickets at reduced rates are available to people attending conferences and their partners who are in Munich for stays of longer than two days.

"Kombikarte"

"Kombikarte" are tickets combining admission to an event with MVV travel to and from that event. This covers events staged by, amongst others, the Bavarian State Opera (Opera Festival, Nationaltheater, Cuvillié Theatre, Prinzregententheater, Theater im Marstall, Residenz Hercules Hall), Gärtnerplatz State Theatre, Bayerisches Staatsschauspiel, Münchner Kammerspiele, and Bayern Munich Football Club.
The blue and white combination ticket ("weiss-blaue Kombikarte") is another ticket for five, this time combining MVV travel with boat trips on the lakes of the Ammersee and Starnberger See between late May and mid-October

The MVV operates 6 late-night bus lines between the city centre and the outer suburbs. Special late night bus and train services also run on New Year's Eve and during Fasching. For times contact the MVV (tel. 23 80 30).

Late-night services

The MVV provides about 15,000 free park-and-ride places at 96 of its rapid transit train stations with the aim of attracting motorists who want to get to town quickly without having to spend time and money on finding and paying for a parking space.

Park & Ride

Bicycles can be taken on S-Bahn and U-Bahn trains during the week outside rush-hours (i.e. not between 6 and 8.30am or 3 and 6.30pm, although the afternoon restriction lapses in school holidays) and at any time holidays and weekends.
Between April 1 and October 31 cycles can also be rented at the following S-Bahn stations: Freising (S 1), Holzkirchen (S 2), Geltendorf (S 4), Fürsten-feldbruck (S 4), Herrsching (S 5), Tutzing (S 6), and Starnberg (S 6) (see Cycling).

Bicycles

Since 1977 all new MVV stations have been built with full disabled access and those built earlier are gradually being brought up to standard. The MVV also publishes a map on which its facilities for the disabled, such as lifts, ramps, etc., are shown in detail. Severely disabled people with the green/orange permit are entitled to travel free on all MVV transport.

Disabled access

Smoking is banned on U-Bahn and S-Bahn trains and Underground stations.

No Smoking

Radio and Television

The Munich area is served by Bavarian Radio (Bayerischer Rundfunk). This has four channels and there are daily broadcasts of the news in English. Most of the information for tourists (weather, road conditions, etc.) goes out on Bayern 3, the third radio channel. In Germany it is also possible to receive the BBC World Service, the American Forces Network (AFN) and Voice of America.

Radio

Munich broadcasts two national TV channels, ARD and ZDF. It also has a regional station (Drittes Programme) which is linked to Bayerische Rundfunk.

Television

Rail Stations

Munich's main railway station, the Hauptbahnhof, is a busy junction for rail travel within Germany and on other trans-European routes on the EuroCity and InterCity lines, as well as for the local rapid transit S-Bahn and Underground U-Bahn lines.
On-station facilities include luggage lockers and left luggage office, post office, catering in the main concourse, Railway Mission and Railway Hotel in the south building, official Bavarian Travel Bureau, exchange bureaus, luggage despatch office, food shops, bookstore and newsagents (German and foreign press and periodicals) and tourist informatiom centres. See also Business Hours.

Hauptbahnhof (main station)

Starnberg station – north wing of the Hauptbahnhof.
Trains to Weilheim (Upper Bavaria), Garmisch-Partenkirchen, Mittenwald. Station restaurant, railway bus station, MVV season ticket office.

Starnberger Bahnhof

Holzkirchner station – south wing of the Hauptbahnhof.
Trains to Wolfratshausen, Bad Tölz, Tegernsee, Schliersee, Bayrischzell.

Holzkirchner Bahnhof

Restaurants

Ostbahnhof	East station – linked to Hauptbahnhof through the S-Bahn tunnel and a line round the city centre. S-Bahn services to Munich's eastern suburbs; trains to Rosenheim, Salzburg, Kufstein, Mühldorf, Simbach. Station restaurant, travel information, bookstore, shops.
München-Pasing Bahnhof	Station in the western suburb of Pasing; S-Bahn station; local and express trains to Weilheim, Garmisch-Partenkirchen, Mittenwald, Kempten, Lindau, Augsburg.
Park & Rail	Most EuroCity/InterCity stations have parking places which passengers can reserve at a reduced charge. These can be booked from the Hauptbahnhof (tel. 1 28–50 34) and München-Pasing (tel. 1 28–66 53).
Rail & Road	Under the Rail & Road scheme it is possible to book hire cars in advance with interRent/Europcar to be collected at the station on arrival. This can be done through German Rail ticket offices or direct with interRent/Europcar, Hauptbahnhof; tel. 55 71 45.

See also Getting to Munich, Lost Property

Restaurants

The following is just a small selection of Munich's 6000 or so restaurants and other eating places. Visitors have a vast choice when it comes to eating out, although it has to be said that quality standards can soon change for better or worse, due in no small measure to the high turnover in restaurateurs. Most hotel restaurants are covered under Hotels.

Restaurants with German and international cuisine

City centre	*Aubergine, Maximiliansplatz 5; tel. 59 81 71 Boettner, Theatinerstrasse 8; tel. 22 12 10 Dallmayr, Dienerstrasse 14; tel. 2 13 51 00 Glockenbach, Kapuzinerstrasse 29; tel. 53 40 43 *Grill Restaurant in the Bayerischer Hof, Promenadeplatz Halali, Schönfeldstrasse 22; tel. 28 59 09 Hundskugel, Hotterstrasse 18; tel. 26 42 72 Isar-Terrassen (in the Park Hilton), Königshof, Karlsplatz 25; tel. 55 13 60 Klösterl, St-Anna-Strasse 2; tel. 22 50 86 La Vie, Ottostrasse 5; tel. 59 34 83 Luitpold, Brienner Strasse 11; tel. 29 28 65 Mövenpick, in the Künstlerhaus on Lenbachplatz; tel. 55 78 65 Pfistermühle (in the Platzl-Hotel) *Preysing-Keller, Innere Wiener Strasse 6; tel. 48 10 15 Ratskeller, Marienplatz 8; tel. 22 03 13 *Sabitzer, Reitmoorstrasse 21; tel. 29 85 84 Spatenhaus an der Oper, Residenzstrasse 12; tel. 22 78 41 *The Marks (in the Hotel Rafael) *Vier Jahreszeiten, Maximilianstrasse 17; tel. 23 03 96 00 Toula, Sparkassenstrasse 5; tel. 29 28 69 *Weinhaus Neuner, Herzogspitalstrasse 8; tel. 2 60 39 54 *Weinhaus Schwarzwälder, Hartmannstrasse 6; tel. 22 72 16 Welser Kuche (Feldherrnkeller, traditional Swabian food, medieval), Residenzstrasse 27; tel. 29 69 73 Zum Alten Markt, Dreifaltigkeitsplatz 3; tel. 29 99 95
Schwabing	Casa Pepe, Klopstockstrasse 4; tel. 36 69 00 *Tantris, Johann-Fichte-Strasse 7; tel. 36 20 61

Bogenhauser Hof, Ismaninger Strasse 85; tel. 98 55 86	Bogenhausen
*Käfer-Schänke, Schumannstrasse 1; tel. 4 16 81	
*Louis XIII, Ismaninger Strasse 71a; tel. 98 92 00	
Prielhof, Oberföhringer Strasse 44; tel. 98 53 53	
Löwenschänke (in the City Hilton)	Haidhausen
Rue des Halles, Steinstrasse 18; tel. 48 56 75	
Zum Gasteig (in the City Hilton)	
Hunsinger, Braunstrasse 6; tel. 26 68 77	Harlaching
Gärtnerei, Schleissheimer Strasse 456; tel. 3 13 13 73	Harthof
Böswirth, Das Kleine Restaurant, Waidachanger 9; tel. 8 11 97 63	Langwied
Königin Elisabeth, Leonrodstrasse 79; tel. 12 68 60	Neuhausen
Schlosswirtschaft zur Schwaige; tel. 17 44 21	Nymphenburg
Weichandhof, Betzenweg 81; tel. 8 11 16 21	Obermenzing
Olympiasee, Spiridon-Louis-Ring; tel. 3 06 13–309	Olymiapark
Olympiaturm-Drehrestaurant, Spiridon-Louis-Ring; tel. 3 08 10 39	
Goldene Gans (Martinshof), Martin-Empl-Ring 8; tel. 92 20 80	Riem
La Marine, Schleissheimer Strasse 19; tel. (0831) 7 25 81	Dachau

Restaurants with Bavarian "Schmankerl" cuisine

Braunauer Hof, Frauenstrasse 40; tel. 22 36 13	City centre
Bürgerhaus, Pettenkoferstrasse 1; tel. 59 79 09	
Nürnberger Bratwurstglöckl by the cathedral; tel. 22 03 85	
Spöckmeier, Rosenstrasse 9; tel. 26 80 88	
Straubinger Hof, Blumenstrasse 5; tel. 60 84 44	

Celebrated Munich inns

Munich Atmosphere

The following small selection is for visitors who want to eat good plain food and soak up some of the local atmosphere.

Augustiner, M 2, Neuhauser Strasse 16; tel. 5 51 99–257
Augustinerkeller, M 2, Arnulfstrasse 52; tel. 59 43 93
Bärenwirt, M 19, Winthirplatz 1; tel. 16 36 16
Donisl (Wirtshaus zur Alten Hauptwache), Weinstrasse 1; tel. 22 01 84
Zum Franziskaner, M 2, Perusastrasse 8; tel. 23 18 12–0
Hackerkeller, M 2, Theresienhöhe 4; tel. 50 70 04
Haxnbauer am Platzl, Münzstrasse 8; tel. 22 19 22
Hofbräuhaus am Platzl, M 2, Platzl 9; tel. 22 16 76
Hofbräukeller, M 80, Innere Wiener Strasse 19 ; tel. 48 94 89
Leopold, M 40, Leopoldstrasse 50; tel. 39 94 33
Löwenbräukeller, M 2, Nymphenburger Strasse 2; tel. 52 60 21
Mathäser-Bierstadt, M 2, Bayerstrasse 5; tel. 59 28 96
Mathäser Weissbierkeller, M 2, Bayerstrasse 1; tel. 59 54 31
Platzl, M 2, Platzl 1; tel. 2 37 03–0
Salvatorkeller am Nockherberg, M 90, Hochstrasse 77; tel. 48 32 74
Spatenhof, M 2, Neuhauser Strasse; tel. 26 40 10
Weisses Hofbräu, M 2, Tal 10

Foreign Specialities

Bohemian	Goldene Stadt, Oberanger 44; tel. 26 43 82
	Praha, Rossmarkt 3; tel. 26 55 27
Chinese	Canton, Theresienstrasse 49; tel. 52 21 85
	Mangostin, Thalkirchen, Maria-Einsiedel-Strasse 2; tel. 7 23 20 31
	Tai Tung, Prinzregentenstrasse 60; tel. 47 83 66
French	Austernkeller, Stollbergstrasse 11; tel. 29 87 87
	Bistro Terrine, Amalienstrasse 89; tel. 6 42 27 78
	Bouillabaisse, Falkenturmstrasse 10; tel. 29 79 09
	Ile de France, Rosenheimer Strasse 32; tel. 4 48 13 66
	La Mer, Schraudolphstrasse 24; tel. 2 72 24 39
	Le Gourmet, Hartmannstrasse 8; tel. 2 12 09 58
	Savarin, Schellingstrasse 122; tel. 52 53 11
Greek	Kytaro, Innere Wiener Strasse 36; tel. 4 80 11 76
	Olympia, Kellerstrasse 29; tel. 48 80 82
Italian	*El Toula, Sparkassenstrasse 5; tel. 29 28 69
	Michelangelo, Leopoldstrasse 87; tel. 33 25 55
	Osteria Italiana, Schellingstrasse 62; tel. 2 72 07 17
Yugoslav	Opatija, Brienner Strasse 41; tel. 59 12 02
Polynesian	Trader Vic's (in the Bayerischer Hof), Paradeplatz
Swiss	Chesa Rüegg, Wurzerstrasse 18; tel. 29 71 14
	Walliser Stuben, Leopoldstrasse 33; tel. 34 80 00
Hungarian	Csárda Piroschka, Prinzregentenstrasse 1; tel. 29 54 25

Shopping and Souvenirs

Shopping streets   Munich city centre is famous as a shopper's paradise far beyond the confines of Bavaria. The pedestrian precinct stretching for half a mile from the Karlsplatz (Stachus) to the Marienplatz contains a wonderful array of big department stores, boutiques and specialist shops, and has recently been extended to take in the Viktualienmarkt and Theatinerstrasse. The best streets and squares for shopping include Karlsplatz, Sonnenstrasse, Brienner Strasse, Sendlinger Strasse and Perustrasse.

Opening hours   Most retailers in the city centre open Mon.–Fri. 9am–6.30pm, Sat. 8.30am–2pm, staying open on the first Saturday in the month until 6pm

(4pm in the summer months). Late-night opening is on Thursdays until 8.30pm (see Business Hours).

The Munich branches of the big German department-store chains such as Hertie, Karstadt/Oberpollinger, and Kaufhof are in the pedestrian precinct between the main station and/or Karlsplatz and Marienplatz.

Department stores

Munich's top shops for luxury items are located in and around Brienner Strasse, Perustrasse, Maffeistrasse, Maximilianstrasse, Residenzstrasse and Theatinerstrasse.

Luxury shopping

Probably the most popular souvenirs of Munich are its famous litre-size beer tankards (Masskrüge). These come with or without pewter lids. In addition to smart fashionwear Munich also specialises in coats, jackets, etc. made from "Loden", waterproof woollen cloth, usually in the traditional green. Porcelain, including pieces from the local Nymphenburg factory, is another good buy.

Souvenirs

Specialist Shops

Beck am Rathauseck, M 2, Marienplatz 11 (clothing)
Bogner, M 2, Residenzstrasse 15 (fashion, sportswear)
Charivari-Kunsthandwerk, M 2, Brunnstrasse 3 (arts and crafts)
Dallmayr, M 1, Dienerstrasse 14 (coffee, delicatessen)
Max Dietl, M 2, Residenzstrasse 15 (fashion)
Geo-Buchladen, M 2, Rosental 6 (maps, travel books)
Gucci, M 2, Maximilianstrasse 32 (women's fashions)
Loden-Frey, M 2, Maffeistrasse 7/9 (Loden and Bavarian costume)
Hallhuber, M 2, Marienplatz (boutique ware)
Gebr. Hemmerle, M 22, Theatinerstrasse 3 (fashion)

A traditional department-store building

A very modern boutique

Hermès, M 22, Maximilianstrasse 22 (fashion)
Hirmer, M 2, Kaufingerstrasse 22 (clothing)
Holy's, M 2, Residenzstrasse 15 (menswear)
Hugendubel, M 2, Marienplatz 22 (books)
Jil Sander, M 2, Maximilianstrasse 21 (fashions)
Feinkost-Käfer, M 80, Prinzregentenstrasse 73
Rudolph Mooshammer, M 22, Maximilianstrasse 14 (fashion)
Nymphenburg Porcelain, M 22, Odeonsplatz 1
Radspieler, M 2, Residenzstrasse 23 (interior design, arts and crafts)
Babette Schweizer, M 2, Maxburgstrasse 4 (pewter figures)
Tiffany, M 2, Residenzstrasse 11 (jewellery)
Seb. Wesely, M 2, Rindermarkt 1 (wax goods)
Sport-Scheck, M 2, Sendlinger Strasse 85 (sports goods)
Sport-Schuster, M 2, Rosenstrasse 3 (sports goods)
Wölfi, M 2, Westenrieder Strasse 20 (Bavarian costume)
Yves Saint Laurent, Maximilianstrasse 21 (women's fashions)
Zechbauer, M 22, Brienner Strasse 13 (menswear)

Sightseeing

Sightseeing Programme

The following programme is intended as a help for visitors in Munich for the first time who want to make the most of a relatively brief stay in the city (places printed in **bold** are covered in the A–Z section under that heading). Otherwise, if it really is a flying visit with only a couple of hours to spare, the best course is to opt for one of the organised tours mentioned later. Some of the highlights can also be seen simply by walking around the parts of the old town in the vicinity of Marienplatz.

One day

Munich city centre is easy to explore on foot. For longer distances there is the excellent MVV public transport system, with its U-Bahn, S-Bahn, trams and buses (see Public Transport), or taxis. Since there is virtually no car parking in the city centre use the Park & Ride (see Motoring) if taking a car, but it is better to leave the car behind for any sightseeing in the city.

The Hauptbahnhof, Munich's main station, is a good starting point for a walk through the pedestrian zone (Schützenstrasse–Karlsplatz/Stachus–Neuhauser Strasse–Marienplatz). The city's top shopping district begins behind the Karlstor on the busy **Karlsplatz**. Places worth seeing here include the **Bürgersaal**, **Sankt Michael** (Church of St Michael) and Deutsches Jagd- und Fishereimuseum (German Hunting and Fishing Museum). Definitely worth a visit is the **Frauenkirche**, its onion domes visible behind the Hunting and Fishing Museum. As the Marienplatz opens up at the end of the Kaufingerstrasse the picturesque **Neues Rathaus** comes into view, dominating the square, and further on the **Altes Rathaus** with the **Peterskirche** (St Peter's Church) nearby. To the south, beyond St Peter's, the **Viktualienmarkt** displays all the colourful bustle of its weekday market.

From Marienplatz it is worth making a detour to the **Münchner Stadtmuseum** (Munich City Museum) and the **Asamkirche** (St John of Nepomuk). Hidden behind the north-east corner of the Rathaus is the medieval **Alter Hof**, first residence of the Wittelsbachs in Munich. Further on, in the same direction, lies the **Residenz**, a great complex of buildings spanning several centuries. Now restored as a museum, this is one of the great sights of Munich and not to be missed, with its three theatres and magnificent staterooms and galleries. Close by the Residenz take a look at the **Theatinerkirche**, **Feldherrnhall** and **Hofgarten**.

To get away from the city traffic go for a stroll in the nearest part of the **English Garden** with the acclaimed **Staatsgalerie Moderner Kunst im Haus der Kunst** (the State Gallery of Modern Art), in the southern corner. One side of the **Königsplatz**, north-west of the old city centre, is taken up by the

Staatlichen Antikensammlungen (State Collection of Classical Art), Propyläen and **Glyptothek**. Further north are Munich's two great galleries of Old Masters and New Masters, the **Alte Pinakothek** and the **Neue Pinakothek**. A day in Munich can be rounded off any way you please, there is so much to chose from – perhaps a concert or an evening at the theatre, a meal in a gourmet restaurant or a night of eating and drinking in a beer cellar, not to mention the more sophisticated surroundings of a smart night club.

Two days

Anyone with two days in Munich can take more time getting to know the major sights outlined in the one-day programme or extend it by visiting some of the city's other attractions.
A good way to spend the morning is a visit to the museum of your choice, whether it be the **Alte** or **Neue Pinakothek**, the **Glyptothek**, the **Residenz**, with its Treasure, the Bavarian **Nationalmuseum**, the **Deutsches Museum** or any of the various art exhibitions. Allow time afterwards for some window-shopping in the exclusive establishments between Kaufingerstrasse and the Theatinerkirche and a glimpse of the cosmopolitan **Maximilianstrasse**.
Use the afternoon to visit one of the palaces such as **Nymphenburg** or **Schleissheim**. It is also worth making a trip to the **Olympiapark** since this can be combined with enjoying the view from the Olympia Tower and having a look at the **BMW Museum**.

Three days

A three-day visit provides time to see some of the attractions on Munich's outskirts. These include **Blutenburg** Palace, the **Botanische Garten** (botanical gardens), **Tierpark Hellabrunn** (zoo), Geiselgasteig, with its Bavarian Film Tour, Grünwald and its Castle Museum, **Westpark**, and Dachau, with its concentration camp memorial.

Excursions further afield obviously require a longer stay. Places worth visiting if there is time include the bishopric of **Freising**, **Schäftlarn** Monastery, the lakes of Tegernsee and Ammersee, with Andechs Monastery, and the town of Fürstenfeldbruck.

Organised City Sightseeing

City tours

Small one-hour tour: 10am and 2.30pm daily
Grand 2½-hour tour: 10am daily (except Mon.), with visit to Peterskirche and Alte Pinakothek; 2.30pm daily (except Mon.), with tour of Nymphenburg Palace.
Olympic Tour (approx. 2½ hrs.): 10am and 2.30pm daily, with trip to top of Olympia Tower only or combined with tour of Olympic site.
Departures from: Bahnhofplatz, in front of the Hertie department store.
Palaces tour (Neuschwanstein and Linderhof): daily 8.30am.
Departure from: Neptunbrunnen, Elisenstrasse.
Operator: Panorama Tours, M 2, Arnulfstrasse 8; tel. 089/120 42 48

Themed city trails on foot, by cycle or by tram, plus special guided tours for children: group tours daily by arrangement. Regular guided tours for individuals: 2.30pm Sat., Sun. 11am and 2pm, holidays 2pm.
Operator: Stattreisen München, M 40, Postbox 40 18 32; tel. 2 71 89 40

City Hopper tours by cycle: daily by arrangement, depending on the weather (inc. cycle). Guided walks on foot also possible.
Contact Stefanie Pokorny, M 40, Hohenzollernstrasse 95; tel. 2 72 11 31

Guided walk round the old town: 10am daily
City tours by cycle: 10.30am Mon., Wed., Fri., daily cycle rental.
Operator: Radius Touristik, meeting point and base at Platform 35, Munich Hauptbahnhof; tel. 59 61 13

Old town guided tours: 10am Mon. and Thu.
Meeting point: Fischbrunnen, Marienplatz.
Operator: Münchner Volkshochschule (Popular University), M 80, Postbox 80 11 64; tel. 4 80 06–2 30

Old town guided tour (alternating northern part and Kreuz district): 10am Sat. Meeting place: Fischbrunnen, Marienplatz.
Operator: Münchner Bildungswerk, M 2, Dachauer Strasse 5; tel. 55 73 31

Taxis

Munich taxis are beige. Tipping is usually done by rounding up to the nearest Deutsche Mark (DM). Taxi rank numbers can be found on the inside front cover of the city telephone directory.

Taxi bookings by phone	Tel. 21 61–0 or 1 94 10
Lady cabs	Angelika's Hexenbesen; tel. 7 55 85 37

Telephone

German telephone boxes are yellow. The sign of a black receiver on a green background means national and international calls can be made. Cheap rate is between 6pm and 8am on weekdays and all day on public holidays and at weekends.

Directory enquiries	Inland: 11 88 International: 0 01 18
International dialling codes	To Munich from abroad: your own international code followed by 49 for Germany then 89 for Munich and the number. From Munich abroad: 00 followed by your own country code (Australia 61, Canada 1, Eire 353, New Zealand 64, South Africa 27, United Kingdom 44, United States 1) and the number.

Theatre

What's On	What's on phoneline: tel. 115 17 (theatre), 115 18 (cabaret, etc.) Listings: Munich Tourist Office official monthly programme, Munich supplement of the Friday edition of the Süddeutsche Zeitung.
	See Music
Drama	Nationaltheater (Bavarian State Opera) M 22, Max-Joseph-Platz 2; tel. 22 13 16
	Residenztheater (national theatre) M 22, Max-Joseph-Platz 1; tel. 22 57 54
	Staatstheater am Gärtnerplatz M 5, Gärtnerplatz 3; tel. 2 01 67 67
	Altes Residenztheater (Cuvilliés-Theater) M 2, Residenzstrasse 1, in the Residenz; tel. 22 57 54
	Prinzregententheater M 80, Prinzregentenplatz 12 Box office: Maximilianstrasse 13; tel. 22 57 54
	Deutsches Theater M 2, Schwanthalerstrasse 13; tel. 59 34 27

Münchner Kammerspiele (theatre)
M 22, Maximilianstrasse 26; tel. 237 21–328

Münchner Kammerspiele (theatre workshop)
M 22, Hildegardstrasse 1; tel. 2 37 21–3 28

Münchner Volkstheater
M 2, Stiglmaierplatz, entrance Brienner Strasse 50; tel. 5 23 46 55

Kulturzentrum Gasteig
M 80, Rosenheimer Strasse 5; tel. 4 80 98–0

Team-Theater
M 5, Am Einlass 4/5; tel. 2 60 43 33

Modernes Theater
M 5, Hans-Sachs-Strasse 12; tel. 26 68 21

Theater rechts der Isar (Isar right bank)
M 80, Wörthstrasse 7/9; tel. 448 36 57

Theater links der Isar (Isar left bank)
M 5, Auenstrasse 19; tel. 4 48 22 61

Kaffee Giesing, M 90, Bergstrasse 5; tel. 6 92 05 79

Theaterclub Off-Off
M 40, Potsdamer Strasse 13; tel. 39 37 29

Theater 44
M 40, Hohenzollernstrasse 20; tel. 32 87 48

Freies Theater München (FTM)
M 2, Landsberger Strasse 79; tel. 50 66 96

Blutenburg-Theater (thrillers)
M 19, Blutenburgstrasse 35; tel. 123 43 00

Theater am Karlshof
M 2, Karlstrasse 43 (entrance Augustenstrasse 4, Karlshofpassage);
tel. 59 66 11

Theater in der Leopoldstrasse
M 40, Leopoldstrasse 17; tel. 39 40 81

Pasinger Fabrik
M 60, August-Exter-Strasse 1; tel. 8 34 18 41

Theaterfabrik Unterföhring
Unterföhring, Föhringer Allee 23; tel. 9 50 56 66

Theater am Karlstor
M 2, Neuhauser Strasse 34; tel. 55 42 00

Theater im Marstall
M 22, Marstallplatz 4; tel. 22 57 54

Kleine Komödie im Bayerischen Hof
M 2, Pranner Strasse (Promenadeplatz arcade); tel. 29 28 10

Komödie am Maximilian-II-Denkmal
M 22, Maximilianstrasse 47; tel. 22 18 59

Theater "Kleine Freiheit"
M 22, Maximilianstrasse 31; tel. 22 11 23

Theater am Sozialamt (TamS)
M 40, Haimhauser Strasse 13A; tel. 34 58 90

Theater Ex Libris
M 2, Guldeinstrasse 47; tel. 50 79 70

Theater in der Westermühle
M 5, Westermühlstrasse 28; tel. 2 01 35 38

Scaramouche
M 40, Hesseloher Strasse 3; tel. 33 45 55

Forum 2 in the Olympic Village
M 40, Nadistrasse 3; tel. 351 37 80

Studiotheater in the "Pep"
M 83, Thomas-Dehler-Strasse 12; tel. 670 60 80

Ludwig-Thoma-Theater
M 2, Ledererstrasse 10; tel. 29 22 39

Das Schloss, Munich music and theatre tent
M 40, Ackermannstrasse; tel. 300 30 13

proT-Zeit
M 80, Steinseestrasse 2; tel. 4 48 66 93

Cabaret, revue

Münchner Lach- und Schiessgesellschaft
M 40, Haimhauser Strasse/corner of Ursulastrasse; tel. 39 19 97

Rationaltheater
M 40, Hesseloher Strasse 18; tel. 33 50 40

Hinterhof-Theater
M 45, Wirtshaus Am Hart, Sudetendeutsche Strasse 40; tel. 3 11 60 39

Theater bei Heppel & Ettlich
M 40, Kaiserstrasse 67

Drehleier
M 80, Balanstrasse 23; tel. 48 43 37

Kunstkeller Neuhausen
M 19, Elvirastrasse 17 A; tel. 18 26 94

Münchner Unterton
M 40, Theater Kurfürstenstrasse 8; tel. 33 39 33

Tangram
M 2, Gabelbergerstrasse 50; tel. 52 23 31

Theater Im Fraunhofer
M 5, Fraunhoferstrasse 9; tel. 26 58 70

Wirtshaus im Schlachthof
M 2, Zenettistrasse 9; tel. 76 54 48

Metropolis
M 2, Zweigstrasse (Mathäser-Festsaal); tel. 76 54 48

Novak's Schwabinger Brettl
M 40, Occamstrasse 11; tel. 34 72 89

Bavarian
folk theatre

Platzl Bühne
M 2, Platzl 1; tel. 2 37 03–0

Weiss-blaue Bühne
M 60, Benedikterstrasse 35; tel. 580 15 23

Münchner Theater für Kinder
M 2, Dachauer Strasse 46; tel. 59 54 54

Puppet theatres

Münchner Puppenspiele
M 2, Stadtmuseum, St-Jakobs-Platz 1; tel. 2 33–48 88

Otto Bille's Marionettenbühne
Ludwig Krafft Theater
M 90, Bereiteranger 15/corner of Zeppelinstrasse; tel. 150 21 68

Münchner Marionettentheater
M 2, Blumenstrasse 29A; tel. 26 57 12

Marionettenstudio "Kleines Spiel"
M 40, Neureutherstrasse 12 (entrance Arcisstrasse; admission free)

Schauburg in der Au, Theater der Jugend
Various venues due to building work on the theatre;
tel. 237 21–363 (box office)

Youth theatre

Time

Germany observes Central European Time (Mitteleuropäische Zeit), one hour ahead of Greenwich Mean Time, six hours ahead of New York Time. Summer Time, in force from April to September, is two hours ahead of Greenwich Mean Time.

Tourist Offices

See Information

Travel Documents

Nationals of European Union countries can enter Germany with an identity card or, in the case of the United Kingdom, a visitor's passport. Other nationals, including those from English-speaking countries such as Australia, Canada, New Zealand, South Africa and the United States, must have a full passport. This entitles them to a stay of up to three months.

Passports

Drivers must have a valid national driving licence or, if they are from Australia, South Africa or the United States, an international driving licence. Anyone bringing in a foreign-registered vehicle should carry the vehicle registration papers and have a Green Card, the international insurance certificate, since third-party insurance is compulsory.

Vehicle documents

Viewing Towers

Bavaria monument (18m/59ft) on Theresienhöhe: access Tue.–Sun. 10am–noon and 2–5.30pm (until 4pm in winter); narrow stairs.

Bavaria

Tower (85m/279ft) of the Neues Rathaus on Marienplatz: open daily 8am–6pm in summer, 9am–4pm in winter; lift.

Rathausturm (City Hall tower)

Tower (92m/301ft) of the Peterskirche on the Rindermarkt, near Marienplatz: open Mon.–Sat. 9am–6pm, Sun. 10am–6pm, closed in bad weather; narrow stairs.

Alter Peter

Towers (98m/321ft) of the Frauenkirche: access by the south tower Apr.–Oct. Mon.–Sat. 10am–5pm; lift.

Frauenkirche towers

Olympia tower (288m/945ft) in the Olympia Park: access in summer daily 8am–midnight (last ascent around 11.30pm); lift.

Olympia tower

When to Go

Although a visit to Munich can be enjoyable at any time of the year, the period from May to September is recommended. However, accommodation in many hotels when trade fairs and other major events are being held (especially during the October Festival) is usually heavily booked. Travel agents will be able to advise their clients.

Young People's Accommodation

Information

Youth Information Centre, Paul-Heyse-Strasse 22; tel. 51 41 06 60
Young People's Guide to Munich: English booklet published by the City of Munich Tourist Office. Its "where to stay" section includes detailed information on how to get to youth hostels, etc.

Youth hostels

Accommodation for young people under 26 holding the International Youth Hostel Identity Card.

Munich Youth Hostel (DJH Jugendherberge), M 19, Wendl-Dietrich-Strasse 20, 510 beds; tel. 13 11 56
Burg Schwaneck (castle), D(W)-8023, Pullach, Burgweg 4/6, 125 beds; tel. 7 93 06 43
Jugendgästehaus Thalkirchen, M 70, Miesingstrasse 4, 330 beds; tel. 7 23 65 50/60

Youth hotels

Youth hotels are slightly more expensive than youth hostels but do not require a special identity card and have no age limit unless otherwise specified.

Haus International, M 40, Elisabethstrasse 87, 480 beds; tel. 12 00 60
CVJM Jugendgästehaus (YMCA/YWCA), M 2, Landwehrstrasse 13, 80 beds; tel. 55 21 41–0
Jugendhotel Marienherberge, M 2, Goethestrasse 9, 24 beds, young women only, age limit 25; tel. 55 58 91

Tent/Youth camp

Jugendlager am Kapuzinerhölzl, M 19, Franz-Schrank-Strasse, 420 sleeping places; tel. 1 41 43 00. Large sleeping tent run by the City of Munich from late June through August. Open 5pm–9am, with canteen, washing facilities, information bureau.

See also Camping

Useful Telephone Numbers

Emergencies
Police	110
Fire	112
Ambulance	1 92 22
Duty chemist	59 44 75
Medical emergency	55 77 55
Women's crisis line	76 37 37

Vehicle breakdown:
ACE	1 92 16
ADAC	1 92 11
AvD	30 45 59
DTC	8 11 12 12
Vehicle insurers	1 92 13

Information
Flight information	97 52 13 13

Road routing pilot stations:
Freimann (Nürnberg autobahn)	32 54 17
Ramersdorf (Salzburg autobahn)	67 27 55
Obermenzing (Stuttgart autobahn)	8 11 24 12

Tourist information centres:
Main station (Hauptbahnhof)	23 91–2 56/2
57	
Airport	90 72 56
Train information	1 94 19
Youth information centre	5 14 10 60

Airlines
Air Canada	28 84 51
American Airlines	2 28 50 18
British Airways	29 11 21

Consulates
Canada	22 26 61
United Kingdom	21 10 90
United States	2 88 80

Lost property
Municipal	12 408
Railway	1 28 58 59
S-Bahn	1 28 84/409
Postal	12 62–5 52

Taxis	21 61–1

Telegrams	11 31

Telephone
Directory enquiries, Germany	11 88
Directory enquiries, international	0 01 18
Exchange for international calls	00 10

Dialling codes:
to Canada, United States	00 1
to United Kingdom	00 44

Weather forecast	1 16 04

What's On
Conferences, fairs	23 91 81
Galleries, museums	23 91 62
Theatres, concerts	1 15 17

Index